A GEOGRAPHY OF OYSTERS

*The Connoisseur's Guide
to Oyster Eating
in North America*

ROWAN JACOBSEN

BLOOMSBURY

NEW YORK · LONDON · NEW DELHI · SYDNEY

The man sure had a palate covered o'er
With brass or steel, that on the rocky shore
First broke the oozy oyster's pearly coat,
And risked the living morsel down his throat.

—JOHN GAY, 1716

Published by Bloomsbury USA, New York

All papers used by Bloomsbury USA are natural, recyclable products made
from wood grown in well-managed forests. The manufacturing processes
conform to the environmental regulations of the country of origin.

THE LIBRARY OF CONGRESS HAS CATALOGED THE HARDCOVER EDITION AS FOLLOWS:

Jacobsen, Rowan.
A geography of oysters : the connoisseur's guide to oyster eating
in North America / Rowan Jacobsen.
p. cm.
Includes bibliographical references and index.
ISBN-13: 978-1-59691-325-7 (hardcover : alk. paper) (hardcover)
ISBN-10: 1-59691-325-8 (hardcover : alk. paper) (hardcover)
1. Cookery (Oysters). 2. Oysters. I. Title.
TX754.O98J33 2007
641.6'94—dc22
2007018823

First published by Bloomsbury USA in 2007
This paperback edition published in 2008

Paperback ISBN-10: 1-59691-548-X
ISBN-13: 978-1-59691-548-0

7 9 10 8 6

Designed by Sara Stemen
Typeset by Westchester Book Group
Printed and bound in the U.S.A. by Thomson-Shore, Inc., Dexter, Michigan

CONTENTS

Contents

HOW TO USE THIS BOOK

THIS BOOK IS designed to make you a more savvy and satisfied eater of oysters. It's divided into three parts. The first, "Mastering Oysters," gives you context. While it's possible to know nothing about oysters and still enjoy them, your experience will be greatly enriched by background knowledge. It's like attending a painting exhibition. Instinctive reactions are important, but most people get more out of an exhibit by reading the accompanying texts and understanding something about the artist, the materials, the movement, and the vocabulary others use to discuss it. Think of an oyster as a minor work of art; knowing something about where it came from, how it came to be, and how it might be described will give meaning to your meal.

The second part, "The Oyster Appellations of North America," provides a guide to the 132 most commonly encountered oysters. It explains the natural and human factors that influence the flavor and appearance of oysters from each area. Rather than reading it straight through, you can use it, along with the Oyster Index at the back of the book, to learn about any oyster you come across in a restaurant or seafood shop. Once you have a few oysters under your belt and are starting to identify the geography of your favorites, use this section to seek out other oysters that have similar provenance, or, better still, to plan your own "oyster crawl" in that area.

The third part, "Everything You Wanted to Know About Oysters but Were Afraid to Ask," helps you put your newfound oyster expertise into practice. It's where you'll find information on shucking oysters, serving them, cooking them, pairing them with wines, and so on. It highlights the best oyster bars and festivals, as well as growers who will pull their oysters straight out of the sea and mail them to your door. It also includes information on safety and nutrition, so you can eat oysters worry-free—and help others to do the same.

INTRODUCTION

I WAS TWELVE years old when I discovered that raw oysters were the best food on earth and not, as I had assumed, the most disgusting. After a day spent bodysurfing the big breakers out beyond the sandbar at New Smyrna Beach, Florida, my family ducked, sunburned and salt-encrusted, into Stormy's—a real bar. While my mother sidled away toward the safety of some mozzarella sticks, and my younger brothers stared at me with "You're going to put *what* in your mouth?" faces, I climbed onto a barstool next to my father, lifted to my mouth an oyster on the half-shell, slurped it in, gave a few halfhearted chews, and left childhood behind.

I matched my dad, oyster for oyster, through a couple of dozen that day. The first had been a dare, no question, and the second was to prove that the first wasn't a fluke, but I ate the third because there was something vital about the experience that I didn't quite understand but wanted to experience again, and I ate the fourth one because I couldn't stop.

Dad and I killed a lot of oysters back then. They were a dime apiece during happy hour at Stormy's. They weren't even especially good oysters, I know now—likely bought on the cheap from some fetid Gulf Coast backwater—but they were my initiation into another way of eating. In an America where we rarely ate recognizable creatures, oysters were the real deal, unadorned and *live*. This food didn't come to you prepped, cooked, and otherwise altered to make it as pleasing and unthreatening as possible. You had to leave your familiar surroundings, cross the cultural bridge, and risk the wild world.

Then there was the taste. Oysters taste like the sea. This fundamental truth has been pointed out enough times that it is easy to forget how extraordinary it is. *Oysters taste like the sea.* No other food does. Not lobsters, not saltwater fish, not scallops or clams or even kelp. Beef tastes meaty, milk tastes creamy, but the comparison for oysters is not a taste or another food but always a place. And a place—the seacoast—for which many of us have romantic associations. From oysters I learned that what's important about good food is not just what it gives you, but where it can take you.

The next step in my oyster odyssey was easy. South of New Smyrna Beach is Canaveral National Seashore, 220 square miles of wilderness surrounding the Kennedy Space Center. The Atlantic flows through Ponce Inlet and into Mosquito Lagoon, an immense estuary protected by Canaveral's mass. I used to canoe there a lot, amid miles of flat green water and egrets and palm trees and marsh—and the occasional column of fire from a NASA launch. And it was there that I noticed the "rocks" sticking just above the water surface at low tide. Florida has no rocks—it's sand, sand, sand—so these were worth investigating. They were beds of oysters, piled on top of each other, revealed at low tide and hidden again at high. I might as well have come across Spanish doubloons.

Soon I was bringing hammers and a plastic bucket, and returning in my canoe with more oysters than I could eat. Some I would whack off with a hammer and open on the spot, returning the empty shells to the lagoon. This was a revelation. No raw bar required! Those oysters took me out of the suburbs and into a relationship unchanged since prehistory. Was I a Florida eighth-grader in an Ocean Pacific T-shirt or a Timucuan Indian boy cruising the coast? You couldn't have told from my meal.

When I think back on those oysters, I'm first and foremost pleased that I'm not dead. Those were risky oysters. *Vibrio vulnificus,* a parasite that infects oysters and is responsible for a few deaths a year, lives only in warm water. Stick to coldwater northern oysters and your risk is virtually nonexistent. I'll bet the water in my lagoon was 80 degrees Fahrenheit.

I didn't harvest another oyster myself for twenty-five years. That one was in Maine, about as far from my warm Florida oysters as I could get. On the frigid shore of the Damariscotta River, I pulled up a thick-shelled oyster, held it awkwardly against my thigh, pried it open with a knife, cut its adductor muscle, and dumped it into my mouth. The meat was cool, briny, and brimming with life. I felt full of well-being and deeply connected to the earth—as well I should have. A mile up the river inlet, a two-thousand-year-old shell midden bore testament that humans had been connecting to the earth in just this spot, in just this way, for a long, long time.

My Damariscotta oyster belonged to the exact same species— Eastern (*Crassostrea virginica*)—as the Mosquito Lagoon oyster I'd eaten a quarter-century earlier in Florida, but it couldn't have tasted more different. Where the Florida oyster tasted a bit muddy and soft, the Maine oyster was fresh, firm, and briny as all get-out. It tasted like, well, Maine. And it drove home a point that is central to this book: More than any other food, oysters taste like the place they come from. Oysters are creatures of bays and tidal pools and river inlets, of places where marine and terrestrial communities collide. While they are creatures of the sea, they draw their uniqueness from the land and how it affects their home waters. They have a *somewhereness* to them, like great wines, and in a mass-produced society where most foods don't seem to be from *anywhere,* this makes them special. You can't look at a grape and tell that it's from northern Chile. You can't taste a supermarket ribeye and say, "Ah, yes, the grasslands of Wyoming." But with an oyster, you can sometimes pinpoint its home simply by looking at it. With a little practice, you can often tell by tasting it. Think of an oyster as a lens, its concave shell focusing everything that is unique about a particular body of water into a morsel of flesh. That's why not only do Florida oysters and Maine oysters taste different, but oysters in one Maine bay taste different from oysters in the next.

The wine term for this is *terroir,* and you'll see it a lot in this book. On one hand, it makes perfect sense to speak of *terroir* with oysters, which exhibit their provenance so precisely. Yet, taken literally, it makes no sense at all. *Terroir,* after all, refers to terra firma, and oysters' terra isn't very firma. But it's a term already familiar to most readers, and speaking of *meroir* would get you laughed out of most restaurants, so *terroir* it is.

So closely is an oyster's flavor tied to its location that oysters are traditionally named for the place they come from. The East and Gulf Coasts, for example, have only one native species of oyster, Eastern, but it goes by many monikers: Pemaquid, Wellfleet, Chincoteague, Malpeque, and Cape Breton, to name just a few. On the West Coast, California's Tomales Bays, Washington State's Hama Hamas, and British Columbia's Fanny Bays are all Pacific oysters *(Crassostrea gigas)*, yet all look and taste different.

This emphasis on provenance is similar to that for European wines. Almost all white Burgundies, for example, are made from the Chardonnay grape, yet a Meursault tastes nothing like a Chablis or a Pouilly-Fuissé. Place is paramount, and the names of both wines and oysters reflect that. Five species of oysters are found in North America, but there are hundreds of appellations. Each appellation produces oysters with distinct characteristics, due to the bay's temperature, salinity, algae, tides, minerals, and many other factors, including the genetics of each bay's population, the age of the oysters at harvest, and the techniques used to cultivate them. Some oysters are insipid, while others dazzle. Learning the geography of all these appellations takes a while, but that's part of the fun. With a little experience, and, I hope, the help of this book, you will soon be navigating oyster lists like an old pro.

It takes great habitat to make great oysters, so when you taste a really superb one, you can take pleasure in knowing that you are tasting the untamed health and beauty of nature. An oyster doesn't taste good because of a food scientist's lecithin; it doesn't taste good because of a winemaker's oak chips; it doesn't taste good because of the chef's sauce. An oyster tastes good because at one spot in the natural world, something went right. A great oyster is an estuary flashing a thumbs-up sign.

Oysters are not mere avatars of their environment, either. They help create it. Scientists refer to oysters as *ecosystem engineers* because they are the key to maintaining estuaries with stable bottomland, clear water, and a flourishing web of life. Supporting sustainable oyster production helps ensure the continuation of that community.

If you only recently started thinking seriously about oysters, you are not alone. We are entering an oyster renaissance in North America. From

Canada to Mexico, from Boston to San Francisco, and even places far from any coast, people are rediscovering that nothing sets the tone for a splendid evening better than a dozen oysters.

It's startling how fast this has happened. Consider Taylor Shellfish, one of the oldest and largest oyster growers on the West Coast. A mere twenty years ago, Taylor sold virtually no oysters in the shell. The entire market was shucked meats. Oysters were something you bought in a can and then fried or stewed. Today, about 75 percent of the oysters Taylor grows are sold live. People no longer want generic oysters in a tub. They want oysters with somewhereness.

With oyster bars springing up on every corner of every metropolis, it's hard to remember that there was a time when most self-respecting chefs couldn't speak knowledgeably about the relative merits of Malpeques and Moonstones. When Tom Madsen of Snow Creek Oysters in Discovery Bay, Washington, started growing oysters in the mid-1980s, he was one of the first to concentrate on the half-shell trade. He went knocking on restaurant doors to try to convince restaurants to try serving oysters on the half-shell. The chef of the local fancy restaurant wasn't swayed. "I think it would look cool," he said, "but it seems like too much trouble." Why? "Well, because first I'd have to take some shells and wash them, then I'd have to take the oysters out of the bucket and put them in the shells." No, no, Madsen explained, he would deliver the oysters *in their own shells*. The chef looked at him, stunned.

Things have changed. Hundreds of varieties of oysters can be had in North America, *in their own shells*. Some are geographical neighbors and taste like it; others are stunningly individual. You may never get to know them all, but there are good reasons to try.

WHY EAT OYSTERS?

Everybody has a first oyster, and it involves gathering courage, overruling one's instincts, and taking a point-of-no-return leap, like jumping into cold water. You psych yourself up, take the plunge, and afterward you pull yourself out and dry your prickly skin and feel sharp and clean and satisfied. Have you ever heard anyone wade out of the ocean and say, "Boy, I wish I hadn't done that"? So it is with oysters. Once you start, you'll be hooked. I can't make you do it, but I can at least anticipate some of your objections:

Oysters don't have much taste. They don't taste like most of our food, it's true. Much contemporary cooking pushes the envelope of sweeter, richer, spicier. Steak with blue cheese on top. Honey in the salad dressing. Wine concentrated to the edge of chewability. If you get used to food that is so desperately eager to please, your palate can become deadened for anything else. Most food is as obvious as a Vegas nightshow: lots of sparkle, lots of jiggle, requiring nothing from us but that we sit back and let it perform. A raw oyster was not designed for our pleasure. Appreciating it is more like catching a glimpse of a fox in the woods: The experience lasts only a moment but leaves us in a fleeting state of grace. Oysters are not easy or obvious, but few foods so exquisitely balance sweet, salty, savory, and mineral. Few foods so reward our efforts.

Oysters are slimy. Guilty as charged. But so are mangos. So is yogurt. In fact, some of the greatest pleasures in life are slimy. Most adults learn to thoroughly enjoy them. So it's simply a question of appropriate slime. A slimy Happy Meal? Very bad. A slippery oyster? Very good. It's the dry ones that are no fun.

Oysters are high in cholesterol. Not so. People used to think all shellfish were high in cholesterol. Now, with better technology for distinguishing cholesterol from other, healthy sterols, we know that only shrimp and squid are high in cholesterol. Oysters, in fact, are astoundingly healthy foods. Nature's multivitamins, they boast an unmatched suite of minerals, vitamins, and omega-3 fatty acids. They are high in protein but low in saturated fat. And, with only about 10 calories per oyster, you'll go broke eating them long before you gain a pound. Considering that you burn almost as many calories shucking oysters as you get from consuming them, they may be the perfect diet food.

Aren't oysters endangered? Wild oyster populations were decimated long ago. Those populations bottomed out in the 1970s, are now carefully managed, and today are creeping upward. But almost all the oysters you find on the half-shell are from oyster farms, which are environmentally benign. The farms actually improve the water quality of their bays, and take pressure off wild stocks. Most environmental organizations put farmed oysters at the very top of their lists of sustainable seafood. See my chapter "Sustainability and the Environment: The Case for Oyster Aquaculture" for more information about this.

Raw oysters aren't safe. Only if you do several stupid things, like eat the wrong kind of oyster from the wrong supplier at the wrong time of year. The microorganisms that hitchhike in oysters and cause people hardship thrive only in warm waters. A Gulf of Mexico oyster consumed in the summer is risky; a Northern oyster from cold fall waters is safe. On top of that, everything from the health of shellfish beds to the temperature at which oysters are shipped and stored (usually around 40 degrees Fahrenheit) is regulated by the FDA.

Oysters are expensive. They certainly are—if you get them in restaurants. They are a sensual splurge. But you can also order direct from growers and save considerably. As live animals go, oysters ship really well. Wherever you live, you can have oysters on your doorstep tomorrow. Better still, hit the road and spend a few days at the source, sampling the coast's oysters and chasing them down with cold local beer. A dozen Olympia oysters from the Olympia Oyster Company costs only five dollars, which may be the most fun you can have for five bucks *anywhere*.

Will they overexcite my libido? Take your chances.

What about that whole *live* thing? We may as well tackle that issue right away. If an oyster's shell is clamped shut, the oyster is the one doing it. (Same goes for other shellfish.) Opening the shell by severing its adductor muscle doesn't always instantly kill it, though the writing is on the wall. Don't fret it. An oyster feels no pain and thinks no thoughts. It has no real brain, just a feeble cluster of ganglia. To an oyster, a housefly is a supergenius.

Pain is a nice evolutionary adaptation that encourages organisms to *get away* from the source of the pain—hot stove, grumpy bear, mother-in-law, whatever. It's a way of differentiating good feelings from bad feelings and acting accordingly. But an oyster can't get away. It has but one muscle and one choice in life: open shell or shut shell? If an oyster feels anything touch its gills other than water and plankton, it shuts reflexively. No mulling over the relative pros and cons of the sensation. In any case, oysters go dormant when temperatures drop to around 40 degrees—the temperature they are usually stored and served at. We can feel fairly confident that the short, happy life of a cocktail oyster ends in cold and blissful slumber.

Left in their natural environment, most oysters would be eaten by something; why shouldn't it be you? For all animals, life involves ingesting other life. That should be celebrated, and oysters are the perfect way to do it. You may not be ready to chase down a rabbit and kill it, but you can shuck an oyster, eat it, and get the primal thrill. It's like going native with training wheels.

Of course, you can also eat cooked oysters. You're still killing them, though your teeth aren't delivering the coup de grâce. For the anti-slime crowd, a few minutes of cooking will firm up an oyster's proteins and turn it into a food that acts, well, more like food. But oysters don't always cook well. When exposed to excessive heat, these most delicate and tender of mollusks lose everything that made them special. The vivacity of the living sea becomes brown, chewy, and dead. You certainly won't taste any *terroir* in an overcooked oyster. Many famous oyster dishes have evolved over time, most of them wretched. If you look carefully, you can find good ones in which the oysters are handled gently so their essence survives. A few of those dishes are in my recipe chapter. The rest of this book is concerned with raw oysters on the half-shell. That is where the fascination and the adventure lie.

MASTERING OYSTERS

A DOZEN OYSTERS
YOU SHOULD KNOW

TO BE A full-fledged *ostreaphile*—an oyster lover—you can't just pound Kumamotos or Wellfleets all the time. You need to explore the full range of styles and varieties. Different oysters, after all, work best as beer accompaniments, culinary stars, or exotic curiosities. This alphabetical list of twelve prominent varieties provides a good representation of the classic types.

BEAUSOLEIL

Néguac, New Brunswick

These small oysters are grown in floating trays in the harsh New Brunswick climate. Always petite and clean-flavored, in classy black-and-white shells, Beausoleils make ideal starter oysters, with the delightful yeasty aroma of Champagne or rising bread dough.

BELON OR EUROPEAN FLAT

Provenance Varies

No oyster comes close to the power of the European Flat (often called Belon, after the famous French oyster of the same species). It is brassy, in every sense of the word. Brassy because it tastes like metal, and because it is shamelessly bold, and because when it hits your tongue it slaps you awake like the opening blast of a bugler's reveille. Try one if you can—just don't make it your first oyster.

COLVILLE BAY

Souris River, Prince Edward Island

Light is a term often ascribed to PEI oysters. Sometimes it's a negative, indicating a lack of body and flavor. Sometimes, as with Colville Bays, it means transcendent. Colville Bays have plenty of body but also an addictive lemon-zest brightness. They are the oyster most likely to make you order another dozen. The dusky jade shells, when piled high, achieve the luminosity of moss on a rain-forest stump.

GLIDDEN POINT

Damariscotta River, Maine

Native Americans ate Damariscotta River oysters for a millennium, as the hill-sized middens along its upper banks confirm. The extremely cold, salty water produces slow-growing oysters with fantastic texture and brine at the upper end of the register. These are the soft pretzels of the oyster world, chewy and salty and heaven with a cold beer.

KUMAMOTO

California, Oregon, Washington, and Mexico

The oyster that put the fruit back in *fruits de mer*. Kumamotos are famously melon-scented, sweet, and firm, with none of the bitter or muddy aftertaste that makes some oysters challenging. Closely related to the Pacific oyster, which also was imported from Japan, Kumos stay small and deep-cupped, and are revered by beginners and pros alike.

MOONSTONE

Point Judith Pond, Rhode Island

Some of the most savory oysters in the world come from a geographical arc running from the eastern end of Long Island, along the ragged Rhode Island coast, to Block Island, Cuttyhunk, and Martha's Vineyard: the line marking the terminal moraine of the most recent glacier. Along that arc, mineral-rich waters produce salty oysters with unparalleled stone and iron flavors, of which Moonstone is the reigning king.

NOOTKA SOUND

West Vancouver Island, British Columbia
An oyster from pristine waters. Ain't nothing on the Pacific side of Vancouver Island except orcas, sea lions, shellfish farmers, and the occasional kayaker. You know these oysters are clean, but clean waters do not necessarily make light-flavored oysters. Art-deco–patterned, lavender-flecked Nootkas, in fact, taste strong, with hints of muskmelon and a flavor of cold, slightly sweet raw milk—animal, but good.

OLYMPIA

South Puget Sound, Washington
The only native West Coast oyster, once found from Baja to British Columbia, but now harvested commercially only in southern Puget Sound. These tiny celadon lockets hold delightful treasures: miniature oysters redolent of morels and butter and celery salt. Maddening to open, and maddeningly good.

PENN COVE SELECT

Samish Bay and Whidbey Island, Washington
Gorgeous, ruffled shells holding consistently plump, white oysters with black mantles. Penn Coves are multiyear winners of the West Coast's Most Beautiful Oyster contest. They are a prime example of the "clean finish" style of Pacific oyster—light, salty, fresh, like a cucumber sandwich rolled in parsley.

RAPPAHANNOCK RIVER

Topping, Virginia
Famous as a Chesapeake oyster river for centuries. Of the twelve oysters on this list, Rapps are the quietest. Extremely mild oysters, exhibiting

a simple sweet-butter flavor, they are easily overshadowed by saltier or fruitier oysters, so they don't fare well in mixed tastings. But on their own, with the most evanescent of wines, they can be delicacy itself—a lesson in the pleasure of minimalism.

SKOOKUM

Little Skookum Inlet, Washington
If Penn Coves exemplify the "light and lettucey" side of Pacific oysters, Skookums show Pacifics at the other extreme. These rich and musky oysters grow fat on the "algae farms"—mudflats—at the head of tiny Little Skookum Inlet, one of Washington's oldest oyster sites. The brown and green algae that thrive on the mudflats, different from deep-water algae species, give Skookums an aroma of trillium and river moss, more earth than sea.

TOTTEN VIRGINICA

Totten Inlet, Washington
The oyster that begs the question: Nature or nurture? By nature, it's a *virginica*, the East Coast oyster, celebrated for its superior texture. But it's nurtured in the gentle algae baths of Totten Inlet, famous for producing full-flavored Pacific and Olympia oysters. The result is an unlikely yet dazzling mutt—fat and round on the tongue, but cleaner and more mineral than a Pacific. If you prefer the Totten Virginica to Pacific oysters raised in Totten Inlet, then chalk one up for the Eastern oyster. If you prefer Totten Virginicas to East Coast *virginicas,* that confirms Totten Inlet's revered status.

THE FIVE SPECIES

THE FIVE SPECIES of oysters cultivated commercially in North America can be thought of as we do wine grapes: Each has classic characteristics, though they can be expressed quite differently, depending on location and growing conditions. The five species are:

- Eastern *(Crassostrea virginica)*—large, firm, briny
- Pacific *(Crassostrea gigas)*—large, soft, sweet, with cucumber notes
- Kumamoto *(Crassostrea sikamea)*—small, creamy, with hints of melon
- European Flat *(Ostrea edulis)*—medium, metallic, with a trace of caviar and hazelnut
- Olympia *(Ostrea conchaphila)*—tiny, coppery, and smoky

These oysters stand in relation to one another a bit like wine grapes do. While their flavors, appearance, and quality will vary depending on where they are grown, they still have certain predictable characteristics. Understanding and describing this territory is a young and evolving art, and comparisons to wine grapes may help:

The **Eastern** is the Riesling of oysters. From the wrong place, it can be simple, one-dimensional, almost flavorless, but when grown in great waters, it can achieve a brilliant subtlety and refinement, a transparency of sea and minerals that some consider unsurpassed. The **Pacific** oyster is more like a Sauvignon Blanc, less mineral but far more fruity and aromatic, often having an aftertaste of cucumber, seaweed, melon, or even bitter walnut. Like Sauvignon Blanc, it can exhibit wildly different personalities in different settings, with occasionally strange and challenging flavors. The **Kumamoto** is the Chardonnay of oysters—buttery, round, and smooth, with all the fruit of Pacifics but none of the bitterness. *Everybody* likes Kumos, causing some oyster snobs to distance themselves from the oyster and the madding crowd, in search of more challenging and exclusive experiences, just as ex-Chardonnay drinkers have done. Eating the **European Flat** will certainly place you far from the crowd. Even most oyster lovers can't stomach its fish-egg-and-metal flavor. For a wine equivalent, look to the tannic Barolo (from the Nebbiolo grape)—complex, tarry, unapproachable. It doesn't want to be your friend. A friendlier version, still metallic but sweeter, is the little **Olympia**, which we might compare to a Gewürztraminer: unusual, mysteriously smoky, and rich.

EASTERN *(CRASSOSTREA VIRGINICA)*

When European explorers first saw the bays and harbors of the New World, they were flabbergasted by the oysters. In both size and number, the oysters far surpassed their Old World cousins. "The oyster bankes," wrote one New England colonist, "do barre out the bigger ships." Partly this was because Europeans had been hammering their oyster populations for centuries, picking off the biggest specimens, while Native Americans had trod more lightly on theirs. But the species differences were also important. The Eastern oysters made the European Flats look like wimps. They grew in massive reefs, stretching for miles and rising twenty feet high. They grew in muddy places that no self-respecting Flat would touch. They thrived in New England cold, Florida heat, and everywhere in between. They fed prodigiously, grew immensely fat, and reproduced at alarming rates.

They were, in short, American.

Europe went bonkers for them. By the eighteenth century, all anyone in London or Paris wanted was an ample American oyster.

Crassostrea virginica does not have the strongest taste of any oyster, but it does have the cleanest. It tastes of the sea and not much else, and for that reason it is the oyster against which others should be measured. Once you get attached to the taste of a particular oyster species, you are as unlikely to shift positions as is an oyster itself. Arguments are not uncommon, though they usually end with the combatants toasting each other's health over shellfish and fresh pints of ale. Pacific oyster boosters generally object to the Eastern oyster's muted flavors, intense brine, and general ugliness. European Flat addicts consider other oysters bland to the point of insignificance. The argument for Eastern oysters goes something like this:

1. They are *terroir* itself. Their taste *is* their environment, plain and simple. Nothing gets in the way.

2. They are native. From the northern reaches of PEI down through Cape Cod and the Chesapeake and on to Apalachicola and New Orleans, they are an essential element of the East Coast. They are far more American than apple pie (apples were brought from Europe by settlers). Aside from the seldom-seen Olympia, the other oyster species—Pacific, Kumamoto, European Flat—are all imports, too. If you want a primordial American dish, unchanged for ten thousand years, it's *virginicas* raw or grilled over coals.

3. They have a little Yankee toughness. Easterners don't always cotton to the way some Pacific oysters fall apart in your mouth. A *virginica* can stand up to a lot of chewing, its flavor evolving all the time. In fact, you have to chew to get much, other than salt, out of a *virginica*.

Now, say I was devoted to Eastern oysters and wanted to present evidence in my argument for their superiority. I'd point to France. The French had enjoyed Flat oysters for millennia, yet when they first got a taste of American oysters in the 1600s, they went hog-wild. Not so Pacific oysters, which had been introduced to the European coast the century before and were considered oysters of last resort. Or I'd point to Washington and California. A few growers there farm *virginicas*, marketing them as the ne plus ultra of oysters. You certainly don't catch

Easterners growing Pacific oysters. Does this mean the Eastern oyster is better, or just that West Coasters embrace change while East Coasters are mired in the past? Then again, East Coast oyster bars almost always include an assortment of Pacific oysters, while West Coast bars stick to their own.

PACIFIC *(CRASSOSTREA GIGAS)*

Look at an Eastern oyster and you see a hard-bitten New Englander. The thick shell and lack of adornment. The simple, salty flavor. Clearly, this is an oyster conditioned by many brutal winters to adopt a viewpoint all too familiar to us Northeasterners: Build yourself a strong house and don't show off too much. The Pacific oyster, by comparison, resembles the pagodas of its original Japanese home, all curves and arches, showy colors, and fancy fruit flourishes. No wonder it took off on the West Coast. For this oyster, the living is easy—maybe too easy.

Eleanor Clark, author of the classic *The Oysters of Locmariaquer*, called Pacifics "a coarse species . . . fast growing and used mostly in canning." It never occurred to her that anyone would eat one given a choice, but then she was a Connecticut Yankee through and through. And at the time and place she was writing (1960s France and New England), not enough attention had been paid to Pacifics. They were still the immigrant oyster that had not yet been granted full citizenship.

Pacifics grow like weeds—and sometimes taste like them. They are the kudzu of oysters, overrunning estuaries with breathtaking speed. They grow twice as fast as *virginicas*, four times as fast as Olympias, Flats, and Kumamotos. They shrug off pollution. Thus, it comes as no surprise that they now supply 75 percent of the world market, including more than 99 percent of that in France, whose culinary connoisseurs sneered at *gigas* until they found that they had almost none of their beloved Belons left, then embraced the immigrant like a long-lost son. Today, so many Pacifics are grown in France that tens of thousands of tons get bulldozed annually to keep the price from collapsing.

A Pacific, left to its own devices, will get huge fast in rich waters.

Its meat will be streaky and watery, its shell thin. It's a bag of saltwater with a crust. But growers on the West Coast, in France, Australia, and elsewhere have discovered that, with proper handling, a Pacific can develop into something with filigreed shells and stylish flavors no *virginica* ever dreamed of. No other oyster has such range, and that makes *gigas* exciting. Will the one before you burst with melon and yuzu flavors, or leave you feeling like you're sucking on old aquarium goo?

Growing *gigas* took some adjustment for farmers used to growing Olympias or *virginicas*. When you grow *virginicas*, the goal is to coax maximum flavor from them. The meats are almost always firm. But *gigas* has an abundance of flavors, some of them strange, and a tendency toward softness, so it needs to be managed for a cleaner flavor and slower growth. When *gigas* was first grown in America, people were put off by its black mantle—the outer rim an oyster uses to filter its food. An early advertising campaign by Washington State's Rock Point Oyster Company tried to turn this into a plus by urging consumers to "Look for the oysters with the velvet rim." There's an elegant yin-and-yang quality to *gigas'* black-rimmed, white-fleshed meat that outdoes *virginica's* gray Atlantic plainness.

The Pacific oyster has taken to its new Northwest home remarkably well. It even grows wild throughout the region. No oyster has benefited so much from modern growing techniques. Today's Pacifics are deeper cupped, smoother shelled, and more refined than their ancestors.

KUMAMOTO *(CRASSOSTREA SIKAMEA)*

I have a love-hate relationship with Kumamotos. I love the taste. I love the smell. I love the extraordinary flourishes of the shells. I love everything about them. And I hate that.

Here's the problem. *Everybody* likes Kumamotos. They are sweet as heck and they smell like honeydew. Their shells are exquisite in adornment and curve, like little geishas. Beginners love them because they are small and don't have challenging aromas or flavors. Seasoned veterans love them because of their unmatched fruitiness and deep cups. It's no fun to like the same thing as everyone else, so I want to hate them. But I just can't.

Although Kumos are often described as mild, they're not. They actually have a lot of flavor, just none of the alien ones that put off some Westerners. Many oysters have passing hints of musk or metal or seaweed that aren't the kind of thing you find at McDonald's—or French restaurants, for that matter. Kumos' flavor profile is much more within the Western comfort zone. Their texture is appealing, too—reliably firmer than that of Pacifics. The meat sits in the shell like a divan, all pillowy flesh. They don't have much liquor, because the meat seems to take up all available space.

Kumos are contrary oysters. They sometimes struggle in algae-rich waters where Pacifics thrive, yet do well in thinner waters. Although they look like mini-Pacifics, they may have a different diet. We know that Olympias, the other small oyster, feed on particularly tiny plankton and reject larger plankton that Pacifics gobble up. Perhaps the same is true for Kumos. Do some of those larger plankton contribute bitter or fishy flavors? And do the thinner waters preferred by Kumos have the smaller algae they like, but not the large kinds? So far, no studies have been done.

We do know that Kumos like it warm. They grow very slowly in cold water. They are from the Nagasaki area in southern Japan, which has much warmer waters than the Miyagi prefecture of northern Japan, from which Pacifics hail.

BELON OR EUROPEAN FLAT *(OSTREA EDULIS)*

Almost everybody who tastes a Belon hates it. Even the people who sell them don't like them. One Rhode Island grower told me, "I personally can't stand the flavor. We got big money for them while we had them, but I can't sell very convincingly what I can't stand to eat. 'Here, buy this expensive oyster. It tastes like sucking on pocket change.'" According to a major shellfish distributor, "The surest way to lose a new client is to ship him some Belons."

Which is why I find them endlessly fascinating.

Belons are off-putting and overwhelming, like an anchovy dipped in zinc. Most people can't take them. But if you *can* take them, you may find that very soon you can't *stop* taking them. You will be on your way to joining the cadre of Belon addicts.

You see Belon addicts at oyster bars on those rare occasions when a bar has them. Somehow, they know. A call goes out, perhaps a phone tree. They appear. They order twenty-four Belons for lunch and another twelve for dessert. Not dainty Belons, either. The true addict wants the platter-sized gaggers, which can run upwards of five dollars apiece and have a crunch like calamari. All the Belons are gone by the end of the day, and the Belon addicts fade into the night, awaiting the next call.

Raw bars that serve European Flats tend to lace their menu copy with coded warnings. "For the adventurous palate!" "A daring and unique oyster!" "The connoisseur's choice!" Buyer beware. It comes down to the Flat's high content of iodine and trace metals, which give it a metallic zing and a stronger flavor than any other oyster. Not everybody wants flavor in their oysters. I do, and I love a good Flat, though I admit I have to work myself up to it. But when your head is in the right place and you are ready to fully commit, an eye-opening experience awaits.

Flats, Europe's native oyster, look very different from Eastern or Pacific oysters, because they didn't evolve for life in the intertidal zone—the area of shore exposed to air every low tide. Flats aren't built to endure long stretches out of the water. Instead of a tear-shaped shell, Flats' are round and shallow. (They don't call them *flat* for nothing.) They hold less liquid, which, along with their weak adductor muscles, means Flats dry out a lot faster than other oysters. (Harvesters ship them with rubber bands around the shells to keep them closed.)

Removed from the narrow and stable conditions for which they evolved, Flats die faster than neon tetras in an eight-year-old's aquarium. If they get too cold, they die. Too hot, they die. Covered with sediment, they die. Exposed for too long at low tide, they die. Out of the water for more than a few days—dead. They also accumulate higher concentrations of red tide (they don't die; you do).

The spawning time for European Flats is longer because, rather than releasing eggs into the water like *Crassostrea* females, Flat females are fertilized in their shells, where the larvae develop for two weeks before being released. Get a Flat at the wrong time of summer and not only will it harbor little black swimmy things that freak you out, but also a granular crunch from all those nascent shells.

As if all those drawbacks weren't enough to discourage growers from cultivating Flats, the oysters are currently being expunged from the planet by a protozoan known as Bonamia, which has the lovely habit of killing Flats just as they reach market size. Brett Bishop, a grower in Washington State, told me that one year he wound up paving his driveway with the shells of the most expensive oyster on the planet. He no longer grows Flats. Few do: In both Europe and the United States, Flats account for less than 1 percent of oyster production.

Fascination with Flats goes far back in European history. Pliny called them "the palm and pleasure of the table," as nice a phrase as you'll find. Apicius, ancient Rome's prolific cookbook author, liked to serve them with a fishy aioli—a no-holds-barred combo I've reproduced in the recipe chapter. Seneca was the first of many epicures to note their "exciting rather than sating" qualities, which explains why they were required fare at Roman banquets and especially orgies. Rome's insatiable appetite for oysters required importing them— packed in snow in winter and in saltwater tubs in summer. Bordeaux had a claim to the best, but Brittany, Normandy, England, Spain, Holland, Greece, and the Black Sea were all conscripted in the effort to keep Rome in oysters.

The Romans liked garum on their oysters, which staggers the mind. Garum was a sauce made by letting salted fish guts ferment in the sun for months, then draining off the black liquid for use. The best, made of mackerel guts, came from Spain. The combo reeks of decadence, a sure sign of a civilization on the decline. Romans, in fact, poured garum on virtually everything they ate, which must have added an unmistakable tang to the air in the Forum.

Flats first acquired the name *Belon* in the nineteenth century when the river of that name, in Brittany, was reputed to have the tastiest variety. Belons became the connoisseur's top choice. The name was soon adopted by all oyster growers in the area who might have conceivably dipped their oysters in the Belon. In the twentieth century, true Belon growers tried to stuff the cat back in the bag and reclaim rights to their name, but it proved impossible, and eventually *Belon* came to indicate any Flat from Brittany. When U.S. growers in the 1980s began cultivating the species, they used the name familiar to connoisseurs.

These are scary times for Flats. Bonamia is wiping them out worldwide. It infects the oysters' blood cells, but stays undetectable until the adult oysters simply start to die. No hatchery in the United States is still working with *edulis* seed, because they fear contamination with Bonamia. One hatchery in British Columbia is trying to develop disease-resistant strains of Flats from survivors of the Bonamia wars. Ireland may also be having some luck in developing Bonamia-resistant Flats. But the future survival of this unique oyster is anything but clear.

OLYMPIA *(OSTREA CONCHAPHILA)*

The little Olympia oyster is special. It's an American native, like the Eastern oyster, but it has a rich, engaging, celery-salt flavor that has earned it the nickname *Baby Belon*. In fact, many connoisseurs prefer the smoky copper flavor of Olympias to the full metal jacket of Belons. James Beard, who especially liked them for breakfast, was a huge Oly fan: "I have tasted many oysters, and, to me, the flavor of the Olympia is one of the finest, if not the finest of all."

If they are so good, then why aren't Olympias more widely known? Because they are also the World's Most Inconvenient Oyster. Like European Flats (with which they share the genus *Ostrea*), Olympias die if you look at them sideways. They are even less shippable than Flats. Elfin oysters not much bigger than quarters, they hold very little liquid and dry out quickly. If you want them, you must head to the source. Working your way through a pail of greenish-gold Olys in some Puget Sound backwater with Mount Rainier towering whitely on the horizon is one of the great experiences in life.

You won't get full, however. Start shucking and eating Olympias and you will be reminded of the "wild blueberry" phenomenon: No matter how fast you work, you can get only so many of the tiny things into your mouth. But that's fine. The intense flavor, seemingly without mass, and the watchmaker's skills needed to unlock the delicate green shells make Olympias more entertainment than meal.

Though Olympias are passing rare today, they once flourished from San Francisco Bay to British Columbia, and were party food for many thousands of frontiersmen. It's hard to believe that an industry survived on the little oysters for fifty years, but it did. Shuckers were clearly cheap back then, because it takes significant time to produce a gallon of Oly meats.

The oysters were so small, and grew so slowly, that they went into decline when the first cities sprang up on the West Coast. Though remnants can still be found hiding out from California to West Vancouver Island, by the 1900s the only commercial crops were in southern Puget Sound. Effluent from a pulp mill on Oakland Bay finished those off in 1927. The mill closed in 1957, but it took decades for the sound to flush itself clean. In the 1980s, the Olys started coming back, reseeded by larvae spawned from a few beds that survived in crooks of the sound that pollution never found, and aided by the Puget Sound Restoration Fund, which restocks native beds. Today, a handful of dedicated growers in southern Puget Sound sells Olys, a labor of love.

OTHER SPECIES

In addition to the five species that can be grown legally in North America, you may encounter four others —at least as rumors.

CHILEAN OYSTER (*OSTREA CHILENSIS*)

Chile is one of the only countries—along with Australia, New Zealand, Mexico, and Canada—that has a trade agreement with the United States so that its live oysters can be imported. A few years back, an oyster known as the Chiloe was a big hit at oyster bars. As you can tell from its genus, *Ostrea*, it is a relative of the European Flat, and it tasted like it. Though small, it was as briny and powerful as they come, as well as plump and firm-textured. Being from the southern hemisphere, it was an ideal oyster to eat during our summers, when other oysters might be offline for reasons of spawning or disease. Alas, the Chiloe hasn't been seen on these shores in several years.

PORTUGUESE OYSTER
(*CRASSOSTREA ANGULATA*)

Despite the hurdles of vast distances and lack of refrigeration, Portuguese merchant ships in the sixteenth century managed to accidentally introduce the Pacific oyster from Asia to their own Iberian coast. In France it became known as the *Portuguese oyster*, sensibly enough, where it supplied a demand for cheaper, less refined oysters. One momentous day in 1868, the Portuguese oyster came to France to stay. A ship laden with Portuguese oysters bound for Arcachon had to ride out a storm in the sheltered mouth of the Gironde River, near Bordeaux. By the time the storm had cleared, too much time had passed, and the oysters smelled very dead. The captain dumped his cargo in the water, where the babies stuck to the adult oyster shells flourished—a feat that Pacific oysters would repeat in Washington state's Samish Bay fifty years later. Soon a massive colony of Portuguese oysters coated the Gironde and spread to other rivers of the French coast, and by the 1920s they had taken over the industry, as Pacific oysters tend to do.

For a long time the Portuguese oyster had its own Latin name and was believed to be a close cousin to *Crassostrea gigas*. Now some people suspect they were originally one and the same, though in isolation the Portuguese developed its own genetic kinks. In any case, with the availability of *gigas* seed, the French oyster industry long ago switched to true Pacifics.

SUMINOE (*CRASSOSTREA ARIAKENSIS*)

This Chinese oyster is sometimes known as the Platter oyster in America, due to its size and flat profile, but considering its Asian name of *Suminoe*, its propensity to get immense, and the popularity of the name *Kumo*, it seems inevitable that the oyster will be nicknamed the *Sumo*. Sumos grows anywhere and seem resistant to MSX and Dermo, two diseases that ravage *virginicas* in the Chesapeake Bay, but that may be all they have going for them. The taste is unimpressive, the shell brittle, and the adductor muscle weak, because Sumos aren't designed to survive long stretches out of the water.

Still, disease resistance has been enough to get the Sumo a lot of attention. West Coast growers are playing around with it, and on the Chesapeake, where native stocks of *virginicas* are virtually nonexistent, baymen are lobbying hard to restock the entire bay with Sumos. So far only sterile and experimental populations are allowed, though escapees are reported frequently. If it does get a foothold, the weak-shelled Sumo will work best in the shucked-meat market.

SYDNEY ROCK OYSTER (*SACCOSTREA GLOMERATA*)

The Sydney Rock Oyster is the native oyster of New South Wales, and it is the Yukon Gold of shellfish. It resembles a Pacific oyster in shell shape and mantle color, but it is smaller, slower growing, and more intensely flavored. Those who dine regularly on Sydney Rock Oysters (something aborigines were doing six thousand years ago) rarely accept anything else. The oysters are rumored to be sweeter and more buttery than any other species—as can be seen in their creamy yellow flesh. The good news? They were just cleared for export to the United States in 2007. The bad news? They are getting muscled out by disease and by faster-growing Pacifics. If you are on good terms with an oyster bar proprietor, it's worth begging him to score some Sydney Rock Oysters to keep you entertained and the industry alive.

HOW TO GROW AN OYSTER

I'M THINKING OF an organism. It is ordered as seed from nurseries. The seed looks like grains of sand and requires lots of fresh water. You plant the organism in the dirt. The organism stays put. Once the organism gets big, you come back and harvest it. Would you guess that the organism is a plant or an animal?

Okay, you knew the answer, but otherwise you'd have guessed plant. Oysters, by virtue of their immobility and their knack for getting all their nutritional needs through water, act more like plants than animals. For that reason, people who raise oysters need to think more like farmers than fishermen. Fishermen and hunters simply need to know how to catch their food. Farmers need to *understand* their food. To farm good oysters, you need to know what makes oysters tick.

BEING AN OYSTER

Say you are an oyster. You and your kin have managed to thrive for several million years with no help from humankind, thank you very much. And, if left to your own devices, that's what you'd keep doing. Here's how you'd do it.

For starters, you wouldn't grow just anywhere. No open sea for you. No, you are a creature of the estuaries, of coves and bays, where fresh river water mixes with the salty ocean, creating a salinity between 2 and 3 percent, and ideally where offshore reefs or barrier islands or peninsulas prevent ocean waves and storms from sweeping you off your perch. Name a protected river mouth in the United States or Canada and you have named a great spot for oysters (pollution aside).

Now, say you are a baby oyster larva, recently ejected from your mother along with a million of your siblings. (At least, if you are a European Flat or an Olympia oyster. If you are an Eastern or Pacific oyster, you were launched from mom and dad as separate sperm and egg that hooked up in the water.) As a larva, you have a few things going for you, along with some serious problems. Your main problem is that you are very small, and pretty tasty, so more likely than not you are going to end your very brief life as lunch. Among the things in your favor are a sticky foot, cilia for swimming, and a rudimentary eye that can sense light and dark. All these things seem very *un*oysterlike, but as a larva you need them all as you swim about, dodging predators, gobbling infinitesimal plankton, sticking close to the surface (hence the eye, for detecting sunlight), and surfing the currents.

After twelve days or so, if all goes well and the planktonic gods are kind, you have grown into a big fat larva, with the beginnings of a shell. Eventually, down you go. Now's the one and only time for your foot to do its thing. As you head for the bottom, bouncing along in the tides, you have a few chances to attach to something with that sticky foot. This is where so many of your siblings go wrong. Only one in ten thousand will find something solid to attach to, or "set," as it's called. The rest will get buried in mud or swept out to sea and end up in any of a thousand hopeless places.

But you are a lucky oyster. You find your favorite substrate: another oyster shell. Rocks and packed bottoms are fine, but nothing attracts you like a shell, occupied or not. It's a good indicator that somebody before you did well in that spot. That's why the first sailors to the New World encountered unfathomable oyster reefs in Chesapeake Bay, New York Harbor, and other estuaries: Generations of oysters had paved the bottom, each generation piling on top of its parents, until the reef rose to the surface and even broke it at low tide.

Once settled in your new home, off go the eye, the foot, the cilia. You'll never travel or see again. As mammals, we have trouble with the concept of jettisoning useful tools as we develop. For us, it's all progress from infancy to adulthood—language, walking, winking, sex. It's hard

A baby Eastern oyster.

to comprehend a creature that voluntarily ditches vision and locomotion. We place a premium on them, but evolution decided such trifles were useless to oysters, and made the cuts. It's a bit like being a Hindu mystic. Your life path involves paring down to the bare essentials, making do with less. You find a nice spot, settle into the lotus posture, and do nothing but eat, breathe, and periodically blow off a third of your body mass in one titanic ejaculation.

Once you've reached adulthood, there you sit, merrily sucking seawater—as much as fifty gallons a day—through your slightly parted shells. As it crosses your gills, you strain out the plankton (algae and other microorganisms) and eat it. If a larger particle hits your gills, you automatically spit it out by clapping your shell shut.

Other than eating and not being eaten, you have only two concerns as an adult oyster: sex and winter survival. Your metabolism has everything to do with water temperature. If you live in the temperate waters of Europe, the Northeast, or the Pacific Northwest, sex begins to cross your mind as the water warms up in late spring. Through May and June, you eat like crazy, generating prodigious quantities of sperm or eggs. With all that gamete in you, you taste pretty gamey. This doesn't stop starfish, but it does dissuade most humans. As the water temperature peaks in late June or July, you shoot your wad. Afterward, you have a wicked case of *tristesse*. You are smaller, flabby, tasteless, and tired. Food is your only solace.

It takes you about a month after spawning to get your life back together. Then, as water temperatures tick downward, you eat like mad. You pack on the pounds, getting fatter and fatter as fall progresses. You start to taste really good, plump and sweet. When the water temperature hits 40 degrees or so (45 in the Chesapeake), you go dormant and don't feed again until the temperature climbs back above 40. (Your digestive enzymes don't work below 40.) In northern waters, that means that from sometime in November or December until sometime in April, five months or so, you don't eat. Even with your slowed metabolism, you need considerable energy reserves to survive that stretch—hence the urgency to get as fat as possible in the fall. It's no coincidence that oysters are traditional food for Christmas and New Year's Eve; that's when they're at their very best—on the East Coast, at least. The Northwest doesn't experience the same brutal winters. Its oysters have shorter dormancy periods and taste best after the two big algae blooms in spring and fall. Gulf Coast oysters never go dormant. Their flavor depends more on spawning (which they do three or four times a year) than on season.

During those cold winter months, your heartbeat slows to just a few beats an hour. You endure the winter with your shell shut tight, parting it for just a few minutes a day to get a bit of oxygen. The rest is darkness.

Until spring. You feel that first warmth on your shell—particularly if you are growing in shallow waters. You open up, start to feed, and, naturally, you consider a sex change. *Crassostrea* oysters begin life as males but many convert to female when they are a year old. *Ostrea* oysters are true switch hitters, changing sexes on a whim many times throughout their life.

BEING AN OYSTER FARMER

Long before humans farmed oysters, of course, they harvested them. For early humans, oysters must have been almost too good to be true—a year-round protein source that doesn't run away. Conveniently stored in waist-deep water, where they could be gathered in baskets or sacks, they helped keep quite a few humans healthy. Alas, as coastal communities grew, wild oyster populations declined, spurring people to begin attempts at cultivation.

The Greeks, Chinese, Japanese, and Mesoamericans all independently hit upon the first step toward farming oysters. They noticed that the same places where oyster seed set well were not necessarily the same places where adult oysters thrived, or tasted best. Salinity and food supply are the major considerations. Oysters grow fastest in areas where strong currents whisk plenty of plankton-rich, salty water over them. However, this is also where oysters' leading predators and diseases ply their trade. Adult oysters are usually tough enough to withstand the assault (though stingrays can crunch up three-inch oysters like popcorn), but tiny seed oysters get gobbled by everything under the sun, swept away in strong currents, and easily destroyed by disease.

The first efforts at farming oysters involved growing seed oysters in gentler and fresher water, where they endured fewer predators. Then, as their shells toughened and their appetites increased, they could be "fattened" in areas with active flow and full salinity. Sometimes this was a simple local operation, as in Long Island's Great South Bay, where oysters were started on the low-salt east side (fed by rivers and protected by Fire Island) and finished on the exposed west side. Sometimes the approach was more elaborate. For decades, most of France's baby oysters came from the protected, brackish Bay of Auray in Brittany, from which they were distributed up and down the coast for *élevage*—fattening—in rougher places less suitable for children.

But how do you collect baby oysters? In nature, only one larva in a million makes it to adulthood, obviously not an acceptable number for a business. You need to get the spat (the baby oyster) as soon as possible so that you can whisk it to safe nurseries. And that's just what the people of Auray did. In the summer, just before spawning time, they would set stakes ringed with ceramic tiles throughout the shallow bay. The tiles were coated with lime, which larvae liked to set on. (It took an embarrassingly long time for people to realize that shells were basically limestone, too, and made ideal spat collectors.) Once millions of larvae had set on the tiles, they could be moved to protected ponds, artificial pens, and other places where they could mature free from predation.

None of this was a recent idea. Way back in 59 B.C., Sergius Orata, a Roman with a knack for turning a buck, was doing pretty much the same thing in Lake Lucrinus, a salt pond near Naples that was a spa destination. Orata had nets of twigs set up around adult oysters. When the oysters spawned, many of the larvae would set on the twigs. Orata could lift the twigs out of the water and transport the crop to other locations for growth, then serve the oysters to rich citizens down from Rome for the week. Very simple. Very lucrative. In Japan, the preferred spat collectors were sections of bamboo, leaves still attached.

In the New World, with its abundance of natural oyster reefs, spat collection was, until recently, a simpler affair. It resembled growing an underwater crop in an underwater field. When it became clear that the wild oyster population was getting ready to spawn, oyster farmers would "till" their section of bottomland, removing whatever soft sediment had accumulated over the year, and then lay down a fresh layer of clean shells, known as *cultch*, for the wild spat to set on. Timing was everything. Spat can attach only to clean shells, so if you set your shell layer too early, sediment ruined it before the spawning. But if you waited too long to put down your shells, you missed the spawn.

A more foolproof, but costlier, option was to buy spat from so-called *buy boats*. Somebody else would do the work of collecting cultch that was already peppered with spat. Small-time oyster farmers would simply motor out to the buy boat when it visited their bay, buy the seeded cultch, scatter it over their bottomland, spend three years guarding their crop from poachers and mopping starfish off the beds, and then scoop up the oysters. On the Chesapeake, this system continued through most of the twentieth century.

The scooping up of the oysters has always been the hard part. The neolithic method—grab them at low tide—works great for oysters growing in shallow water, but most oysters are farther out. One traditional method for harvesting them—still used in the Canadian Maritimes, where quaintness seems to be a guiding principle—is tonging from flat-bottomed boats. Oystermen reach into the water with gigantic hinged salad tongs whose teeth close to form a basket. If they're

Scallop and oyster shells seeded with spat (the white spots), Japan. (Photo courtesy NOAA)

lucky, they scoop up a few choice oysters. Tonging makes for exhausted, patient, and buff oystermen.

But tonging is *so* nineteenth century, and in any case it's limited to harvesting oysters in less than fifteen feet of water, so by the mid–twentieth century dredging had become the dominant East Coast method of harvest, and remains so today. Wide, shallow baskets are dragged along the bottom by boats, scooping up oysters and anything else that happens to be at the bottom. The baskets are then hauled to the surface and emptied. Dredging is efficient. On long-cultivated bottomland, it doesn't do much damage—no more than any other farmers do when they till their fields. But dredging for wild oysters is like dragging a plow through the wilderness—it destroys the natural community.

BEACH CULTURE

The East Coast is a land of meager tides. It has a small *intertidal zone*—the area that is underwater at high tide, high and dry at low. There isn't much appropriate land for intertidal oyster farming. Even where the tides are large, like Maine and Wellfleet, the harsh winters would kill the oysters. Except in the gentle Southeast—where intertidal oysters are more protected from disease and predators than their subtidal

Hand-picking oysters in Willapa Bay, Washington, in 1969. (Photo courtesy NOAA)

neighbors—*virginicas* tend to grow in deeper water where they are covered 24/7.

The West Coast, however, is a different story. Tremendous tides and the temperature-moderating influence of the Pacific make intertidal culture—or *beach culture,* as it is often called—not only possible but preferable. Acres of gently sloping beach are uncovered at every low tide, and hard freezes are rare. The native West Coast oyster, the Olympia, is well adapted to beach culture, and the introduced oyster, the Pacific, loves it. What could be easier and more pleasingly low-tech than walking the beach at low-tide and tossing the biggest oysters into your bucket? That is how the Pacific Northwest tribes harvested oysters for centuries, and it's how some oysters are still harvested. Larger-scale operations really make the tides work for them. At low tide, their harvesters walk out and collect oysters, but rather than hauling the heavy cargo by foot, they toss the oysters into giant tubs that have flags on them. When the tide comes in, barges visit each flag, haul up the tub, and collect the oysters. The best of both worlds—no dredging, no schlepping.

Equally important, beach life makes oysters harden their shells, which improves their shelf life and makes them easier to shuck. If you are an oyster living underwater all the time and you have a few tiny holes in your shell, who cares? But if you are exposed at low tide and your precious water starts dribbling out, you mortar up those holes pretty fast. Your adductor muscle gets stronger, too, from clamping down for hours at a stretch, which helps you "hold your liquor" and gives you a much longer life in your final journey from farm to plate. Think of beach culture as Pilates for oysters.

AQUACULTURE TECHNIQUES

Hand-picking, tonging, and dredging can be used with either wild populations or farmed. But most of the oysters encountered in raw bars today are creatures of more sophisticated aquaculture, which long ago revolutionized West Coast oystering and is in the process of doing so in the East. In fact, most oysters destined for half-shell service begin life far from the sea.

HATCHERIES

Rare is the terrestrial farmer who still saves seed from year to year. The vagaries of nature are too unpredictable, the skills required to make good seed too specialized. Most farmers prefer to purchase seed from experts. Today, the same is true for most oyster farmers. Why risk some freak storm or heat wave or disease that leaves you with no crop for the coming year? You no longer have to. Put in your order with the shellfish hatchery for a million seed in May and you are covered.

Hatcheries function as oyster love motels and birthing centers rolled into one. Instead of letting oysters cast their sperm and eggs into the great blue and hoping for the best, hatcheries let those sperm and eggs mix in a safe tank where their odds of getting together are exponentially higher. Those larvae spend their first weeks of life in tanks with awesome food, cozy temperatures, and no bad guys.

A huge advantage offered by hatcheries is that they can provide seed that has already set—perfectly. By introducing shells crushed to particles smaller than sand grains into the larval tanks, the hatcheries force the larvae to set on individual grains. In the wild, spat will set close together on any available surface. As they grow in clumps, they squeeze each other into tangled, asymmetrical shapes. Spat "singles" from a hatchery develop into the perfectly shaped oysters that wow you in the oyster bar. Attached to nothing heavy, they must be kept in bags or nets until they are large and heavy enough to stay on the bottom on their own—though some growers keep them in bags or lantern nets their whole lives.

Just as garden seed companies offer multiple strains of a particular vegetable, some oyster hatcheries have become sophisticated enough to offer a choice of genetic stocks. You can order stocks selected to thrive in cold-water areas or stocks with some resistance to diseases such as MSX. Many oyster farmers send their own broodstock, which has already proven itself well-adapted to its particular waters, to the hatchery to seed the next generation. This fairly recent phenomenon means that in coming years we should see even more diversity and geographic specificity in oysters, as the populations of certain appellations become genetically unique.

Farmers can also order sexless oysters from a hatchery. Expose an oyster larva to certain mutagenic chemicals or to intense atmospheric pressure and it will develop three sets of chromosomes instead of two, making what is known as a *triploid* oyster. Normal oysters are diploids, and so are you. Cast your mind back to high school biology and you may recall that if you have XX chromosomes you produce eggs, and if you have XY chromosomes you produce sperm. Triploids, like gelded steer, produce neither sperm nor eggs. Having no sex drive, they think about nothing but food. They get fat and sweet. Triploid oysters have an obvious advantage—no spawning, so no R months to worry about (see the chapter titled "Safety")—and a huge PR disadvantage (mutant freaks!). The public doesn't warm to the idea of eating mutated oysters, so the industry tends to keep pretty quiet about the whole triploid thing. Still, triploids are safe. We have been eating them for years. In fact, many of the vegetables we eat are also triploids.

Triploids now account for the majority of the Pacific oyster industry, and are making inroads in the East. And they are no longer created through exposure to chemicals. Today, they are produced by breeding a tetraploid male (yes, four sets of chromosomes, and no, I have no idea how they make that one) with a regular old diploid female. Triploids tend to have larger adductor muscles, giving them a more clamlike chewiness (good or bad, depending on your taste). And some claim that their shelf life is inferior. But there is an additional argument in favor of triploids: Sometimes normal oysters will prepare for spawning in summer by producing lots of gamete, but then for whatever reason—say, unusually cool water—they never manage to pull the trigger. They are stuck with lots of bad-tasting gamete, which they try to reabsorb, with varying degrees of success (females do better than males). The off taste lasts well into fall and even winter, when no one expects to encounter a spawny oyster. Triploids don't have this problem. They are far more predictable, as indeed we all would be if sex weren't involved.

FLOATING NURSERIES

Consider the plight of the poor oyster baby. It cannot move. It is at the mercy of the tides and fate to bring it food and not predators. Its chances are slim to laughable, at best, because *everything* eats it. And even if it somehow escapes all those hungry mouths, has it cemented itself to a spot where not much plankton comes by? The deck is most definitely stacked against it.

Many oyster farmers start their seed oysters in a FLUPSY (FLoating UPweller SYstem). Think of these floating nursery trays as marine greenhouses. In a terrestrial greenhouse, seedlings can stay warm through cold spring nights, don't get nibbled by pests, and get exactly the water and nutrients they need. By the time they get transferred to the great outdoors, they are considerably larger, more developed, and more numerous than their wild peers. The same is true for oyster seed in nursery trays. It begins life in barrels or mesh bags where it is completely safe from predation and where it enjoys the warm and algae-rich summer surface waters. Motorized upwellers constantly pump fresh water over the seed, maximizing the food supply. As their size and nutritional requirements increase, oysters may be moved to larger and less crowded living spaces several times over the summer and fall. Maybe they're not as tough as those wild oysters who fought their way up on the streets, but they are certainly bigger. By the time winter hits, the young oysters are big and strong and ready to face life on the bottom, or whatever home awaits them.

BOTTOM CULTURE

Even with all the technological advances in aquaculture, most oysters eventually meet the mud—or gravel, sand, or shell. There is something

Oyster seed in a below-dock
FLUPSY.

reassuring about this. What kind of bottom-feeder doesn't spend life on the bottom?

After spending their first few weeks in a hatchery, and their first summer in floating nursery trays, oysters destined for bottom culture get thrown from a boat and fall to the bottom, where they spend a year or three growing to market size. It takes a lot of money and maintenance hours to grow oysters inside equipment their whole lives, so the bottom is a more viable option for most farmers—assuming, of course, that you have a viable bottom. It must be packed hard enough that the oysters won't sink into the sediment and suffocate. With bottom culture, some oysters are lost to predators, but no equipment is necessary. Equally important, oysters that live on the bottom get regular workouts. They are strong. They taste stronger, too. In areas with firm bottoms, bottom culture is the way to go, though harvesting is still a question.

OFF-BOTTOM CULTURE

Life isn't easy for bottom-dwelling oysters. Packed cheek-by-jowl with their mates, they struggle to suck a little water that hasn't just come out of some other oyster. Twice a day the tide washes through and unceremoniously dumps dirt on them. Even if they manage to get enough food and stay above the mud, they are likely to get picked off by a

Starfish attacking Eastern oysters. (Photo courtesy NOAA)

stingray or a starfish or a crab, which will worry away the soft growing edge of an oyster shell and scoop it out like a soft-boiled egg. It's a marginal existence.

Some pampered oysters, however, get a little lift. The farmer places them in mesh bags and sets them in huge cages that are lowered to the bay bottom. The cages have multiple racks where the oysters sit, a foot or two from the mud and hoi polloi on the bottom, enjoying the best food that the water column has to offer. It's a cushy life; all they have to do is eat and look good doing it, thumbing their noses at the drooling starfish plastered against the cage. (Though the occasional acrobatic starfish has been known to stick its stomach *through* a cage to digest an oyster externally.)

Oysters raised in off-bottom cages grow significantly faster than their bottom-dwelling kin. Given enough elbow room, they don't get long and skinny and curved in an effort to stay above the fray. Trees in a forest grow long and thin, fighting to stay atop the canopy, their only living branches where the light is. Trees that grow in a field have the plush and symmetrical shape that appeals to us. Same for properly spaced oysters. They get plump and pretty.

They also don't require dredging or hand-picking. Oyster farmers

Eastern oysters growing like trees. (Photo courtesy NOAA)

Hauling up oyster cages.

love this. No culling the dredged oysters and throwing back the small ones. Just haul up a cage full of same-age oysters. Cages have made it possible to grow oysters in bays that could never support bottom culture.

One obstacle to farming oysters in cages is the significant investment in equipment. You need to buy a lot of expensive cages and a boat with a winch capable of hauling the heavy cages to the surface. A more affordable variation, perfect for growing areas that are accessible from shore, is "rack and bag"—mesh bags of oysters are attached to rebar "tables" that sit a foot off the bottom on metal legs.

BAG-TO-BEACH

The ascendant method of oyster culture in the Northwest is a combination of rack-and-bag and beach culture. The combo avoids the main problem associated with each technique. Seed a beach with baby oysters and you may as well ring the undersea dinner bell: Crabs and other predators come lumbering from far and wide to pick it clean. Keeping the seed in bags protects it from predation, but if you leave it in those bags all its life the shell stays thin and brittle, and shuckers everywhere will curse you. The solution is to let the seed stay in bags until it gets pretty big, perhaps two inches in size, at which point it is safe from most predators, then scatter it on the beach for six months to a year, where waves and currents knock it around, and predators and low-tide exposure force it to clamp its shell shut. Such harassment makes for tougher shells and stronger adductor muscles, which means longer shelf life on the way to the oyster bar and happier shuckers once there.

LONGLINE CULTURE

Another off-bottom variation is longline culture. Long ropes are seeded with spat and staked perhaps a foot off the bottom of a bay, separating the oysters from silt. This is a wonderfully low-tech method that doesn't require much investment in equipment. It also produces fairly tough oysters, since they are exposed to the natural pressures. The real beauty comes at harvest time, when, instead of spending many hours gathering your oysters, you just detach the ropes and carry them to shore, where the oysters can be separated at your leisure. Longline culture works best with massive operations, and requires long, relatively flat bottomland.

SUSPENDED CULTURE

Who else but the Japanese would think of hanging oysters in deep water in nets that look like immense Japanese lanterns? It must be perplexing to be an orca and come across a thousand oysters swaying in a giant mesh cylinder in thirty feet of water. These are the astronauts of oysterdom, floating in an environment their brethren could never imagine.

The Japanese have contributed much grace to oyster aquaculture, including the original longline technique of hanging spat-covered ropes, and later strings of spat-covered scallop shells, from long bamboo poles, but it's their hanging lantern nets that revolutionized the

West Coast industry. It took a mental leap on some genius's part. Oysters, after all, seem inextricably linked with *bottoms*, with reefs or sand or ledge. But what are an oyster's actual requirements? Nothing but temperate, plankton-rich water. Take young oysters, hang them in some channel with good flow, and they will grow fast and fat, living out their lives without ever knowing the taste of grit.

Suddenly, the world of oyster farming opens up. No longer are we limited to places with good bottoms. We could grow oysters in the middle of the Pacific if the algae were right and there were a way to keep the floating lantern nets stationary.

The first person in the United States to capitalize on the possibilities of lantern nets was Bill Webb, who in 1979 began growing European Flat oysters in them in Westcott Bay, off the coast of San Juan Island in Washington State. Westcott Bay is still one of the leading West Coast oyster farms. Today, many growers use suspended culture, either lantern nets or floating trays. Some raise oysters nearly a mile out to sea.

As you would expect for an oyster that never wallows in the mud with the sea slugs but instead soars with the eagle rays, a lantern-raised oyster is a beautiful thing to behold. Its shell is gemlike in form and delicacy—a delicacy that finds its way to the meat as well. Like milk-fed veal, these oysters have tender flesh that comes from lack of use. Some prefer the lighter taste and texture of a lantern oyster, some don't. But all agree that the fragility of the shell is a problem. Without tumbling in the waves and sand, or constantly opening and closing to escape danger and expel grit, lantern oysters have thin shells and weak adductor muscles. This is a problem for the guy shucking and serving them, who has to worry about broken shells and reduced shelf life. But it is not your problem if you order them at a restaurant. In fact, lantern oysters' shells display stunning patterns and delightful pastel colors.

Ways of dealing with the brittle-shell problem are just starting to emerge. Some growers periodically bring their oysters to shore and tumble them in big metal cylinders to rough them up. When tumbled, oysters go into repair mode, reinforcing their shells and building up their glycogen reserves for extra energy. Hugely labor-intensive, tumbling also manages to kill a fair number of oysters. Stellar Bay Seafarms, in

British Columbia, has invented specially shaped floating trays that fit right into a mobile tumbler, making the process faster and less stressful for the oysters. A lower-maintenance solution, invented in Australia and now being explored by Northwest growers, involves attaching weighted floats to spinning oyster bags. The floats go up at high tide, down at low, turning the bags of oysters gently, without human labor.

As these and other new methods take hold, expect to see deeper-cupped, harder-shelled oysters in the future—oysters that combine the best qualities of the farm and the wild.

HOW TO GROW A PEARL

For starters, *do not* grow a North American oyster. They don't make pretty pearls. Those are made by the pearl oyster, a creature of South Asian seas that bears as much resemblance to a true oyster as a flying fox does to a fox. In fact, pearl oysters are more closely related to mussels—which themselves can make freshwater pearls. There are numerous species of pearl oysters, the best being in the genus *Pinctada*, which includes the traditional pearls of Japan's Akoya oyster, as well as the silver and gold pearls of Australia's silver-lipped oyster and the famed black pearls of Tahiti's black-lipped oysters. All these pearls are cultured by inserting a tiny shell bead into the oyster—near its genitals, for maximum discomfort. Less than half the oysters survive this "insemination." The oyster coats the irritant with nacre, the same mother-of-pearl stuff it uses to line the inside of its shell. As the coats build up, a beautiful, perfectly spherical pearl forms.

What happens if you stick a shell bead in a true oyster? It will be irritated just as much as a pearl oyster, and will coat the bead with something, but you wouldn't call it a pearl. The difference is in the composition of the nacre. Both pearl oysters and true oysters use calcium carbonate to form their nacre (and their shells), but in structures that crystallize differently. True oysters produce calcite (common limestone), which makes dull whitish or brownish "pearls"; pearl oysters produce aragonite, whose crystal structure creates incredible iridescence as light breaks up in its depths. (Of course, creating beautiful gems is not the goal of the pearl oyster. Aragonite makes extremely fibrous, pliable shells, almost more like a plant fiber than the glassy, easily shattered shells of *Crassostrea* oysters.) The dull brown pearls from North American oysters make great mementos, but generally have no value. One exception occurred a few years ago, when a Connecticut oyster managed to make a black pearl that sold for thousands of dollars at Sotheby's.

THE TASTE OF AN OYSTER:
A PRIMER

AN AMAZING AMOUNT of ink has been spilled over the years in an effort to nail the taste of oysters. The essayist Michel de Montaigne compared them to violets. Eleanor Clark mentioned their "shock of freshness." M. F. K. Fisher was one of many to point out that they are "more like the smell of rock pools at low tide than any other food in the world." To the French poet Léon-Paul Fargue, eating one was "like kissing the sea on the lips." For James Beard, they were simply "one of the supreme delights that nature has bestowed on man. . . . Oysters lead to discussion, to contemplation, and to sensual delight. There is nothing quite like them." Something about them excites the palate, and the mind, in a way that other shellfish don't. You don't see cookbooks devoted to scallops, and you'd never have found M. F. K. Fisher writing *Consider the Clam*.

Yet something about oysters resists every attempt to describe them. If we didn't love them so, it wouldn't matter, but there's a tension and energy in the fact that we adore them, many others do not, and that we struggle to explain this mysterious love. The proliferating category of oyster adjectives—cucumber, citrus, melon, copper, smoke—is useful, but doesn't cut to the core. At some level, it's not about taste or smell at all. Because an oyster, like a lover, first captures you by bewitching your mind.

The Oyster Conversion Experience is remarkably consistent among individuals, genders, and generations. You are an adolescent. You are in the company of adults, among whom you desperately want to be accepted. You are presented with an oyster, you overcome your initial fear or revulsion, take the plunge, and afterward feel brave and proud and relieved. You want to do it again. Many authors have told their own version of the experience, including Anne Sexton in her poem "Oysters": "there was a death, the death of childhood/there at the Union Oyster House/for I was fifteen/and eating oysters/and the child was defeated./The woman won."

Some pleasures in life are immediate. Ice cream, sex, and crack all plug straight into our limbic system and get those dopamine centers firing. We don't need to think about whether we're having a good time. In fact, no thought is required at all. Other pleasures sneak up on you. Poetry, cooking, cross-country skiing. They may even feel like a challenge at the time. Only afterward do you realize how alive and satisfied you felt. Oysters belong to the latter club.

When you eat oysters, you wake up. Your senses become sharper—touch and smell and sight as well as taste. You carefully unlock the oyster, then make sure it is good before eating it. Like a hunter, you stay focused, alive to the world and the signals it sends you. You are fully present and engaged, not watching football while absentmindedly slapping nachos in your mouth.

Many oyster lovers mention the importance of ritual: the shucking of the oysters; the anointing with sauces; the lifting and tilting of the shells; the drinking of the liquor before, during, or after; and then the laying of the downturned shells back on the plate. Done properly, ritual still serves its ancient purpose—to raise awareness. Like the Japanese tea ceremony, a good oyster ritual has a Zen spirit. It allows you to mask the world and live briefly in the here and now.

And, like the Japanese tea ceremony, it is art as much as consumption. Its sensual pleasures go beyond taste. There are the soft purple, green, and pink watercolors of the shell; the need to read its geometry in order to open it easily. And once open, there is the absolute contrast of the oyster and the shell. Such softness within such hardness.

Art is something we experience not to fill any basic needs but instead to learn about ourselves and our connections to the world. Food is rarely art. We eat to fill our bellies. We eat to sustain ourselves. We eat because we must. Oysters come pretty close to breaking this connection. No one fills up on them. They are taste sundered from satiation. We do not eat them to satisfy any needs—except for our need to *experience*.

That's why, to me, there's something distasteful in the stories of Diamond Jim Brady downing three hundred oysters in a sitting, of Brillat-Savarin watching his dinner companion polish off thirty-two dozen. Part of the pleasure in eating an oyster is paying attention to this other creature, respecting it. It's a one-on-one relationship. By the time you have shucked the oyster, examined it, and slurped it, you have gotten to know that oyster pretty darned well. As with lovers, you can only shower that kind of attention on so many.

BUT WHAT DOES AN OYSTER TASTE LIKE, REALLY?

To understand the nuances of oyster flavor, it's necessary to unlearn the bad culinary habits America has taught us. Oysters don't taste like bacon double-cheeseburgers. They don't taste like Chinese barbecue. They don't even taste like grilled swordfish. They don't cater to our basic childhood preferences for sweet and fatty tastes, as so much contemporary food does. They are quietly, fully adult.

If you like sushi, then you are well on your way to liking oysters. Sushi has surely been a factor in the current oyster renaissance. It got a whole generation of Americans comfortable with the idea that their seafood need not be cooked, and that strong flavors were not automatically better ones.

Texture is a big part of sushi's appeal, and so it is with oysters. They are firm and slippery at the same time. Or should be. The farther south you go and the warmer the water gets, the softer the oyster becomes—*listless*, as M. F. K. Fisher put it. An oyster from very cold water, on the other hand, can be described as crisp or crunchy.

But we are getting ahead of ourselves, because oyster flavor, like perfume notes, comes in three stages, and texture is part of stage 2. The first stage involves salt, the second stage body and sweetness, and the third floral or fruity finishes.

Salinity is what hits immediately when you tilt an oyster into your mouth. It can be overwhelming, unnoticeable, or anywhere in between. Oyster blood is seawater, more or less, so oysters take on the salinity of their environment, which can range from 12 to 36 parts per thousand (ppt). In the role of primordial bar snack, to accompany a pint of lager, a fully saline oyster can be great. Crisp, crunchy, salty—all the same adjectives that typify a bag of potato chips can likewise apply to a plate of Maine oysters. But if you plan to have more than a few, you may soon feel like a kid at the beach who has gulped too much seawater. Salt overload. It's worth pointing out that salt and acid cancel each other on the tongue, so a squeeze of lemon or a touch of mignonette will substantially reduce the impression of salt.

Oysters with very low salinity, on the other hand, can taste flat, like low-sodium chicken broth. We have grown accustomed to a certain level of salt in almost all our food. People who grew up eating low-salinity oysters, however, prefer them, insisting that too much salt masks the buttery seaweed tastes that make oysters unique.

Most people prefer the midrange of salt. Such oysters provide plenty of taste interest up front, but allow the body and finish of the oyster to come through.

After the initial sensation of salt, you will sense the body of the oyster. For this, you will have to chew. Some squeamish eaters don't like to chew their oysters. I'm sorry, but chewing is where all the toothsome pleasure of the oyster comes out—the snappy way it resists your teeth for just a moment before breaking, like a fresh fig. Chewing also begins to release an oyster's sweetness.

In wine terminology, *body* refers to the way a flavor fills the mouth, and that's an important part of the pleasure of an oyster, too. Some just seem to vaporize. Others are dense with sweetness or savory richness. This doesn't always correlate with size. A tiny Olympia has plenty of body, while a large Gulf oyster can leave your mouth with very little sensation other than a compelling need to swallow. But, in general, a larger, older oyster is more likely to have a full body and an interesting palette of flavors.

Those flavors will be encountered during the third and final stage—what is generally known as the *finish*. These are the impressions that linger after you have chewed and swallowed, and sometimes they are truly surprising. Cucumber is the flavor most frequently cited, by which people mean the fresh, green, slightly bitter flavor of a garden cuke. Melon is another common note—not surprisingly, since cucumbers and melons are in the same family and share some aroma compounds. Of the oysters I've tasted, only Kumamotos have a true, sweet honeydew note. Many Pacifics have a hint of melon gone murky, as if you stored cantaloupe slices and sardines in the same refrigerator container. Some have a delicious finish that people call watermelon, but it's really the spicy, herbal taste you get from watermelon rind—unmistakable, but quite distinct from the taste of watermelon flesh. One of my favorite descriptions of oyster aroma comes from Luca Turin, the perfume expert, in *The Emperor of Scent*, and it isn't even describing an oyster. It's Calone, a molecule developed by French perfumers in the 1960s and described as "oysterlike." Turin, on the other hand, labels it "halfway between the apple and the knife that cuts it, a fruity turned up to a white heat." That nails the aroma of Pacific oysters.

All the fruity flavors ascribed to oysters belong to Pacifics and their little cousin the Kumamoto. Eastern oysters taste of the salty sea and various minerals, not fruit. Olympias and European Flats taste metallic and smoky. There are also various nutty, buttery, musky, algal, fungal, citrus, seaweed, black tea, and grainlike flavors that turn up in particular oysters.

Don't expect to identify these flavors the first time you taste an oyster. Think of the novice wine drinker in *Sideways* who, when asked to describe the flavor of a wine, says "fermented grapes." At first, oysters taste "oystery." But the more you taste them side by side, the more obvious the differences become. A world of wild and fascinating flavors opens up.

THE IMPORTANCE OF SEASON

The first Tatamagouche oyster I ever had was lousy. It had a big barnyard flavor, and I regretted having choked it down. After that I steered clear of Tatamagouches for a while. But then I was with some friends, and they were eating Tatamagouches and didn't look miserable, so I tried one. It was fantastic—plump, juicy, salty, and sweet with nutty petrol notes.

While it is possible to generalize about the taste of an oyster from a particular body of water—eat enough Hama Hamas, for example, and you will start to recognize certain shell patterns and flavor notes—any single oyster can deviate significantly from the norm. It may be noticeably different from its neighbor only a foot away, due to either genetic or environmental differences. It is an individual creature, and there is always some excitement and mystery as you unveil it in all its half-shell glory.

This is different from wine, where the grapes are all harvested in the fall, and the entire year's harvest gets mixed together. There can be considerable variation from year to year, but within a vintage each bottle holds the same mix. But every oyster is its own entity, and oysters are harvested to order. They will vary in flavor and appearance through the course of a year, depending on water temperature, algae availability, spawning, and other factors.

Enjoying a wine at its peak is like robbing a slow-moving train: You know when it will arrive, because of previous trains that were on the same schedule, so it is just a matter of being in the right place at the right time. You won't always time it right, but your odds are pretty good. Catching an oyster at its peak is more like trying to shoot a bat: There are short-term cycles and longer arcs, and it requires some skill and faith and luck. But when you hit it, you are giddy with excitement.

The biggest factor is season. The same oyster will taste different throughout the year. Those Hama Hamas, for instance, will taste sweet and salty in fall, buttery and fresh in spring, when months of rain have swelled the Hamma Hamma River, and thin and salty in summer, after they have spawned. (Some growers, in an effort to achieve product consistency, will "follow the salinity": upriver during droughts, down toward the sea when rivers are full. This only works if your oysters are in portable cages.) Chances are, the main difference in my two Tatamagouches was season.

Many oysters are referred to as sweet. No, oysters are never going to make it onto the dessert course. Sometimes *sweet* in regard to oysters is a euphemism for "not salty." It sounds better than calling an oyster "bland." But some oysters have a discernible sweetness, and most people, but not all, agree that a sweeter oyster is a better oyster. And sweetness is driven by season.

Ask an oyster farmer what makes his oysters sweet and he will say glycogen—the starch that oysters store as an energy supply. Ask any food scientist, and she will tell you that glycogen is tasteless. It might add body to an oyster's taste, but not sweetness. How to explain this disconnect? Well, starches are long chains of sugar molecules. Glycogen is made from glucose—the same kind of sugar we use in our muscles for energy. So while glycogen itself is tasteless, it can be broken down so that its glucose molecules fit snugly onto our taste buds that detect sugar. Voilà, sweetness! Our saliva is filled with enzymes that break down food (that, in fact, is saliva's job), and oysters themselves have enzymes that will start to break down their tissue once they are dead. The question is this: How much time does it take?

Most people don't chew their oysters long enough to get more than a whisper of sweetness on the finish. If you have an oyster fat with glycogen, and you chew *a lot*, you can get some real sweetness. But chewing an oyster twenty or thirty times is kind of like brushing your teeth for five minutes—it may sound like a good idea, but few of us are willing to do it.

A second source of sweetness in oysters may be glycine, the substance that gives shrimp and crab its sweetness. Glycine isn't a sugar, but it's one of several amino acids (protein building blocks) that taste lightly sweet to us. We may even have separate taste receptors for it.

An oyster stores food in two ways. In the fall, as the water cools, it eats as much food as it can, transforming that food into the glycogen that will keep it fueled through the dormant winter months when it doesn't feed. An oyster in December will be at its fattest, and then will slowly thin through the winter as it lives off its reserves. By April, it is pretty thin. But then the water warms up and swollen rivers pour nutrients into the estuaries, fueling the spring algae blooms. The oyster feeds again, but this time, instead of storing its food as glycogen, it stores much of it as lipids—fat—which is necessary for producing sperm or eggs. It will taste buttery and rich for a brief time, until those lipids get converted to sperm or eggs, at which point it develops more of an "organ meat" flavor. (Some people like the taste of a spawny

Eastern oyster. Nobody can stomach a spawny Pacific.) Depending on the warmth of the water and the type of oyster, spawning can take place anywhere from May to August. In the Gulf of Mexico and other points south, where cold water is not an issue, and where there is plenty of plankton year-round, oysters never go dormant. They will often spawn in sporadic trickles over months, rather than in a single spurt. They also don't need to store much glycogen, so they never get as firm and fat as a cold-water oyster in the fall.

When an oyster is full of glycogen and lipids, it looks plump and creamy white or ivory. That's what you want to see. It will taste firm, springy, and delicious. Transparency is a sign of a lack of glycogen— either it recently spawned or it just survived a long winter. At that time, it will taste like little more than a bag of saltwater. If it looks veiny, with bluish or whitish channels through the flesh, that's a sign that it's getting ready to spawn and is filled with gamete, not glycogen. Prick a spawny oyster and its liquid will look milky. Eat a spawny oyster and it will burst in your mouth like a greasy raw egg yolk.

On rare occasions, the water an oyster feeds on is so dense with a particular algae that it turns the oyster liquor blue, green, red, even gold. American restaurants don't bother trying to serve these, especially the reds, which make it look as though the shucker has cut himself. The enlightened ostreaphile, however, knows that the famous Marenne oysters of France are finished in shallow saltwater basins dense with a blue navicule algae that turns their liquor and their mantles green and gives them a singularly rich flavor. No doubt exotic flavors lurk in the blue, red, and gold oysters, too, but don't expect a wave of interest in the States. If you are French and you get a green or gold oyster, you squeeze yourself for joy, thank the gastronomic gods for delivering such a prize, and dig in. If you are American, you call the HazMat squad.

Not everyone prefers the algae-plumped oysters of spring and fall. A cadre of contrarians favor thin ones. Judy Rogers, for example, of San Francisco's Zuni Café, says, "I know I like 'leaner' oysters— literally, not full of food, stored as creamy glycogen, which is chemically equivalent to cornstarch. Leaner oysters have clearer, smaller meat and bright flavor notes, and they don't coat your mouth."

What Rogers may be responding to in leaner oysters is *umami*—a fifth category of taste, separate from the familiar quartet of sweet, salty, sour, and bitter. Umami is perhaps best described as savory. It's what makes chicken broth, soy sauce, and anchovies taste delicious. As with the other four tastes, we have taste buds specifically tuned to umami. If you love tea and tomatoes, you love umami.

The term *umami* comes from the Japanese word meaning "the essence of deliciousness." Most eaters would have no quibble with that claim. Free amino acids, especially glutamate, are responsible for umami. Since amino acids are the building blocks of protein, umami tends to be found in abundance in meat and fish products that are cured, aged, dried, or otherwise abused so that their protein breaks down into its constituent amino acids. Parmesan cheese, Prosciutto ham, and smoked salmon are umami powerhouses. So are oysters. When an Olympia or European Flat is compared to caviar or anchovies, that's the umami talking. When a Moonstone oyster is called brothy, that's umami. A thin oyster may not have much sweet, starchy glycogen, but it can still have plenty of umami.

We don't yet know what factors influence umami content in oysters. One may be minerals and metals. Ions of certain metals are known to break apart molecules in food. The most famous example of this is the copper kettles used to make Comte, Gruyère, and other cheeses, because the copper breaks the milk fat into delicious flavor compounds. Similarly, cast-iron pans and clay pots have long been known to impart good flavors to certain foods. Oysters are high in copper, iron, and other metals, and extraordinarily high in zinc (by far the highest of any food), so perhaps something similar happens in them.

One surefire way to increase umami in oysters is to let them sit in the fridge for a while. At 40 degrees Fahrenheit, they are dormant, but metabolizing ever so slowly, digesting their fats and glycogen in the effort to stay alive. As they metabolize without oxygen, they develop more propionic acid (found in milk and charcoal) and more amino acids—more umami. So an oyster that's been out of the water for a week will be more savory, and have different flavors, than one that was pulled out that day.

For most people, that isn't enough of a reason to let oysters sit.

Virtually everyone agrees that an oyster pulled straight out of the sea tastes better. Freshness, in fact, is the single most important factor. To get that fresh sea taste we all covet, the oyster's liquor must still be seawater, still alive and vibrating with microscopic life. After a couple of weeks, that liquor has been through the oyster a few times. It ain't bad, but it ain't seawater.

SUSTAINABILITY AND THE ENVIRONMENT: THE CASE FOR OYSTER AQUACULTURE

HUMANS AND OYSTERS have tangoed for a long, long time. Invariably the oyster comes out the worse for these encounters, whether we're talking the individual (eaten), the local population (evicted), or the species as a whole (decimated). The notion that this was an oyster's lot in life was already established in a French text of the 1400s, where the inhabitants of Orleans, under siege, lament, "Must we suffer these tribulations, like Cancale oysters?"

Europeans aren't the only offenders. All around the world, wherever oysters have grown, we find middens—vast shell mounds, the garbage dumps from prehistoric feasts or preserving operations. Some middens on the East Coast go back nearly ten thousand years, and some of these were in use for a thousand years. That's a long time to keep harvesting a resource from one place. Invariably, the middens contain larger oyster shells on the older, bottom layers and smaller shells on the more recent upper layers. The biggest, choicest oysters were eaten first, at a rate faster than they could be replenished. Then the biggest of the remainders were eaten, and on down through the generations, until, more often than not, no oysters were left at all.

Scroll through histories of the world's oyster hot spots and you will find eerily similar statements. In 1681 the French government declared France's natural oyster banks to be "inexhaustible." A mere seventy years later, they were quite exhausted. The same was true throughout Europe. On the west side of the Atlantic, explorer Henry Hudson in 1609 discovered a New York Harbor that was virtually paved with living oysters, 350 square miles of them, literally billions. In the Chesapeake Bay there were even more—so many that the residents

55

A vast shell pile in Long Island in the 1930s. (Courtesy Long Island Maritime Museum)

complained when forced to eat them. (Much as Down Easters considered lobster trash food until the twentieth century—and some still do.) But by 1891 the Maryland scientist William Brooks could already write, "The oyster property of the state is in imminent danger of complete destruction unless radical changes in the methods of managing the beds are made at once."

No one listened. New York's natural beds were gone by 1870, and even its cultivated beds were destroyed by 1920. Chesapeake Bay continued to produce three-quarters of the U.S. oyster supply, over one hundred million pounds in 1880. Then the collapse began. Fifty million in 1920, forty million in 1930, twenty million in 1960, and now far fewer than one million pounds. Only the Gulf of Mexico has managed to produce a steady twenty million pounds or so a year every year since the 1920s, and it continues to do so, interrupted only by the occasional hurricane.

On the West Coast, San Francisco forty-niners discovered the native Olympia oyster coating San Francisco Bay and attacked it with the same enthusiasm they showed for gold-bearing hillsides. In a handful of years the oyster was gone, and the miners cast their lusty eyes and bellies north. They found a mother lode in Shoalwater Bay (now called Willapa Bay), a shallow, perfectly protected estuary in Washington State, where no one but a few natives was plying what *The Fishing Gazette* later called "a table 24 miles long" piled high with oysters—again, literally billions of them. From 1850 to the 1890s Shoalwater Bay supplied most of San Francisco's oysters. Then they were gone. In the labyrinths of Puget Sound, Olympias held on until 1927, when floods of sulfites from a new pulp mill poisoned the species to the brink of extinction.

If this was simply the case of a particularly fantastic food source disappearing, it would be indictment enough. But it's more than that. We are only now understanding that oysters were the lynchpins of entire coastal ecosystems. Once they were pulled, the systems fell apart.

If you ever waded into Chesapeake Bay, or were cavalier enough to try the same thing in New York Harbor, you noticed that your foot disappeared by the time your knee was getting wet. You were in murkworld. You probably assumed that that is what water was supposed to look like in the mid-Atlantic. You were wrong. That murk was the sign of a very sick bay.

The early European explorers were blown away by the clarity of America's waters—including New York Harbor, Boston Harbor, and the Chesapeake—which stood in sharp contrast to their already mucky waters back home. That clarity depended on several factors. Mature forests and riverbank vegetation formed an interlocking mesh of roots that held soil in place, as well as a canopy of leaves that sheltered the ground from hard rains. As a result, very little sediment eroded into streams and made its way to estuaries. Logging and agriculture had not yet exposed vast acreage to erosion. Humans were not yet populous enough to contribute their own murk in the form of sewage and industrial pollution.

So the water that entered America's estuaries three hundred years ago was not nearly as high in sediment and nutrients as it is today. Those nutrients feed single-cell algae, which is as responsible for the opacity of our waters as is the sediment itself. There was less algae centuries ago, and what did exist must have been filtered by the oysters as soon as it reached the coast—they waited, lining every river mouth like a gauntlet, sucking in whatever came downstream. By filtering as much as fifty gallons of water per day, and cleaning that water of plankton and other microparticles, each oyster improved the clarity of its bay.

Clear water isn't just more pleasant to swim in. It allows sunlight to penetrate all the way to the bottom so that eelgrasses and other aquatic plants can grow. And those plants provide a host of benefits, stabilizing the bottom with their roots, creating shelter for juvenile fish and crustaceans, and providing food for larger fish. The grasses had the oysters to thank for the sunlight, but also for providing a firm and craggy substrate in which their roots could take hold.

The oyster reefs of the New World turned out to be the coral reefs of the temperate zone. Like the coral reefs, they were a skin of life atop a ledge of dead calcium carbonate. They harbored the same breathtaking diversity: a single square meter of oyster reef provided fifty square meters of surface area in the form of tiny folds and crevices. And they were just as sensitive to destruction. And they disappeared first, because people can't eat coral.

THE CASE FOR AQUACULTURE

The combination of overharvesting and increased erosion finished off virtually every natural oyster bed in the United States. As the beds emptied—Wellfleet, 1775; Manhattan, 1820; Narragansett, 1830; San Francisco, 1870; Long Island, 1870; Willapa, 1900—aquaculture stepped up to replace them. Leases of bottomland for oystering were first granted by New York State in 1855. Other states followed. This farming style of oystering came to dominate the industry by the 1880s, taking over for the fishing free-for-all that had preceded it. The transition was not smooth. Since the time of the earliest colonists (indeed, long before that) oysters had been a wild, public resource. All you needed was a skiff and a pair of tongs and you could be a bayman. An oyster farmer, however, needed to know that the seed he planted wasn't going to be fair game for any bayman who came along. The issue of private property reared its head. The baymen objected strenuously to any underwater areas being marked off-limits to them. They also worried, rightly, that powerful individuals and corporations would take over the business.

As a way to appease the baymen, states initially limited leases to a few acres per individual, and to this day they allow leases only on bottomland that doesn't have existing natural beds (a moot point). But by the 1890s commerce had run its ineluctable course, leases had changed

Shoveling fresh cultch from a barge onto oyster grounds in Long Island Sound, early 1900s. (Photo courtesy Long Island Maritime Museum)

hands and pooled in the largest hands, and a few corporations based in Connecticut and New York City came to own tens of thousands of acres of leases and dominated the industry north of the Chesapeake.

The baymen went down fighting. Their natural beds destroyed, their resentments high toward the corporations they believed had stolen their waters, they turned to piracy more than once. In 1893 five sloops appeared three nights in a row on the leased beds near Blue Point in Long Island and dredged thousands of bushels of oysters. Though security guards launched a steam-powered boat and actually rammed one of the sloops, the pirates fired back with pistols and the security guards had to retreat.

That was the baymen's last hurrah. Thankfully so, because the only hope for oystering in America depended on the transition from a hunter-gatherer mind-set—get the resources before your neighbor does—to a farming one, where an individual was invested in a particular place and had an incentive to manage the resource so it could produce in perpetuity.

To be a good steward, you need to understand the needs of your flock. Oyster businesses on both coasts, as well as in France and Japan, spearheaded the science of oyster cultivation, learning a few things about oyster biology along the way. Modern aquaculture was born.

The first thing most people do upon being told that 95 percent of oysters are farmed is to wrinkle their noses. "Farmed? I don't want farmed oysters. I want the wild ones." An understandable reaction, particularly in this era of factory farms. We don't want a chicken from a factory because it's been tortured—debeaked, stuck in cages so small that it can only stretch one wing at a time, shot with antibiotics, and so on—and because, due to lack of exercise and a grain diet, it doesn't taste much like a chicken, or anything else for that matter. We want a free-range chicken that got to use its muscles and to eat grass and grubs and a variety of natural foods that help give it, and its eggs, flavor. I'm in full agreement. But there are no free-range oysters. Oysters don't range.

Today, the primary difference between a wild oyster and a farmed one is that the wild oyster led a fairly miserable existence, stuck in the mud, gasping for breath, while the farmed one was lifted out of the mud—at least in its youth—where it could get the best food in the water column. Centuries ago, wild oysters weren't growing in the mud; they were growing on the reefs of their forebears, which served the same purpose as aquaculture equipment does today—to provide structure. If you want to eat an oyster that lived under conditions similar to those that made oysters famous in the early days of America, you need to look to aquaculture.

But *aquaculture* is a dirty word, thanks to salmon farms. The biggest problem is the feed. Fish meal—a mix of ground fish, grains, and, frequently, antibiotics—gets dumped into the salmon pens in vast quantities. Some of it goes into the salmon, some settles to the seafloor, and even most of what goes in the salmon eventually comes out the salmon. This feed, like fertilizer, lawn runoff, or sewage, is full of nitrogen and phosphorus, the nutrients that promote algae growth and toxic algae blooms, leading to turbid water where plants can't get enough sunlight to grow. The decaying algae, in turn, uses up the oxygen in the water, leaving "dead zones," which are becoming all too common along the world's coasts. In North America, at least, salmon farms have lately cleaned up their act, reducing antibiotics use and improving their food conversion ratio from 5:1 to 1.2:1. Today shrimp farms, a huge industry in Asia, are worse offenders.

Not oyster farms. With fish or shrimp farms, you pour tons of nutrients, in the form of feed, into the water, remove a portion of those nutrients in the form of fish, and leave the rest. The end result is a steady dumping of nutrients into the sea. With oysters, the equation is reversed, for the all-important reason that oysters don't need to be fed. Oyster farmers don't put anything into the water except oysters, and they don't take anything out of the water except bigger oysters. Think of oysters as nutrient sponges: You dip them in the water, they soak up nutrients and get plump, then you take them out.

Over its lifetime, a three-inch Eastern oyster is responsible for removing about 2 grams of nitrogen from the water. In Chesapeake Bay, a billion harvested oysters (a shadow of the historical number) could remove about 4.4 million pounds of nitrogen per year—only a fraction of the hundred million pounds a year that still needs to be reduced to restore water quality, but a huge help all the same. The Chesapeake Bay Foundation, working with oyster farmers, such as Travis and Ryan Croxton and Tommy Leggett, sponsors programs encouraging individuals, schools, businesses, and anyone else with water access to grow oysters, with the goal of increasing the population to the point where natural sets in the billions are once again possible.

As a group, oyster farmers are rabid about water quality. Their livelihood depends on it. Bad water equals no oysters or oysters that can't be sold. Oyster farmers end up devoting a lot of time, energy, and money to improving water quality in their area. Thus, an indirect product of oyster farms is often the improved conditions of the watershed. Oysters are the canary in the coal mine. If you can eat the oysters, the watershed is doing pretty well. If you can't, work needs to be done.

For inspiration, consider Drayton Harbor, a well-sheltered horseshoe of tideflats straddling the Washington/British Columbia border. The city of Blaine dominates Drayton Harbor and is an old oystering town. The 1909 edition of the *Blaine Journal* included this poem:

> *The oyster beds on Jersey's Coast*
> *Have justly won a name.*
> *But we grow better flavored ones,*
> *Yes sir, right here in Blaine.*

But by 1999, sir, they didn't grow *any* oysters in Blaine. All of Drayton Harbor had been closed to shellfish harvesting because of

Oyster restoration project on the Chesapeake's York River. (Photo courtesy NOAA)

poor water quality. A citizens group called Farmers of the Tideflats, led by Geoff Menzies, decided to change that by starting a Community Oyster Farm. In 2001 they planted Pacific oyster seed on two acres of tideflats. For those oysters to be approved for harvest in the future, water quality would have to be significantly improved, which made a palpable goal for spurring local citizens, corporations, and the city of Blaine to clean up their act. Studies were commissioned to find the sources of pollution. The Blaine sewer system was repaired. The twenty dairy farms in the watershed adopted manure-control systems. And water quality quickly recovered. In 2004, 575 acres of Drayton Harbor were approved for shellfish harvesting. Most of the oysters from that first harvest, growing since 2001 in rich waters, were already seven inches long—too big for American consumers—so they were sold to China, where large oysters are popular. As of 2006, the Community Oyster Farm has harvested 65 tons of oysters. Proceeds from the sales are funneled back to the oyster farm and the ongoing watershed-improvement projects.

I feasted on Drayton Harbor oysters in 2006, and they were some

Joth Davis, grower of Baywater Sweet oysters, spraying shell into the water for the Puget Sound Restoration Fund's habitat enhancement project. (Photo courtesy Puget Sound Restoration Fund)

of the best Pacifics I've ever had. Rich and sweet, they demonstrated the potential of Drayton Harbor—and the potential of oyster aquaculture to help build a clean, sustainable, and profitable future along our coasts.

The bottom cages used by some oyster farmers can also improve the ecosystem. They serve as artificial reefs, providing shelter for numerous small critters and footholds for aquatic plants. Juvenile lobsters, crabs, and fish love to hang out in the cages. Striped bass, winter flounder, and shad are attracted to the area. Oyster farmers have noticed that sport fishermen tend to congregate around their lease sites, because that's where the fish are. And the fish are there because the small fry are there. And the small fry are there because the oyster cages are there.

But cages are still in the minority of aquaculture techniques. Bottom culture dominates. And its overall impact depends on how the oysters are harvested. The hand-picking and tonging methods that have been discussed are ecologically benign, but they are limited to shallow-water sites. In other areas, including most of the East and Gulf Coasts, a dredge must be used. In addition to the big metal baskets dragged behind a boat on cables, there are vacuum dredges that suck the contents of the bottom up to the boat in tubes. Dredging will destroy a thriving seabed.

This sounds bad, but few, if any, oysters are being dredged from pristine bottomland. Most remaining undisturbed bottomland in North America is already in marine parks and other conserved areas. Oyster dredgers are often working marginal habitat—land that has been hammered for generations and has little but mud on it. Places like Long Island Sound and the Louisiana coast.

Complaining about an oyster farmer working the same leases he has for decades is a bit like objecting to the local farmer planting another corn crop on the family field. Sure, he could stop farming, let those acres go wild, and improve the habitat. But we don't think that way about terrestrial farming. After all, we gotta eat. Returning America's agricultural land to wilderness and growing less food is not realistic. The goal is to grow food lightly on the land.

All sources of food have their costs. Terrestrial farming, even organic, involves huge expenditures of fertilizers, water, electricity, and fossil fuels. Poultry, pig, dairy, and cattle farms produce tremendous amounts of nitrate pollution. Commercial fishing has decimated species after species. Compared to any of these, oyster farms are a godsend. They use amazingly little energy, leave the environment cleaner than they found it, and produce a delicious food of the highest nutritional value.

WHAT KIND OF OYSTER EATER ARE YOU?

DIFFERENT OYSTERS SUIT different occasions and different people. If you haven't yet been wowed by oysters, you may well have been dallying with the wrong ones. Maybe you hate the mouthful of salt you get with Eastern oysters and love supersweet Kumamotos. Maybe you like bold, gourmet oysters with brassy, lemony finishes. Or maybe that's not you at all. Maybe, for you, heaven is a plate of petite oysters accompanied by Champagne, candlelight, and the perfect dinner companion. Don't endure the duds in your search for a compatible oyster. Save yourself time, money, and heartbreak by picking your profile below, then finding your matches.

THE SHRINKING VIOLET

You're not sure about this whole oyster thing, and need some convincing, preferably with the lightest-flavored, smallest, least intimidating oysters possible.

Beausoleils are the East Coast model—delicate, salty, with a fresh biscuit aroma. Many other New Brunswick oysters, such as **La Saint Simons** and **Caraquets**, also have a small size and a clean finish. On the West Coast, **Kumamotos** are every beginner's favorite oyster, and **Kusshis** are reliably small, pretty, creamy, and mild.

THE BRINE HOUND

Bring on the salt! Chips, pickles, olives—you love 'em all. If you could drink seawater, you would.

Look for oysters grown in or near the open ocean. Maine and Massachusetts provide some of the briniest, with **Pemaquids, Glidden Points, Wiannos,** and **Wellfleets** leading the pack. **Island Creeks,** from Duxbury, can be extraordinarily salty, and **Cuttyhunks** come from an island off the coast of Cape Cod that has no rivers. **Olde Salts,** grown near Chincoteague Bay, are one of the few briny Virginia oysters. Pacifics tend to be less salty than Eastern oysters, but **Snow Creeks** fit the bill, and **Willapa Bay** is famous for its salty oysters. **Bahia Falsas** and **El Cardons**, from Baja California, may be the saltiest oysters on the planet.

THE SWEET TOOTH

Salt? Yuck! But there is nothing quite so divine as the creamy sweetness of a superplump oyster.

Forget Eastern oysters. The kind of sweetness you're looking for can only be found in a **Kumamoto**—sweetest of the sweet—and some Pacifics. **Totten Inlets** are reliably sweet, **Baywater Sweets** and **Hog Island Sweetwaters** amazingly so. **Nootka Sounds** and **Chelsea Gems** also deliver the goods.

THE GRAIL SEEKER

Wellfleets? Westcotts? Been there, done that. You've had all the common oysters and want to taste new ones no one has heard of. And you're willing to travel.

If you haven't yet had the unique **Olympia**, that should go to the top of your list. It doesn't travel well, so you'll probably need to visit Washington State. **Colville Bays** are easy to find in PEI but rarely seen elsewhere. Sweet **Drayton Harbor** oysters aren't sold commercially; you'll need to visit the Community Oyster Farm in Washington State. **Whale Rocks** are rare Connecticut oysters from the Mystic River. **Chiloes** made some brief appearances in the United States but now are hiding out in Chile. **Sydney Rock Oysters** are the favorite Down Under and may begin appearing in the United States. To find the real grail, go to Brittany and get yourself a bona fide **Belon**.

THE CONNOISSEUR

You want the best oysters in the world, price be damned.

Tiny, intense **Olympias** are the demiglacé of oysters, a perfect reduction of tasty flavors. **Penn Cove Selects** and **Hama Hamas** are more satisfying in size, with the bright green flavors that mark the best Pacifics. **Kumamotos** have unmatched fruitiness—though **Hog Island Sweetwaters** give them a run for their money and balance the fruit with perfect brine. **Westcott Bay Flats** deliver a refined, metallic zing that can be found only in a European Flat. Among Eastern oysters, **Colville Bays** have full citrus flavor and perfect salinity; **Glidden Points** are big and briny. For mineral-rich, savory intensity, **Moonstones**, **Oysterponds**, and **Widow's Holes** are your best bets. Some feel that a **Totten Virginica** combines the best of both coasts in one oyster.

THE WILD ONE

Forget those hatchery-raised wimps. You want a natural-set oyster that survived the one-in-a-million journey from egg to adult.

Olympias are natural-set—and native, of course. **Hama Hamas** are still grown from natural sets in Hood Canal. Most **Apalachicola** oysters are completely wild, born and raised in the flats of Apalachicola Bay and harvested with tongs. **Gulf** oysters are generally wild, as are many **Malpeques, Caraquets, Tatamagouches, Bras D'Ors, Martha's Vineyards,** and **Chesapeakes**. But if the call of the wild is what you're after, consider harvesting your own. Many state parks, particularly in Washington State, have oyster seasons.

THE WINO

Those potent, briny, musky oysters are as overblown as an Australian Shiraz.
You like to savor oysters with wine, so you want subtle mineral flavors,
not metal and salt and mud.

Kumamotos are Sauvignon Blanc's best friend; their clean melon flavors bring out its fruitiness. **Westcott Bay Petites** and **Stellar Bays** are both creamy and mild, not too salty, with no clashing bitterness. Eastern oysters are tougher matches for wine, but buttery **Watch Hills** have a full-bodied flavor that can be terrific with sharp, flinty wines, and **Rappahannock Rivers** bring out the minerals in some white wines. **Beausoleils** have a supreme lightness that is heaven with Champagne.

THE BOLD

Bring on the tangiest, muskiest, biggest, most challenging oysters possible.
You don't scare easy.

Damariscotta Belons are your Everest. **Snow Creek Flats** are your K2. Any European Flat is going to test you. Large Pacifics can also have intense and exotic flavors, particularly those from southern Puget Sound. **Skookums** will push the musk as far as you want to take it. **Hammersley Inlets** aren't far behind. Any extra-large oyster will deliver sheer chewing intimidation.

THE CLEAN FREAK

You prefer filter feeders from pristine waters.

Two Canadian oysters from opposite ends of the country grow in national parks: **Raspberry Points** in Prince Edward Island National Park and **Imperial Eagle Channels** in Pacific Rim National Park. **Nootka Sounds** grow in an area of British Columbia *less* populated than Pacific Rim National Park. **Canoe Lagoons** hail from Alaska's seventeen-million-acre Tongass National Forest, where the bears outnumber the people. **Drake's Bays** are screened from all of California by the bulk of Point Reyes National Seashore. **Cuttyhunks** live in solitary splendor on the deserted west end of Cuttyhunk Island, ten miles off the Massachusetts coast.

THE JEWELER

You eat with your eyes as much as your belly, and you love the gemlike shells of some oysters.

Suspended culture—floating trays or lantern nets—is the best way to preserve the colors and patterns some oysters develop on their shells. **Carlsbad Blonds** display black-and-white fan patterns. **Kusshis, Stellar Bays,** and **Hog Island Sweetwaters** have smooth, deep, purple-black shells. **Imperial Eagle Channels** and **Nootka Sounds,** two oysters from West Vancouver Island, have art-deco swirls of pink, purple, and green. Oysters from **Samish Bay,** including **Penn Cove Selects** and **Naked Roy's Beach,** have impressively fluted shells.

THE MINISTER OF SILLY NAMES

For you, half the fun is the goofy things oysters are called.

Naked Roy's Beach and **Moonstone** are named for nude beaches. **Fanny Bays** might as well be. **Tatamagouche, Malagash Thrumcap, Nootka,** and **Hama Hama** are just plain fun to say. **Tomahawk** has a certain retro charm. A **Stingray** is cool, a **Kusshi** is cute, and who could forget their first **Carlsbad Blond**?

THE APHRODISIAC ANGLE

SURE, THEY TASTE great and they're fun to eat. But let's cut to the chase: Will oysters inflame desire? The Romans certainly thought so. Oysters were standard fare at orgies, and Galen, the second-century physician, prescribed them for impotence or flagging desire. Casanova liked eating them raw in the tub with a lady friend—or two. But where did this idea come from?

There's no denying that some oysters, shucked properly, can look more than a little labial. Does this excite anyone? Apparently so. The thrill, I suppose, is in coaxing the creature, breaking down its resistance, and then savoring the goods. It's ritualistic foreplay. A drunken *bon vivant* in a Montreal oyster bar once held forth on this subject for quite some time, and ended by telling me passionately, "There is no bigger turnoff than taking your date out for a nice dinner and discovering that she won't eat oysters!"

Oysters have been pegged as erotic food for millennia, and originally it had to do with their lifestyle. To get to the root of this notion, we need to talk about pomegranates, another ancient aphrodisiac. Consider the structure. Open them up, and red, ripe seeds come bursting out. Most of their mass is devoted to reproduction. Thus, following the classical belief that Like Makes Like, if you eat them, they will help you reproduce, too. (Some other Like Makes Like aphrodisiacs include figs, which resemble seed-filled testicles, and a tiger's penis, which is fairly self-explanatory.) So it was with oysters. They are copious reproducers. A female can produce millions of eggs, a male more than a billion sperm. They expend themselves fully during reproduction. Many die afterward. A creature so devoted to sex made more than one person think, "Whatever they've got, I wanna get me some," and oysters' reputation was sealed.

Is there any truth in it? Oyster experts tell me they're not sure, but have volunteered to collect more data. Science-minded types attempting to justify the "Viagra in a shell" legend always fall back on zinc. Zinc is a mineral the body requires for all sorts of functions, including the generation of testosterone and sperm. Oysters are zinc superstars. They are the Lance Armstrong of zinc—so far ahead that the second-place guy isn't even in sight. So, yes, if you have a zinc deficiency (common among vegetarians) and you eat a heap of oysters (uncommon for vegetarians), you might start to behave more manly and make a whole bunch more sperm. Maybe Galen was onto something. But if you are a typical red-meat-eating, testosterone-making male, extra zinc won't do a thing for you. And consider this: that distant second-place finisher in the *Tour de Zinc* is liver, not exactly everybody's favorite aphrodisiac.

Still, the anecdotal evidence is strong. A certain oyster bar proprietor tells me that a certain famous reporter credits the conception of her twins to a meal of oysters she had at his bar that night. Many people know that an evening of oysters and Champagne often ends amorously. There *is* something about oysters. Those of us who eat them regularly have all observed their druglike effect. Down a dozen oysters, and you start to feel a surge of well-being. It's not subtle; you feel as if you could run a marathon—or pin your dining companion to the wall in a potent embrace. No zinc is responsible for this. To explain it, I'm going to have to get all New Agey on you.

Asian medicine, which had been successfully healing people for thousands of years when Western doctors were still bleeding patients with leeches, is based on the concept of *chi*—the invisible life force that flows through all living things. The food we eat plays a huge role in keeping our *chi* healthy and balanced, but the food itself doesn't have much *chi*—that disappeared shortly after it was killed or harvested. Oysters, however, are like little *chi* bombs. Perhaps that surge we feel is a temporary explosion of life force, and those desires we feel a quite natural wish to share the wealth.

Or there may be an even simpler explanation. Who out there is eating raw oysters? It isn't the middle-management paper-pusher picking up a burrito on his way home. It's the experimenters, the explorers, the risk-takers, the people who want to know the world and all the things it has to offer. Eating a raw animal pushes the envelope of what most Westerners consider normal. It's borderline taboo, so only taboo-breakers need apply. Which makes raw-oyster-eating a beautiful selection process. Just go to an oyster bar, look around, and know that you are among the other sensualists, those who love delight and aren't bashful about embracing it.

THE OYSTER
APPELLATIONS
OF NORTH AMERICA

NAVIGATING THE WORLD
OF OYSTER NAMES

ALTHOUGH WINE HAS been made in France since Roman times, not until the 1920s was a system created for establishing name and quality control. Before that time, certain wines had established strong reputations for themselves, but nothing stopped unscrupulous growers from appropriating those names for their inferior products. It took crises—the phylloxera epidemic of the nineteenth century, World War I, and the economic ruin and ensuing fraud triggered by both—to spur growers and the government to work together to create rules governing wine's geography and growing practices. After the *Appellation d'Origine Contrôlée* regulations passed in 1935, one knew that a Volnay, for example, came from the Burgundy village of that name and was made from Pinot Noir grapes, not Gamay or any other. The result of the appellation system is that the name of a French wine is much more than just geography. It is a (theoretical) guarantee of quality.

The oyster world is just beginning to sort this out. Everyone recognizes that particular places produce oysters with certain characteristics, but there is no consensus about what to do about it. There are unwritten laws—name your oyster for its home waters—but few written ones. Thus, there's nothing to stop John Doe of Florida from calling his oyster a Wellfleet, except the ire of the Wellfleet Chamber of Commerce and, one would hope, the undying scorn of ostreaphiles everywhere.

The few laws that have been created have proved ineffectual. New York State passed a law in 1908 stating that an oyster must spend at least three months in Long Island's Great South Bay to be called a Bluepoint—the most marketable name. But no other states paid attention, and today a Bluepoint has little geographic meaning. This situation will be familiar to anyone who was drinking wine in the United States in the 1970s, when any jug of cheap red wine would be labeled "Burgundy," and any cheap white would be called "Chablis." Things got straightened out with wine, and they will with oysters.

Fortunately, the abuse of the Bluepoint moniker is the exception to the rules. Most oyster growers are proud of the local flavor of their oysters and eager to trumpet that in the name. You can trust that a Quilcene came from Quilcene Bay and a Wellfleet lived its life on the Cape Cod flats. As more people learn to recognize oyster *terroir* and develop personal favorites, the naming system should become more regulated. For now, it's best to follow rules similar to those for choosing wines:

LOOK FOR PRODUCERS YOU TRUST

Wine drinkers know that even within a well-respected Burgundy appellation, you can get a good bottle or a boring one. So, in addition to the area, they learn to look for particular producers who do things right. With oysters, one producer in a bay may use different culture techniques from his neighbors, or may let his oysters get larger and more flavorful. Some producers may crowd their oysters more than others. Some are far more rigorous about culling ones that don't meet specific size and shape requirements. These producers are generally going to trademark their product as a way of distinguishing it. As you parse an oyster list, some oysters will be listed by geography, and some by brand. For example, a Stingray is grown in the Chesapeake and could be labeled as such. Unlike most Chesapeakes, however, Stingrays are grown from selected seed in off-bottom cages and culled to high standards, so the name has more meaning than *Chesapeake* would. In this book I list oysters by trade name, if they have one.

SMALLER APPELLATIONS CAN EXIST WITHIN LARGER ONES

The basic French appellation Bourgogne (Burgundy) covers an area 180 miles long from Chablis in the North to Beaujolais in the South.

Any wine in that region can call itself *Bourgogne,* yet within the region are at least seventy-five smaller appellations that are generally considered better, and growers will use one of those labels if they qualify. The same is true with oysters, though it's all self-policed. Any oyster from Hood Canal might be labeled as such, and an unknown grower could get some instant name recognition by using that name, but growers in Hood Canal's Quilcene or Dabob Bays will likely use those names, which have more specificity. And growers who have monopolies on certain Hood Canal river deltas, such as Dosewallips and Hamma Hamma, will take advantage of those unique names.

MICROCLIMATE MATTERS

So you once ate a British Columbia oyster and it sucked. Does that mean you write off BC oysters forevermore? Certainly not! It could have been one bad oyster, it could have been the season, or it could be that you don't care for oysters from that area of BC.

With oysters, microclimate matters. A stream emptying into one corner of a bay can change all the conditions of the local oysters' lives—temperature, salinity, food supply, mineral concentrations. Willapa Bay has one salty end and one sweeter end. Salinity on the Chesapeake ranges from less than 5 ppt near Baltimore to well over 20 in Virginia. You can generalize about macro regions like the Chesapeake or British Columbia the same way you can about large wine regions like Burgundy or Mosel: Broad statements about the species and style of oyster will hold, but hiding out in unknown inlets may be gems, or duds, that break all the rules.

When it comes to finding these unknown great oysters, we are still on the frontier of a New World. Legions of wine writers have trampled every corner of the globe, stomping out all wine secrets. With oysters, much mystery remains. This book provides some initial maps and impressions of the geography, but it's like the early explorers' maps of America: It might help you get your bearings and chart your course, but you never know what you'll find until you start navigating those bays, rivers, and fjords for yourself.

* * *

A practical note: The species of oyster is not always stated in the appellation listings, but it is simple to determine. All East Coast and Gulf Coast oysters are *virginica* unless they are called *Belons* or *Flats,* in which case they are *edulis.* All West Coast oysters are *gigas* unless they state their species in their name: *Kumamoto, Olympia, Flat,* or *Virginica.*

MARITIME PROVINCES

NEW BRUNSWICK

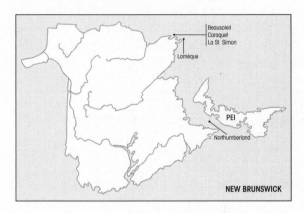

The granite and sandstone coastlines of New Brunswick make for gritty beaches and well-nestled bays that warm the cool St. Lawrence waters as the summer sun hits their shallow, sandy bottoms. For a brief stretch, water temperatures climb to swimmable levels, and oysters can spawn. There are only a few places in eastern Canada where the water gets warm enough to support natural colonies of oysters. Caraquet Bay has been New Brunswick's best for centuries. The two great names in Canadian oysterdom are Caraquet and Malpeque, the provinces' answer to Bluepoint and Wellfleet.

But Caraquets are not Bluepoints or Wellfleets. They are small, and that smallness is what distinguishes New Brunswick oysters. You don't eat New Brunswick oysters because they are big, powerful, briny, or unusual. You eat them because they are delicate and dainty and in-offensive.

Who wants a dainty oyster? Well, a lot of people. Think back. Even if you are an intrepid eater of fat oysters redolent of algae and manganese, there was a time when you had to work up the courage to slip one into your mouth. I don't know what oyster started your career, but how nice for you if it was a crisp and blameless little two-inch Caraquet, instead of some monster Elkhorn staring you down.

Caraquets are the oyster next door. In fact, most New Brunswick oysters fit that bill. Cold brackish waters with moderate levels of algae and a long, long winter keep them that way. They're a cheap date, too. For half the price of more sophisticated oysters, you can get a little ex-perience under your belt. If you haven't been around much, and the music and mood are right, you just might fall in love.

THE NEW BRUNSWICK OYSTERS TO KNOW

BEAUSOLEIL

Beausoleils are farmed in three bays of northern New Brunswick: Shippagan, Néguac, and Richibuctou. Basically, they are suspended Caraquets, never touching the seafloor. In fact, Maison Beausoleil col-lects the seed from the wild waters, so some Beausoleil oysters are in-deed Caraquets by birth. Half the year they grow in floating bags near the surface, enjoying as much warmth and food as the Canadian coast has to offer. When Canada's dark winter sets in, they are suspended in deeper waters to ride out the ice.

Because of their carefully controlled, uncrowded environment, Beausoleil shells are always perfect. Not big—it still takes them four years to reach a 2½-inch cocktail size—but well groomed, and so uni-form they almost look stamped out by machine. The white shells have a classy black crescent. The flavor is refined and light, like a Caraquet, but with a bit more brine, and something of the yeasty, warm-bread aroma you get with good Champagne. This makes them the perfect starter oyster. If I had a novice oyster eater in my care and wanted to guarantee a successful first experience, I'd order a dozen Beausoleils.

Beautiful Sun is a lovely name for an oyster that does all its growing in the short and sweet Canadian summer of seventeen-hour sunlit days, but it draws on history, too. *Beausoleil* was a leader, actual name Joseph Broussard, in the Acadian Resistance against the British in the 1750s. He captured many British ships on the St. Lawrence before himself being captured. Eventually, he was allowed to lead his people to Louisiana, where no doubt he was demoralized by the quality of the oysters.

CARAQUET

The famous oyster of the Maritimes, a staple among fishermen and loggers forever. In fact, if you want to look like an old-timer, stomp into a pub, the rougher the better, slide a plateful of shucked Caraquets into your pint of beer, and chug it. I guarantee that interesting conversation will ensue.

Caraquet is still a traditional fishing community. That, along with its excellent beaches, is a good reason to visit. You can enjoy beachcombing and boat-watching, along with top-notch seafood and tourism kept down to a dull roar.

The Caraquet grows wild in Caraquet Bay in northern New Brunswick, where the cold waters and short growing season mean that it takes about four years for a typical oyster to reach a mere 2 to 2½ inches in size. It's small, but mature, and has the firm texture and deep cup (for its size) typical of slow-grown oysters. You can also find fancier Caraquets that are farmed in suspension—generic Beausoleils. In flavor, the Caraquet flirts with nonexistence: a hint of brine, a tickle of amino acids, and it's gone.

LAMÈQUE

Lamèque Island forms the eastern boundary of Caraquet Bay. That makes Lamèque oysters slightly more exclusive Caraquets. Like Caraquets, they are small and delicate, with pretty white-and-green shells. In my experience, they are a bit brinier than Caraquets, perhaps because they are a bit closer to the sea. Nice little oysters.

LA SAINT SIMON

Refined, brown-shelled, light-bodied oysters from Shippagan, one of Beausoleil's homes. It would be easy to mistake these clean 2½-inchers for Beausoleils. They seem equally uniform in their smooth teardrop shapes. Tray-cultured in similar ways, they make decent substitutes, though their gray flesh is more salty and less creamy. Still, they have genuine sweetness and make excellent ambassadors to the land of the oyster-shy.

NEW BRUNSWICK FLAT

European Flat oysters are few and far between these days, so jump on any chance you get to sample these. Then you can curse me, because the metallic, citrus-and-fish-sauce flavor is not many people's cup of tea. (Come to think of it, "oversteeped tea" would be a fair description of their tannic nature.) The texture is remarkably firm.

NORTHUMBERLAND

The Northumberland Straits separate Prince Edward Island from the mainland of New Brunswick. So the *Northumberland* appellation could fall under either New Brunswick or PEI jurisdiction. Either way, it's not a great oyster. Harvested wild from the straits, it's very mild in flavor, long and skinny, and much bigger than other New Brunswicks, usually hitting at least four inches. According to Canadian fishery regulations, it's graded *standard*, which is one grade below *choice* and one above *don't be a fool*.

PRINCE EDWARD ISLAND

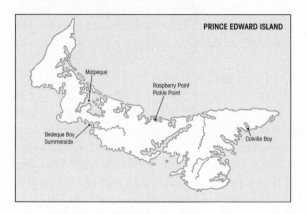

It's early morning on Malpeque Bay, PEI, and through the soft fog you hear the sound of two-stroke engines hacking to life. You ride out of the harbor in a fifteen-foot dory that seems too small for commercial use. Everything in the dory is quickly soaked by the mist, but then the air clears and beneath you, through ten feet of water, you see them, as if a wrecked treasure galleon had spilled gold coins across the bay: oysters everywhere. You anchor and get out your tongs—fourteen-foot, hinged wooden poles with teeth at the ends for grabbing oysters. Slowly, painstakingly, you fish up oysters, a handful at a time, and deposit them in your boat. Across shallow Malpeque Bay, as the rising sun beats the water blue and silver, a hundred fishermen in a hundred dories like yours are making their living, tonging gold from the bay.

This is the essence of the Malpeque oyster, Canada's most famed. Malpeques are some of the finest wild oysters on the East Coast. At first the story of their success and failure has a familiar ring to it, but then it takes a surprising and inspiring turn.

Jared Diamond's best-selling book *Collapse* is subtitled *How Societies Choose to Fail or Succeed*, and in it he offers portraits of many societies that collapsed under the weight of poor environmental choices, as well as a few that teetered at the brink and managed to turn themselves around. Most societies that have faced ecological doomsday, such as the Maya, the Anasazi, and the Norse Greenlanders, saw the edge of the cliff and ran off it without even slowing down. The same could be said of the New York and Chesapeake oyster fisheries, as well as the New England cod fishery, which sped up their rates of harvesting even as the problems became clear, and ran their fisheries into extinction as fast as they could.

But a few societies managed to change their ways as things got bad, and that was the case with the PEI oyster fishery. PEI is at the very northern tip of the Eastern oyster's range, so the same oyster that reaches three inches in a year in the Chesapeake or two years in New York takes four to seven years in PEI. You'd think if any oyster population were the first to go, it would be the slow-replenishing PEI one. But PEI also had a few things going for it, namely a small, manageable number of fishermen and a forward-thinking regulatory agency.

Still, things did get bad. The early peoples of PEI feasted on the native oysters, and the Acadian settlers of the 1700s followed suit. By the 1800s Malpeque oysters had a reputation throughout Quebec. The industry got serious, and what a perfect setup it had. No braving the rough seas in big, expensive ships, just row your dory into your local bay, pull up some oysters, row them back to the nearest cannery, and you've made your nugget for the day. By the turn of the twentieth century PEI oystermen managed to do what oystermen everywhere have done: The fruitful waters of Bedeque Bay were empty, and Malpeque Bay wasn't far behind. The solution was the same hit upon by baymen to the south, with the same disastrous results. Seed oysters were brought up from New England to restock the local beds, bringing with them a disease that Maritime oysters had never seen before, forever after known as Malpeque disease.

The mortality rate was 90 percent, and for two decades the oyster industry in PEI was dead. But by the 1920s evolution had taken its course. Disease-resistant oysters began to appear. Careful coddling of these hardy survivors produced a population that began to thrive. It also produced a new emphasis on cultivation and conservation that continues to this day.

For instance, those dories. You won't see big dredges plying the waters of Malpeque Bay as you do on Long Island Sound, Chesapeake Bay, the Gulf of Mexico, and Willapa Bay. You won't even see the little dredges used by smaller oyster operations. Wild Malpeque oysters are harvested by tongs from a dory. Not even *hand-picking* is allowed. It sounds crazy for a twenty-first-century industry, but it works. Besides, it makes the photo-snapping tourists delirious.

In addition to the regulations, the PEI oyster fishery is aided by strong cultivation techniques. Yes, these are wild oysters, but they are given a lot of encouragement to make more wild oysters. During the summer spawn, ships drag special collectors behind them in the water, catching as many larvae as possible. Beds of clean shell are laid down (about one hundred acres a year of bottomland are improved this way) for the spat to nestle on. And small oysters are often relayed to better grounds as they mature. So Malpeque oysters are natural, yes, but not ferociously wild.

All this help explains why PEI oyster landings have taken off in the past twenty years, from three million pounds in the 1980s and 1990s to four million in 1998, six million in 2000, and more than seven million now. PEI produces 80 percent of eastern Canada's oysters.

Not all are wild. Oyster farming is going strong in PEI, too, using some suspension culture but mostly bottom-planting. No matter what technique is used, farmers and fishermen alike must face a cold fact of life about PEI, indeed about all the Maritimes: They are going to be iced in from December through April. Not just the bays and harbors, but the surrounding ocean, too. The public fishery in PEI ends in November. Aquaculture operations have no such regulations, but many farmed PEI oysters are available only into December or January, when harvesting becomes too difficult or risky. Other operations cut the ice with chainsaws and keep on harvesting. Virtually everyone shuts down in April, when the ice is still too thick for boats but too soft to walk on.

That cold climate has many advantages. PEI oysters mature slowly and have good firmness because of that. And PEI waters are so cold that the oysters rarely spawn before mid-July, meaning that if you want to eat oysters in May or June, PEI should be near the top of your list.

THE PEI OYSTERS TO KNOW

BEDEQUE BAY

This open bay on PEI's Northumberland Straits coast may be PEI's best oyster region. In addition to providing the excellent Summerside oysters, it's responsible for Bedeque Bays, harvested from the sheltered waters of Salutation Cove. Oysters in Bedeque Bay grow faster than any others on PEI—two or three times faster! Partial thanks for this goes to the strong tidal surge that comes around Cranberry Point and replenishes the bay twice daily, as opposed to the slower-flushing Malpeque Bay. Bedeque must also have dense algae populations for PEI, which would explain the stronger flavor of Bedeque Bays and Summersides—compared to the uncommonly light flavor of most Maritime oysters.

CANADA CUP

Canada Cups are actually a brand created by American Mussel Harvesters, a large shellfish distributor based in Rhode Island. They deal with many oyster growers in PEI, and select from them all for their Canada Cups. What defines a Canada Cup is not place but characteristics: three inches in size, a decent cup shape, a nice clean shell. That makes Canada Cups consistent, reliable, and affordable, but not exhibitors of any particular *terroir*.

COLVILLE BAY

If I could eat any oyster from PEI, it would be a Colville Bay. Sometime-lobsterman, full-time-oysterman Johnny Flynn grows Colville Bays near his home, where the mouth of the Souris (that's "Surrey") River empties into Colville Bay on the southeast coast of PEI. They are unparalleled oysters. Stunning teardrop-shaped, jade shells let you know they are different right away. Delightfully crunchy texture and sweet meat confirm their excellence. A Colville Bay starts off with medium salt, then fills your mouth with nutty, popcornlike flavors, and finishes with a lingering floral lemon zest.

Johnny Flynn with his oyster racks
at the edge of the Souris River.
(Photo by Marialisa Calta)

For those flavors, thank the plankton-rich Souris River, which constricts just before entering Colville Bay and acts like a natural up-weller, aerating the water and churning it before shooting it over the oyster beds. The phytoplankton fuse to the growing oyster shells, which can be emerald in fall or aquamarine in summer. The river mouth is rich in eelgrass, too, and everywhere you find good eelgrass, you find scrumptious oysters. (And often vice versa.) Flynn grows the young oysters on French Tables—ten-foot rebar "tables" set off the bottom on short legs. Each table can hold about twenty bags of oysters. The oysters spend two years or more on the French Tables, then are broadcast on the bay bottom where they spend at least another two years. They are harvested by tong at a size of three to five inches—choose the larger ones if you can—and an age of four to five years.

Colville Bays travel well. They are one of the few PEI oysters with a part-time intertidal life, growing shallowly enough that on the strongest tides, around the full moon and new moon, they are exposed for hours. They clamp down hard to protect themselves, and a lifetime of this gives them massive, stratified shells and Arnold Schwarzenegger adductor muscles—contributing to their firm texture and their ability to survive for weeks out of water.

Alas, if you can find Colville Bays in the United States, you are having a very lucky day. Boston-based Legal Seafoods used to buy three thousand a week, but Flynn tired of the customs paperwork and no longer ships his oysters out of Canada. And there's your excuse to go to PEI. Rent a cabin on the pounding north shore, spend the day touring the lush green pastures of the interior, and then, toward evening, swing by Johnny Flynn's farm and let him rustle up a few dozen jade gems. Then it's back to the cabin to sip some ale and shuck your Colville Bays and send the shells hurtling back into the sea from which they came.

MALPEQUE

Malpeques have taken the world by storm in the past twenty years, and now rival Bluepoints as the most common restaurant oyster, partly because they are affordable. As such, they have been great ambassadors, convincing many a diner that oysters were more exciting than she'd realized. They are good transitional oysters, bigger and bolder than Beausoleils or Kusshis, but still light-bodied and clean on the finish. Easy to eat, with the perfect balance of sweetness, brine, and picklelike liveliness, they make great accompaniments to a pint of lager. Part of their appeal is due to the nature of Malpeque Bay. The bay is not great oyster habitat, if by great habitat you mean warm water and plenty of food. Getting bigger is a struggle for oysters in Malpeque Bay, not just compared to New England and points south but even compared to other PEI oysters. An oyster in Bedeque Bay, on PEI's southern, Northumberland Straits side, can grow an inch and a half per year, while the same oyster in Malpeque Bay will grow less than half an inch. That's why Malpeques come to market at a minimum of four years of age and more commonly six. They are old oysters, with the pleasant concentration old oysters usually have, but with none of the powerful, exotic flavors you find in Pacific and some East Coast oysters.

At least, the good ones are like that. Malpeques vary. Many

oystermen and purveyors sell Malpeques. Unless you know your source, you can never be sure exactly what you're getting. Many Malpeques, in fact, are fished from Bedeque Bay or other more fecund grounds and relayed to beds in Malpeque Bay or elsewhere. All the name *Malpeque* really signifies is that the oyster is from PEI.

Wherever they were born, Malpeques can be anywhere from three to six inches in size, from relatively flat to deep-cupped, from nice and round to banana-shaped. The whitish shells are touched with green and brown and always sturdy. Sadly, in the past few years, some lesser Malpeques have been appearing. As more people in the United States ask for Malpeques, harvesting pressure grows. And with so many people harvesting and selling Malpeques, it becomes nearly impossible to control the quality. Even if you are an oysterman with the highest standards and you toss back all but the best, somebody else will come along beside you, scoop up your rejects, and sell them.

In Canada, all oysters in the public fishery are graded. The two top grades are *choice* and *standard*. There are lower grades, but you don't want any part of those. Go for *choice* if you have any choice; those have the deep, round cups that give you enough meat to know what you're tasting. The *standards* have good flavor but less meat and curvy shells that are more difficult to shuck.

Malpeques have great availability in the spring, summer, fall, and early winter, then become more scarce in January as ice seals off the bay.

PEI SELECT

These are the oysters that get cut from the Raspberry Point team (see below). A lesser—but more affordable—oyster, ideal for cooking.

PICKLE POINT

An oyster farmed by the same two men, James Powers and Scott Linkletter, who grow Raspberry Points. Pickle Points, which, like their namesake, have a lovely green sheen, are grown right around the corner in PEI National Park. In that pocket, oysters grow at glacial speeds, contributing to Pickles' wonderful bite and heft.

RASPBERRY POINT

Raspberry Points are one of the great success stories in oysterdom. Fifteen years ago who had heard of a Raspberry Point? Now they are everywhere. You will encounter them often, and they are worth trying. They are consistently good—salty like a Malpeque, but always nicely rounded and substantial. Raspberry Points are famed for their clean finish. Once my novice oyster eater had enjoyed some Beausoleils, I'd move him up to a Raspberry Point—a bigger mouthful, more crunch, lots of salt, and it goes down so easy. Think of a Raspberry Point as a medium-sized Malpeque that's perfect every time. You'll pay more for that assurance, but you'll never get a disappointing oyster, which you can't say about Malpeques anymore.

It's hard to imagine a more pristine spot than Prince Edward Island National Park, on the chilly north shore of PEI, and that's where Raspberry Points grow in off-bottom cages. Keeping them off the bottom gives them lighter flavor and nicely manicured shells. But it's cold up here at the northern tip of the oyster's world, so Raspberry Points take a whopping six to seven years to reach their standard 3 ¼-inch size.

The same guys who grow Raspberry Points also grow Pickle Points and PEI Selects, but Raspberries are their flagship oyster, and those are the ones to try.

And no, they do not taste like raspberries.

SUMMERSIDE

A great oyster from PEI's southern side. As briny as a Malpeque, but bigger, deeper-cupped, and more satisfying. The aptly named town of Summerside is on PEI's summery south side and is the second-largest city on the island—though, PEI being PEI, it still has only fifteen thousand people. Summerside's leafy streets and stately homes look out on Bedeque Bay, prime oyster habitat.

You may encounter oysters called *Sunnysides*. These are grown in the same bay as Summersides, but are a trademarked name.

NOVA SCOTIA

Nova Scotia is not a leading producer of oysters, but it certainly leads in the category of Silly Oyster Names. Pugwash? Tatamagouche? Malagash Thrumcap? Blame the Mi'kmaqs, the Maritimes' first resident oyster aficionados. *Tatamagouche* means "meeting of the waters" in Mi'kmaq. *Pugwash* means "deep water." *Malagash* means "ruffled water." Pretty much everything in Mi'kmaq seems to refer to water, which tells you a lot about their interests.

But we can't blame the Mi'kmaqs for Lady Chatterley and French Hooter. (*Huitre* is French for oyster, thus "French Hooter.") Folks in

Nova Scotia are having some fun, and why stop them? I myself am not going to be ordering a Lady Chatterley anytime soon, but who can resist a Tatamagouche?

Nova Scotia has two very different coastlines, producing different styles of oysters. Its northern coast is a continuation of the Northumberland Straits that run between New Brunswick and PEI, and the oysters share the clean and mild characteristics of those coasts, though the harvesters tend to let them get bigger in Nova Scotia. It's a pretty land of saltwater marshes and wheat and corn fields.

The other oystering hot spot is Cape Breton Island, the rough and ready "lobster claw" of Nova Scotia, thrusting its tangled forests and thousand-foot cliffs into the Atlantic. Cape Bretons are true ocean oysters, higher in brine, with less of the mineral subtleties of their Northumberland cousins. They also come from perhaps the cleanest waters in the Atlantic, with nothing but miles of rock and woods in all directions.

THE NOVA SCOTIA OYSTERS TO KNOW

BRAS D'OR

The immense saltwater Bras D'Or Lakes nearly turn Cape Breton Island into a doughnut shape, with them as the doughnut hole. The channel to the sea is small, but the lakes aren't fed by any sizable rivers, so the oysters stay brinier than you might think. Other than brine, they are very light in body—a quintessential Maritime oyster. The lakes themselves are stunning, but there's *nothing* there. Just seventy-one miles of forests and sheep, windswept meadows, and a few minor villages. Such untrammeled nature is good for oysters, though perplexing. This should be Lake Tahoe East. Thank God it's not, for the sake of the oysters and everyone else.

Chances are your Bras D'Or oysters will be from Alba Oyster Farm, where Melissa and Bill Maclean collect their own wild spat in May and grow the seed oysters for a full year in floating trays, near the surface in summer and down below the ice that covers the lakes the other half of the year. The oysters are gently placed on the bottom of the lakes, where they spend three more years slowly marinating in the Atlantic brine.

CAPE BRETON

Cape Breton is a catchall name for any oysters coming from the island. They can vary from medium to full brine, from medium to large in size. No guarantees.

CAPE NORTH

Grown by Scott Brown at the northern extreme of Cape Breton Island, these are very unusual oysters. The four-inch emerald shells are almost clamlike in appearance: spade-shaped, smooth, rock-hard, and oddly symmetrical for an oyster—it can be hard to tell which is the "flat" side. I don't know how you get shells like these, but I know it doesn't happen quickly; Cape Norths can be eight years old at harvest. They are briny, as you'd expect coming from a spot sticking out into the North Atlantic, very meaty, and otherwise light in flavor.

MALAGASH THRUMCAP

Malagash Thrumcap sounds like something that comes up at an Audubon Society outing: "Hey, is that a scarlet tanager?" "No, by golly, it's a Malagash Thrumcap!" But Malagash is a village, on the tongue-twisting highway between Pugwash and Tatamagouche, and it's my favorite oyster name to say. The oyster itself is secondary to the name. It's another of those wild, mild, bottom-grown Northumberlandy oysters, big and long with a greenish-white shell and an irregular cup. It's firm, as all the slow-growing Canadian oysters are, with a mild vegetal flavor.

NOVA SCOTIA BELON

A farm-raised European Flat oyster. The East Coast equivalent of Westcott Bay Flats, this "Belon" has the lighter brine and gentler flavor of its French namesake, due to being kept off the bottom. With no East Coast hatchery currently selling Flat seed, it's unclear how long this oyster will be around.

TATAMAGOUCHE

A big, sandy-colored oyster that is gaining in popularity, no doubt because of the lively name. Tatamagouche is a charming little fishing village on the Northumberland Straits, and I suspect its oysters are all wild, because they rarely possess the perfect almond shape of farmed ones. In fact, they are often long, skinny shoehorns, and the meat can be watery and tasteless. It can also, however, be extremely choice, ivory-colored and nutty, with a lot of body and medium brine. Tatamagouches are available May through early winter, but avoid them in summer, when they can be spawny. Oddly, this village of six hundred hardy souls hosts the second-biggest Oktoberfest in all of Canada. If you don't think that's a reason to end up there in October, with nothing to do but eat the freshest oysters and drink the freshest beer, then you may want to reconsider your value system.

MAINE

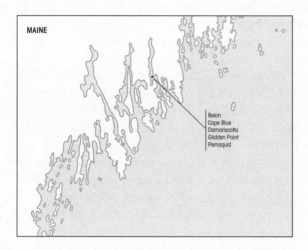

MAINE

Belon
Cape Blue
Damariscotta
Glidden Point
Pemaquid

In most people's minds, Maine is lobster country. But the same frigid ocean, terminal moraine, and unpolluted coastline that grows such happy crustaceans also makes for beautiful bivalves. Maine is geologically distinct from the rest of New England, as a quick glance at a map will prove. Instead of the many south-facing saltwater "ponds" that line the coast of Massachusetts, Rhode Island, and Long Island, Maine has innumerable fingers of land reaching into the Atlantic. Between these thin fingers run the famed rivers—Androscoggin, Kennebec, Sheepscot, Damariscotta. In these estuaries, fed by Maine's robust tides, grow oysters that are distinctly Maine, as salty as a Camden sea captain.

Maine waters are *cold*. Not only are they colder than southern New

England waters, they are sometimes even colder than the waters of the Maritime Provinces to the north. They get no help from the warm Gulf Stream (as do Nova Scotia oysters), from shallow straits (Northumberland oysters), or from large, sheltered bays (PEI and New Brunswick). Summer waters in PEI can be *ten degrees* warmer than summer waters in Maine.

Maine oysters grow slowly, though not as slowly as their PEI counterparts. While Southern oysters can reach market size in a year or less, a Maine oyster needs three years minimum. A four-year-old, cold-water Maine oyster has a glorious depth of texture and flavor, a deep cup, and a beautiful green-and-white shell, sometimes edged with purple, that can be remarkably tough and hard-bitten, like Down Easters themselves.

The Maine Coast is a land of tenacious traditions, and so far Maine has produced traditional oysters. Yes, aquaculture has been embraced, but within certain bounds. You won't see any of the suspended culture techniques used on the West Coast; Maine oysters are predominantly bottom-planted in estuary basins. You won't see any beach culture, either. Though you'd think intertidal culture would be the perfect method for Maine, where ten- or twenty-foot low tides commonly reveal quite a bit of real estate, it just isn't done. A few factors work against it. One is the weather: A clam that buries itself in the muck can survive a few hours of brutal midwinter cold, but an oyster will freeze. A still bigger factor is politics: Those clams are an archetypal part of Maine, and the last thing a lot of people want to see is oyster farmers squeezing out the clams. The state controls subtidal leases and encourages oyster aquaculture, but individual towns control intertidal leases and are more conservative. For now, at least, the oysters get the depths and the clams get the mudflats.

The Damariscotta River estuary, midway up the Maine coast, has been ground zero for oyster lovers for thousands of years. High up the estuary sits the Glidden Midden, an enormous hill of oyster shells dating back more than two thousand years. The mound is thirty feet high, runs along the river for 150 feet, and contains some oyster shells a foot long. It took Native Americans a thousand years of tossing shells on the scrap heap to create it. If people come back to the same spot for its oysters for a thousand years, that's a pretty good testament to the quality.

That quality still exists. Among Maine's string of finger estuaries, the Damariscotta River stands out. It's the best spot in Maine for growing oysters, and contains three of my favorites: Glidden Point, Pemaquid, and

The town of Damariscotta at the head of the Damariscotta River, within sight of the floating nurseries of several oyster farmers. (Photo by Bill Kaplan)

the rare Damariscotta Belon, perhaps the strongest-flavored oyster in North America. Virtually any oyster from the Damariscotta is going to be tasty, thanks to the shape of the basin. The Damariscotta runs wide and deep fifteen miles inland to the town of Damariscotta and beyond to Damariscotta Lake, giving plenty of room for growing oysters. Cruise the jade-colored river and you will see buoys marking leases lining both shores, with a tight navigable channel in between. Within a stone's throw of each other you'll find the growing areas of Glidden Point, Pemaquid, Dodge Cove, Hog Island, Mook Seafarms, and many other leading oyster producers. This river is the Northeast's Cote D'Or.

That wide, flat basin makes for plenty of brine, too: The estuary is less than 1 percent freshwater, so its oysters have the full salinity of the open sea. Stand at the bridge in Damariscotta, fifteen miles upriver, as the tide comes in, and you can see that ocean surging under you and continuing powerfully upriver.

Unlike most Maine and Maritime Province oysters, which would be overwhelmed by such salinity, Damariscotta oysters have the body and sweetness to balance the brine. We may have clay sediment to thank for that. In bygone days the Damariscotta was a brick center; at least four major brickyards operated on its shores. You see their work in the handsome redbrick downtown of Damariscotta and in the many bricks still tumbled in its waters. You even find wild oysters that have set on bricks. The clay that fueled those brickyards may contribute to tasty oysters; everywhere oysters are grown in clay-rich substrate, they seem to be full-bodied.

Other estuaries in Maine resemble the Damariscotta from the

Four Maine oysters (from left): Glidden Points, wild Damariscottas, Sheepscots, and scallop-shaped Belons. (Photo by Bill Kaplan)

surface, but oysters from their waters look and taste very different. The Sheepscot, for example, the next estuary to the south, produces oysters with less brine and body than the Damariscotta, and with a powdery shell, perhaps due to freshwater acidity.

Even wild oysters, which disappeared decades ago, are making a comeback on the Damariscotta. Maine's wild oyster population went extinct by the 1950s. Historically, the waters in Maine were too cold, even in high summer, for farmed oysters to spawn much, if at all. (For this reason, triploid oysters have never been used in Maine.) But as cold-water broodstock has been developed, and especially as global warming has brought record-warm waters to Maine, spawning has become more common, and many of those spat have set up shop along the river. The first strong wild set occurred ten years ago. Now all those wild oysters spawn, too. A healthy rebound seems under way. It's worth looking for the ridged shell pattern of wild Damariscotta oysters for sale if you're in the area.

The Damariscotta feels deeply Down East. Gray, shingled cottages peek out from the unspoiled banks. Bald eagles fish from its pine-lined promontories. Horseshoe crabs scuttle over the oyster-tiled bottom. The brown heads of curious harbor seals pop to the surface and follow the oyster boats. Visit in summer and the cool green water is a pleasant relief from the heat. Other times of year the Damariscotta is cold, foggy, isolated, and foreboding—for city-dwelling *Homo sapiens*, at least. For an oyster, it's heaven on earth.

THE MAINE OYSTERS TO KNOW

BELON

Belon is a river in France famed for succulent oysters. Belon, you will point out with a pinch of Gallic disgust, is *not* in Maine. No, but the oyster that made Belon famous—the European Flat—is. Scientists brought European Flats to Boothbay Harbor, Maine, in the 1950s to see if the skinny oysters would grow there. They wouldn't, at least not while the scientists were watching, so the scientists gave up. The oysters, however, did not. Enough escaped (for an immobile animal, oysters have escape rates that rival Houdini's) to establish pocket colonies from Kittery to Ellsworth. Over the years a few farmers have grown European Flats from seed and marketed them as Belons or Maine Belons, because nobody knew what the hell a European Flat was. Barb Scully of Glidden Point used to plant 400,000 Belon seed every year. Today, no hatchery is selling Belon seed, so no farmers are growing them, but the descendants of the escapees are still out there, battling the cold and sediment and Bonamia. These wild oysters are as powerful as any on the planet, redolent of fish and zinc and umami—not for the faint of heart. They tend to be on the chewy and dry side, but that goes with the *edulis* territory. They are also the favorite oyster, bar none, of Sandy Ingber, executive chef at the Grand Central Oyster Bar. A minuscule five thousand Belon a year are pulled in Maine and sold, making them one of the rarest oysters in the world. If you are lucky enough to get your hands on a few, savor them. You may hate them, you may love them, but they will definitely make an impression.

CAPE BLUE

There is a little point in the Damariscotta River called Hog Island, and there is a little aquaculture firm there called Hog Island Shellfish. Problem is, one of the best-known oyster companies in the world is California's Hog Island. Confusion reigns. To avoid trouble, Maine's Hog Island is sold under the name Cape Blue. So a Cape Blue is a Hog Island is a Damariscotta. Got it?

DAMARISCOTTA

An oyster labeled simply *Damariscotta* (or, occasionally, *Dam River*) could be coming from many different small-time harvesters. It could even be wild. It should be salty, full-bodied, and clean finishing, but there are no guarantees.

PROFILE

Glidden Point

THE OYSTER

Glidden Points stand out on raw-bar lists for their size, crispness, brine, deep cup, and rock-hard shells. What I always notice is their weight. Hold a Glidden Point in one hand and a different oyster in the other and you will immediately notice the heft of the Glidden Point. Both the shell and the meat have a density that comes only from slow growth in cold water. They are four years old when they reach market size, unusually rich and springy.

Glidden Point shells are a natty white and black. The greenish algae that colors many shallow-water oyster shells can't thrive at the depths where Glidden Points grow. Due to their size and thickness, the shells seem daunting, but they are among the easiest to open. Once an oyster reaches a certain size and age, a notch forms between the hinges that is made-to-order for an oyster knife. And the strong shells aren't prone to break.

Given their size and intense brine (about 32 ppt), Glidden Points do *not* make good starter oysters. I once made the mistake of offering one to an enthusiastic and curious eight-year-old boy. The oyster filled his mouth and his cheeks bulged. He worked gamely at it, chewing for a good minute. But at some point something changed on his face, enthusiasm faded, and I saw it just wasn't going to happen. Out came the oyster. Save Glidden Points for those veteran eaters who know they are getting a rare and spectacular jewel from the Maine sea.

THE PLACE

Most farmers grow their oysters in just a few feet of water; Barb Scully grows hers forty feet down in the Damariscotta, making them perhaps the deepest- and coldest-grown oysters on the East Coast. "My bottom sites are deeper and colder than most growers would find tolerable," she says. "I chose my sites just for that reason, because it was doing something different from what everyone else was doing. It could have sunk me." The basin has plenty of deep holes where oysters do well, growing slowly but steadily, protected from the heat of summer and the deadly cold of winter. The basin features four constrictions from its mouth to its headwaters, where a huge volume of water is forced through a small space. In places, the water seems to boil. This upwelling effect mixes nutrients and oxygenates the water, allowing oysters at the bottom of the Damariscotta to get more food than they normally would at that depth.

Barb Scully's children, Morgan and Ben, getting ready to turn floating bags of Glidden Point seed on the Damariscotta River. (Photo by Bill Kaplan)

THE PRODUCER

Barb Scully is a straight shooter. She looks you right in the eye when she talks. And what she talks about is the challenge of growing the perfect oyster. "I can grow an oyster right here in my cove from seed. It will take five years to reach market size, but it will be the roundest, plumpest, coolest-looking oyster. It will be perfect. But I'd starve. . . . The other extreme is people who grow oysters in suspension the whole time. Yes, they can get a four-inch oyster in eighteen months, but it's brittle, so it's hard to shuck, and it doesn't have a cup. In essence, it's large seed. The trick is to balance the two. You need to get a quicker return on your investment than five years, but not so fast that quality suffers. It doesn't make a lot of sense to me to devote my life to doing something mediocre."

In her quest to grow the best oyster, Barb does everything by hand. Pure muscle and sinew, as you'd expect from somebody who has been at this for twenty years, she is the only oyster farmer in the country who harvests her oysters primarily by diving. Hand-picking off the bottom is gentler on the oysters, preserves the bottom ecology, and doesn't disrupt oysters that aren't yet market-sized. Of course, forty feet down in frigid water murky with plankton means zero visibility; the harvesting is all by feel. Sound fun? Barb used to do it all herself, and used to do it year-round. Once, diving in midwinter, she came to the surface and discovered that an ice sheet had drifted down the river and taken her boat with it. She had to swim to shore and walk home in a frozen wet suit. Another time, she rose from the bottom with her oysters and hit her head on an ice sheet that had drifted over her dive site. She had to scramble to find a new hole.

Even when things went well, winter harvesting in Maine was a stretch. People don't like that weather, and outboards don't like that weather. If in January your boat is filled with five thousand oysters and suddenly your motor won't start, you have about twenty minutes before your oysters freeze. Barb now stops harvesting from January through mid-March.

Barb Scully started her oyster farm in 1987. A job with the Department of Marine Resources required her to travel the entire Maine coast, and she fell in love with the Damariscotta River as soon as she saw it. She lives right at the oyster farm in a classic gray Maine house, with several million oysters in her backyard. She purchases cold-water oyster seed from local hatcheries in May, then grows these seed oysters in floating trays on a two-acre lease in the warmest surface waters of the Damariscotta estuary, within sight of the town of Damariscotta itself. As late in fall as possible, usually around the first of November, they are bottom-planted on a ten-acre and a five-acre lease in the deepest parts of the estuary for the next three years or more.

Barb keeps 15,000–20,000 oysters—what she ships in a typical week—in "wet storage," floating in trays in her cove. Because they are bottom-cultured, they need about a week in wet storage to purge themselves of sediment. They are brought ashore to fill orders.

Glidden Points are well established as one of the world's great oysters. They are a mainstay at many leading oyster bars, and are one of the better summer oysters to choose, since the cold water keeps them crisp and sweet.

The most satisfying way to score Glidden Points is to visit Barb Scully's tiny honor-system store right next to her house, five miles down the River Road from Route 1 in Newcastle. Inside you will find a cooler with perfect Glidden Points ready for the taking. Pick out your oysters, leave your money in the basket, drive a mile up the road to Dodge Point Public Lands, find yourself a good spot on the banks of the Damariscotta, and swallow your oysters within spitting distance of where they grew.

PEMAQUID

Another brilliant oyster from the deepest holes of the Damariscotta River. *Pemaquid* means "long finger" in Abenaki—a fitting name for the ten-mile peninsula that forms the Damariscotta's east bank and ends with the iconic Pemaquid Point Lighthouse. You could shout back and forth from the Pemaquid and Glidden Point shellfish lease sites and be heard clearly. The oysters are equally close in character. Pemaquids are even brinier than Glidden Points, very firm, deliciously lemony and light, with a rock-hard brown-and-white shell. Sometimes you'll encounter three-inch Pemaquids, which have less flavor; ask for the more interesting four-to-five-inchers. It's hard to believe an oyster that substantial could taste so clean.

SPINNEY CREEK

A company that specializes in relaying oysters from elsewhere and depurating them in special equipment. Very safe, but very mild, oysters.

MASSACHUSETTS AND RHODE ISLAND

MASSACHUSETTS AND RHODE ISLAND

Duxbury
Island Creek
Wellfleet
Plymouth
Rock
Cotuit
Wianno
Naragansett
Quonset Point
Umami
Martha's Vineyard
Cuttyhunk
Tomahawk
Whale Rock
Moonstone
Watch Hill

Mention the state of Massachusetts, and just one name surfaces in the mind of the typical oyster eater: Wellfleet. Wellfleet is a noble name in the lineage of oyster towns, and rightly so: The shallow bays of that famous Cape town produce the same excellent oysters they have for centuries. Wellfleets appear on virtually every raw-bar menu, and will deliver an ultrabriny mouthful every time.

But the intrepid oyster eater will certainly want to explore the geography of New England oysters beyond Wellfleet's well-mapped shores. Wellfleet is actually an anomaly. We have to leave the Outer

Cape entirely to find the other jewels—oysters that rival any in the world—which come from the southern salt ponds of Massachusetts and Rhode Island.

Why southern? To understand that, we need to detour by way of Geology 101.

The story of New England is the story of ice. From the valleys of Vermont to the peninsulas of Maine and the tumbled coastal islands of Massachusetts, Rhode Island, and New York, glaciers have been the dominant shaping force of the past eighty thousand years.

When we think of glaciers, we tend to picture cute little rivers of ice, but the most recent glaciers covered northern New England in an ice sheet a mile high. Every feature you can think of was buried under this ice. A mile of ice is pretty damned heavy, and the ice had quite an impact on the ground beneath it. The weight and force of the creeping glacier scraped the bedrock like a bulldozer plowing a field, ground it up, and pushed this layer of rock and sediment with it, sometimes hundreds of miles.

The ice pushed past the New England coast, where warming temperatures finally halted its advance about eighteen thousand years ago. The bulldozer paused, then slowly backed up. You can see exactly where the ice stopped advancing because it left a wall of rock and gravel, called a terminal moraine. We call this wall Long Island (especially Montauk and the South Fork), Block Island, Martha's Vineyard, and Nantucket. As temperatures fluctuated, the bulldozer returned a second time with a new wall of material, but didn't get quite as far. This second wall became the North Fork of Long Island, the coast of Connecticut and Rhode Island, the Elizabeth Islands, and the Upper Cape.

Sea levels were lower in that cold time, so the terminal moraine of Long Island and the Massachusetts islands formed a dike, inside of which were freshwater lakes in the area now filled by Long Island Sound, Narragansett Bay, and Buzzards Bay.

The tongue of any glacier is a torrential river of meltwater carrying the sediment the glacier has picked up on its journey. When that outwash hits a lake or sea, its movement stops and the sediment filters out. Throw a handful of dirt and rocks into water and the big rocks drop immediately, the sand takes longer, and the tiny clay particles take forever to settle out. That's just what happened as those glacial rivers funneled sediment into the lakes. The layers became stratified, with the heaviest sediment on the bottom and the smallest—clay and silt—on top.

As global temperatures warmed over the past fourteen thousand years, the seas rose and eventually breached the dike of the moraines, filling Long Island Sound and the other coastal bays with saltwater. Suddenly, those nutrient-rich, south-facing bays and ponds became ideal oyster habitat—except that young oysters couldn't survive in the soft clay bottoms. The bay waters continue to be filled with calcium for shell growth and other minerals for flavor, and with perfect salt levels, but they now require humans to nurture oysters until they are large enough to make it on the bottom on their own.

The Lower Cape, however, from the elbow and up, is another story. It was formed by extensive glacial runoff over dry ground, and later by wave action, forming deep, sandy soils. This sand had fewer minerals to impart to the water and contribute flavor to the oysters, but it did form a wonderfully gentle gradient of nice, hard bed. Wellfleet's reputation as an oyster mecca was made in this pre-aquaculture era when a suitable bottom was a prerequisite for growing oysters. Today, it still grows lovely oysters with a lighter body and the full salt of the ocean, since there is little freshwater that far out on the Cape, but without the rich minerality of some other New England oysters.

Before we leave geology, it's worth pointing out that the coast of eastern Connecticut, all of Rhode Island, Massachusetts other than Cape Cod, southern Maine, and Nova Scotia is actually part of Africa. Or Proto-Africa. Way back, before dinosaurs had even thought of evolving, the east coast of Proto–North America was about where the Hudson River is today. Then a hunk of drifting continent, known as Avalonia, came spinning off Proto-Africa and slammed into North America. The seabed that was squeezed in between the collision got pushed up onto North America and became Vermont, New Hampshire, most of Maine, and western Massachusetts and Connecticut. When the landmasses later separated, a strip of Avalonia got left behind and became the New England coast.

Look at a map and you can see that the old land of Avalonia is pretty much a spot-on map of the best oyster *terroir* on the East Coast. Don't overlook the importance of the ancient seabed that forms the mountains of New England. Because it was once seabed, that land is rich in limestone, the calcium-rich rock formed by ancient microscopic shellfish as they died and settled to the seafloor. The rivers draining those limestone mountains—and filling the oyster-growing bays of New England—are constantly supplying calcium, along with other minerals, to the oysters.

What happened to the rest of Avalonia? It slammed into Proto-Europe, where it became Ireland, England, Wales, and parts of the coast of Northern France, Belgium, Holland, and Germany. Yes, again, we are talking about some of the best oyster *terroir* on the planet. Obviously, many factors affect the flavor and health of oysters, and things such as climate and human influence have changed greatly over the eons, but the next time somebody objects to calling a Maine oyster a Belon, or claims that a Flat from Nova Scotia could never taste like the original French, you might want to quietly mention that the bedrock is one and the same. The two oysters may indeed have more in common than a French Belon would with an oyster from, say, Bordeaux.

We can thank the jumbled geology of Massachusetts and Rhode Island for the amazing variety in the oysters found there. There are the light-bodied salt bombs of Wellfleet and Cape Cod Bay, the richer oysters from the south-facing ponds and islands, and the earthier oysters of the big bays—Buzzards and Narragansett. Only Washington State can boast a wider range.

As the area awakens to the glory of its local oysters, more and more growers are investing the time and energy to grow premium oysters, knowing that the market will reward them. Quite a turn-around from the DOA status of the New England industry just decades ago.

THE MASSACHUSETTS AND RHODE ISLAND OYSTERS TO KNOW

COTUIT

Cotuit oysters, tucked away on the south side of Cape Cod, may be the "separated at birth" twins to Johnny Flynn's sainted Colville Bays from Prince Edward Island. Both come from clear, cold coves matted with verdant eelgrass and bountiful with a particular algae that turns the oyster shells jade. People have been farming Cotuit oysters for a while—the Cotuit Oyster Company, the oldest in the United States, has been at it since 1837. A few things have changed since then. Seed now comes from a hatchery and is raised in a FLUPSY and in floating trays before being bottom-planted. But unspoiled Cotuit Bay has changed little, and the oysters still have the bright and briny flavor they are famous for.

CUTTYHUNK

The Elizabeth Islands push out from Woods Hole like a strong, straight arm guarding Buzzards Bay, and the fist is Cuttyhunk Island. It has been Seth Garfield's family home for generations, and it was there that he returned after a stint at Fisher Island, a hatchery off the Connecticut coast started by Carey Matthiessen, brother of the writer Peter Matthiessen. Fisher Island has been one of the main suppliers of oyster seed for decades, as well as something of a grad school for oyster growers. Some of the most perceptive minds in the industry worked on Fisher Island before starting their own farms. Joth Davis wound up in Washington State, where he now grows Baywater Sweets. Bob Rheault moved up the coast to Rhode Island, where he grows Moonstones. Seth Garfield came back to Cuttyhunk. There, in West End Pond, the unspoiled edge of an already remote island, he grew European Flats from 1981 until 1989, using Japanese lantern nets. In 1989, after a mysterious disease wiped out 90 percent of his Flats, he switched to *virginicas*. To my knowledge, these are the only *virginicas* being raised in lantern nets. Unlike Pacific oysters raised in nets, their shells are strong and muddy. This may be because their estuary is only six feet deep, so there is plenty of bottom contact.

Cuttyhunk Island has a year-round population of only forty, and West End Pond is on the *quiet* end of the island. Surrounded by nothing but bayberry and sumac, it is where researchers come to learn what water with zero human influences should be like. The pond is crystal clear in winter, but in summer it *louches* like absinthe, turning milky-green with marine algae. Oysters grow fast in this environment, some reaching a hefty four inches in less than a year. The flavor is mild sea, all light and sparkle, and the brine is intense (33 ppt).

Cuttyhunks are seasonal—late summer to early winter—and uncommon: Garfield grows less than 100,000 per year. He ships to a handful of restaurants and direct to consumers. Or you can go to the source: Cuttyhunk Harbor is a popular stopover for yachts on the way to Martha's Vineyard, and each evening Garfield's Floating Raw Bar makes the rounds, delivering oysters harvested that morning right to the boats.

DUXBURY

Unusual southwest winds in Duxbury Bay, forty miles south of Boston, sometimes create a natural upweller effect, blowing warm surface waters across Cape Cod Bay to Wellfleet and drawing up cold water from the bottom. This water is filled with heavy nutrients that settled to the bottom, including the iron that fuels plankton growth, making for a rich feeding environment. More notably, In July, when the wind is right, water temperatures can plunge from 70 to 54 overnight. When other Massachusetts oysters go offline for spawning and general flabbiness, Duxburies are still cool and crisp. They are also extremely salty, since whatever freshwater accumulates in Duxbury Bay floats on top of the denser saltwater and gets blown out to sea by the winds. The plain white shells attest to life in off-bottom bags and cold, hypersalty environments. If you like brutally briny oysters, Duxburies (and Island Creeks, below) will be among your favorites.

ISLAND CREEK

Island Creek is the brand name for a cooperative of Duxbury oyster farmers, and they have the classic butter-and-brine, uncomplicated Duxbury taste. One of the saltiest oysters you'll ever find, they are also many people's favorite. I've never been disappointed by one. Often noted for their al dente bite, they were the oyster used by the French Laundry's Thomas Keller for his Oysters and Pearls, a decadent concoction of oysters, caviar, and tapioca.

MARTHA'S VINEYARD

A century ago, the island of Martha's Vineyard sported a thriving wild oyster fishery. That fishery still exists in much reduced numbers, but now aquaculture is picking up the slack. Both wild and farmed oysters appear under the appellation Martha's Vineyard, so it can be hard to generalize. The wild ones will have irregular shells and even concave marks where other oysters set on them. Wild or tame, I've yet to encounter a bad MV oyster. The geography is ideal. The terminal moraine of the glaciers of eighteen thousand years ago left rich clay deposits that sweeten the waters and the oysters, the sandflats provide nice firm bottoms for growout, and the numerous natural salt ponds shelter the oysters and get clean, oceanic flushes twice a day. I've had some Martha's Vineyards that were on the salty side, typical for an island oyster, and others that were nearly saltless, though big and creamy with glycogen. The ones nestled in the salt ponds—often in bottom cages—can be less briny than those out on the bays. A wild MV oyster tends to be about three years old at harvest, at least three inches in size, with a gnarly sage-green shell, a huge adductor muscle from all the working out, and a mild, clean seaweed flavor, no doubt deriving from life on the bottom. Farmed oysters are a bit younger, cleaner, and milder.

Moonstone

THE OYSTER

Moonstones are nicely sized oysters (at least four inches) with full-bodied flavor and unusually deep cups. They come in classy evening attire: white shells with black stripes and trim. The brine is strong—higher than a Gulf or Big Bay (Chesapeake, Long Island Sound, Narragansett) oyster, but not quite as overwhelming as a Wellfleet, an Island Creek, or a Damariscotta. What jumps out at you is that full body; the taste fills your mouth with minerals and brothy umami richness. Copper, iron, clay—it's all there. In fact, the stony, tannic flavors can make some wines taste almost bitter; your best bet is something exceedingly dry and simple, like Muscadet or Chablis, or a martini. Get that right, and you will discover why I love Moonstones' fine, flinty flavor and long finish.

THE PLACE

Point Judith Pond is an oval bit of loveliness on the Rhode Island coast just around the corner from Narragansett Bay. That corner makes all the difference. The pond has none of the industry lining its shores that Narragansett Bay does. Half the volume of the shallow pond, which averages just six feet in depth, disappears twice daily in the three-foot tides, and is replaced by fresh sea, ensuring clean water and salinity that is nearly oceanic. But the shallow waters and steady supply of nitrogen from the swampy watershed (this is cranberry country, after all) ensure excellent plankton growth and great food for the oysters. That could be responsible for Moonstones' richness, but the clay bottom and high mineral content also contribute. The area was chosen by Bob Rheault after he tested many sites throughout Rhode Island as part of his doctoral thesis and found that Point Judith Pond had the fastest-growing oysters. Chefs confirmed that it had the best-tasting.

And the name *Moonstone*? Borrowed from a nearby nude beach. Also a semiprecious pearl-like gemstone.

THE PRODUCER

Bob "Skid" Rheault's sister says that he is the only person she knows who had career ambitions at age thirteen and stuck with them. He learned to dive at age sixteen, worked at Woods Hole after college, took a summer job managing the Fisher Island oyster farm, and has been in the industry ever since. He is everywhere. He's a marine biologist. An oyster grower. He's president of the East Coast Shellfish Growers Association and serves on the board of the National Aquaculture Association. He used to run a hatchery called Spatco and designed the underdock Floating Upweller System (FLUPSY) now common throughout the industry.

Rheault provides his own broodstock, which is now well-adapted to Point Judith Pond, to a number of different hatcheries and they produce his seed. He then grows the seed from sand-grain size in upwellers right under the dock of the Point Judith Marina. The seed is stirred twice daily to break off the new growing edge; this prevents the oysters from getting long before they have a chance to "cup up." When the seed is about a month old and half an inch in size, it is transferred to off-bottom cages in eight to ten feet of water. Rheault used to keep his oysters in cages all the way to market size, but that changed after a surprising discovery. A few years back, he didn't have enough cages for all the large seed coming out of his upwellers, so he threw a few hundred thousand of the half-inch oysters to their "certain death" on the bottom—certain death because Point Judith Pond has a soft, muddy bottom, and conventional wisdom says that oysters will suffocate in such an environment. Recently, he was diving on the spot and saw that it was paved with beautiful oysters. He pulled out 160,000 by diving. Not only had the oysters survived down in the mud, with just their bill end sticking out, but they had thrived. Their shells were thicker, with none of the plague of boring sponges and mud-blister worms that had marred the off-bottom oysters. Moonstones now spend the last year-plus of their lives nestled safely in the muck of Point Judith Pond.

Rheault harvests with a scallop dredge, using a unique oyster boat that was custom-built to his specifications. Steel-clad, it has a World War II–surplus feel to it, and includes slick features like a hole in the middle through which oyster cages can be raised and lowered, relieving the backbreaking work of leaning over the side to grab three-hundred-pound cages. Moonstones are held suspended in a tray for a few days to spit out any mud they have ingested, and then brought ashore only to fill orders—which can run as high as ten thousand a day.

NARRAGANSETT

Wild oysters dredged from Narragansett Bay. They tend to be mild, without much brine, and are often long and skinny with shallow cups, due to the challenging conditions on the bottom of the bay. Considering the large city of Providence looming at the head of the bay, these wouldn't be my first choice.

PLYMOUTH ROCK

It's a testament to the ineptitude of the Pilgrims that many of them managed to starve in those first lean years in the New World when a few feet under their bobbing ship lay millions of the most nutritious creatures on the planet. It's not as if those oysters were particularly

A massive, and old, oyster from Narragansett Bay. Like tree rings, you can see the cycles of growth on an oyster's shell. (Photo courtesy NOAA)

elusive, either; even a Pilgrim should have been able to catch one. But for whatever reason, they didn't much, and no one has since; still clinging to that famous rock are descendants of the original colony (of oysters, not Pilgrims). These may be the tastiest wild oysters left on the East Coast.

Threateningly briny—this end of Plymouth Bay is subject to the same upweller effect as Duxbury, just to the north (see Duxbury, above)—they are also lively and clean and wonderfully chewy. Note the goosefoot pattern of raised ridges on the green shell—sign of an oyster exposed to fluctuating tides and temperatures in its youth. A final Pilgrim note: If you've read the geology brief that begins this chapter, you'll understand why, when these English refugees hit the Massachusetts coast, they thought it felt pretty homey. Perhaps the land, only recently (in geological terms) separated from England, resonated for them in some deep way.

QUONSET POINT

Grown by Bill Silkes, who also runs American Mussel Harvesters, one of the major oyster distributors. Quonset Points are part of the biggest farm in Narragansett Bay, fifteen acres of leased bottomland containing two million oysters, so Quonsets are a staple of many New England raw bars from September through January. Quonsets are farmed in suspended cages, developing a consistently deep cup and mild, sweet finish that is very popular with those oyster eaters who don't like to choke on salt. The bottom shells have an extraordinary orange color that makes for gorgeous presentation.

TOMAHAWK

Menemsha Pond is a large bay that nearly severs Gay Head from the rest of Martha's Vineyard. It is the ancestral home of the Wampanoag Tribe, and still claims about 350 tribal members. Middens around Menemsha Pond testify that oysters have been a part of the tribe's traditions for at least five thousand years. In 2003, the tribe decided to reembrace that tradition—and they did everything right. They chose a site where development was limited, and they also redirected road runoff away from the pond. They developed a solar shellfish hatchery so they wouldn't have to rely on seed from the mainland and could develop their own unique strain of oyster. They adopted cutting-edge West Coast growing techniques, tumbling and grading their oysters constantly to produce deep cups and plump meats. Most important, they grow their oysters solely in clean Menemsha Pond, where the four-knot currents wash the oysters with fresh phytoplankton constantly. Even the freshwater springs in this area are famed for their curative powers—who knows what impact this has on the oysters? Certainly the ocher-streaked cliffs of Gay Head help imbue the water with clay and minerals. Briny oysters with a bright, lemony finish unusual in New England, Tomahawks are pricey, but worth it if you care about clean oysters, native traditions, or flavor.

UMAMI

Salt Water Farms calls their second-string oysters Umami. Oysters *are* high in umami content (see "The Taste of an Oyster: A Primer"), so I suppose this name follows the "Chincoteague Salts" tradition of naming an oyster for its flavor. Umamis will have less attractive shells and shallower cups than Quonset Points. Go for the Quonsets for half-shell presentation, the Umamis for cooking.

WATCH HILL

Watch Hill's stock went way up a few years back when *Bon Appetit* magazine named it one of the best oysters in America. Then Sansom Street Oyster Bar in Philadelphia called it "the sweetest, most flavorful oyster on the market." This was grower Jeff Gardner's NC State Wolf-pack moment, the unknown trouncing the big boys, and for all I know he ran around Rhode Island like Jim Valvano looking for somebody to hug. White-shelled Watch Hills are grown off-bottom in waist-deep water on a five-acre lease in Winnapaug Pond, near Westerly. They are unusual for being mild in salinity but full-bodied, with strong "oyster-ness" and an addictive sweet-butter flavor that is especially apparent in winter. That combination makes them perhaps the best *virginica* with wine.

WELLFLEET

Wellfleets were big before the United States was. The explorer Samuel de Champlain didn't name the area "Port aux Huitres" in 1606 for nothing. Wellfleet rose to prominence as an oyster center in the 1700s, once Boston had exhausted its own beds, and the last native Wellfleet disappeared down some Brahmin's gullet in 1775. That's right, the last Wellfleet vanished hundreds of years ago. After that, Wellfleet was more of a relay station where uninteresting oysters from Buzzards Bay or Narragansett Bay (or, by the 1840s, the Chesapeake) would be planted in the spring to "salt up" through the summer. In fall, they'd be shipped to Boston and sold as Wellfleets—which had that pretzel-like saltiness everyone wanted. Nineteenth-century Boston was known for its oyster peddlers, who would go door to door with bags of Wellfleets over their shoulders, calling, "Oys! Finey oys! Buy any oys?"

Wellfleet had a few things going for it, one of which was its shallow, firm, calm harbor, guarded by the extended arm of Great Island—perfect for planting vast quantities of oysters and retrieving them later, no boats or tongs required. Ten-foot tides and two freshwater streams kept the oysters bathed in a rhythmic, brackish flow. The harbor is also

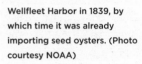

Wellfleet Harbor in 1839, by which time it was already importing seed oysters. (Photo courtesy NOAA)

Northern view of Wellfleet Harbor.

an easy, protected sail up to Boston, and, prerefrigeration, proximity was a major consideration for live oysters.

Chesapeake oysters don't spawn well in the cold waters of New England, so Wellfleet relied on seed oysters from the south for a long time. Today, most seed comes from hatcheries. Though the beaches are still viable (and, with a permit, you can still harvest your own oysters), most Wellfleets are kept in bags and staked in the Wellfleet Harbor shallows, far enough offshore that the tourists won't get into them. In flavor, Wellfleets resemble Malpeques in their light body and clean finish, but they are even saltier. They scream out for a pint of Sam Adams Lager and some sandy dunes to enjoy them on.

WIANNO

Wianno is a townlet on the southern Cape Cod coast within spitting distance of Cotuit. Same bay, similar oysters. Wiannos are grown in racks and bags just off the bottom and are exposed at low tide. This helps them cup up into very pretty oysters. Always three inches, they are brown on top, green and white on the bottom. The whitish-pink meat is slightly sweet and profoundly salty. If you like Wellfleet-style salt blasts, these make a good alternative. Apparently, they are grown on both the Wianno side of the Cape (Nantucket Bay) and the north side (Cape Cod Bay), and one wonders how similar the two populations are.

NEW YORK, NEW JERSEY,
AND CONNECTICUT

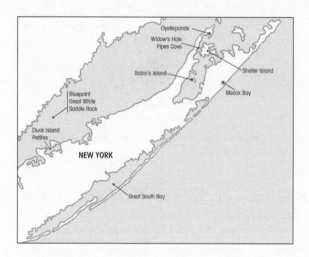

In the minds of many people, oysters and Bluepoints are synonymous. They feel that New York is the only city that counts and Bluepoint the only oyster worth asking for. The funny thing is that, in the two centuries since Bluepoints' reputation was forged, everything about the oyster has changed—except the name, which was always the most important part of its success.

The original Bluepoints were, apparently, great oysters. They had Long Island's Great South Bay to thank for that. Shielded by Fire Island and with an average depth of only six feet, the bay formed a vast and shallow estuary, ideal for oystering. Spat grew well and safely in the river-fed east end of the bay, while adult oysters thrived in the warmer,

Floating oyster houses on the Hudson River in Manhattan, 1912. (Photo courtesy Long Island Maritime Museum)

saltier west end. Bluepoints really did taste better than oysters from the East River or Raritan Bay.

Once the Bluepoint craze took off in the early 1800s, everybody in New York who wanted an oyster wanted a Bluepoint. Mysteriously, they got them. More and more Bluepoints became available. How? Because everybody began calling their oysters Bluepoints. First, any wild oyster in the vicinity of Blue Point, a town on the Great South Bay, was called a Bluepoint, then any wild oyster from anywhere in Great South Bay was given the name. By the 1870s the wild oysters were gone and Chesapeake seed was being planted in the Great South Bay and sold two years later as Bluepoints. One of the first tasks of the Long Island Railroad was to send four trains a day into New York City laden with fresh Bluepoints.

Name control arrived in 1908, when a state law designated that an oyster must spend a minimum of three months in Great South Bay to be called a Bluepoint. Of course, that law only had jurisdiction in New

York, so Connecticut oystermen continued to call their oysters Blue-points. (Today, you may see Connecticut Bluepoints listed on menus, which is fair enough. But you'll also see New Jersey Bluepoints, Virginia Bluepoints, and oxymorons from even farther south.)

When you order a Bluepoint today, one thing you can be sure of is that the oyster has not spent a single day of its life in Great South Bay. Today, a Bluepoint is usually an oyster from Long Island Sound, the opposite side of Long Island. Today's Bluepoints have the mild flavors of the sound—quite the opposite of the original Bluepoints, which must have been salty. The change came because the oyster industry in the Great South Bay died, the hurricane of 1938 delivering the coup de grâce. Not only did the hurricane bury the existing oyster beds under sediment, but it also punched some new inlets through the barrier islands, allowing the Atlantic to penetrate the bay. With that oceanic salinity came oyster drills and other predators that hadn't been able to survive in the brackish bay. New oyster seed was wiped out. Adult oysters could still grow in the bay, but the 1940s brought a number of duck farms that drained into the bay, creating a nitrate soup garnished with algae blooms that choked out the shellfish.

By then the Bluepoint name had already migrated to Long Island Sound, as New York growers decided that if they couldn't beat their Connecticut neighbors, they would join them. All the surviving New York oysters were in the sound, particularly Oyster Bay, where Frank M. Flower and Sons, one of the primary suppliers of Bluepoints, survives to this day.

Long Island history abounds with oyster names that caught fire and quickly vanished in a conflagration of overconsumption. Rockaway, East River, Saddle Rock, Shelter Island. Huntington Bay yielded a trove of exceptionally tasty morsels in 1859, and was instantly picked clean by every oysterman on the coast. To see illustrations of that frenzy, depicting 215 oyster sloops packed cheek-by-jowl in the small bay, is to witness the Tragedy of the Commons at work.

Of course, the biggest name to suffer such a fate was New York itself. As Mark Kurlansky expertly details in *The Big Oyster*, his oyster-tropic history of New York City, one of the first things the colony of New York became famous for in Europe was the quality of its oysters.

Nineteenth-century ad for Bluepoints.
(Courtesy Long Island Maritime Museum)

These oysters were bigger, fatter, and brinier than the oysters known in Europe at the time, and they quickly developed an unrivaled reputation. They also grew everywhere—in Raritan Bay, in the East River, up the Hudson, around Liberty and Ellis and Governor's Islands, along the shores of Manhattan itself.

Today, no one associates Manhattan with oysters—oyster bars, perhaps, and indeed there were more than eighty in the city at last count, but good oysters don't come from Manhattan or nearby. They do still come from New York, however, if you know where to look. The same conditions that made Bluepoints famously succulent still exist; you just need to move farther away from the population centers.

Snuggled within the forked fishtail of Long Island's East End are Peconic Bay, Noyac Bay, and Gardiner's Bay. A hundred years ago, after the prodigious oyster beds of the Great South Bay were destroyed, the East End waters took up the slack, harvesting mountains of oysters from the clean waters of Greenport and Shelter Island. The oysters were as sweet as could be, and grew justly famous. In 1936, the *Brooklyn Daily Eagle* called Greenport "the heart of Long Island's famed oyster industry." At one time Greenport hosted thirty canneries churning out

Colville Bays, Eastern oysters from PEI famed for their
green shells and bright, lemony flavor.

The showy pink, purple, and cream colors of British Columbia's
Nootka Sounds and Imperial Eagle Channels.

Tiny, green-gold Olympia oysters (Washington) are dwarfed even by these extra-small Skookums.

Three regions, three diverse Pacific oysters: Carlsbad Blonds from Southern California (top), Emerald Coves from British Columbia's Straits of Georgia (right), and Imperial Eagle Channels from Pacific Rim National Park (left).

Three Chesapeake Oysters: Rappahannock Rivers, Stingrays, and Olde Salts.

An assortment of oysters: plain white and green Easterns in the foreground, and colorful, shapely Pacifics and Kumamotos in back.

Rappahannock River oysters served three ways. (Photo courtesy Rappahannock River Oysters)

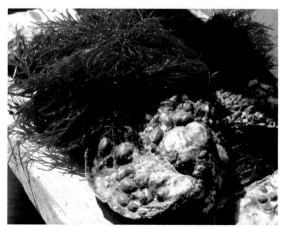

Widow's Hole oysters (Long Island) and the telltale red seaweed that grows with them and indicates fine flavor.

Twentieth-century Long Island oyster ad. (Photo courtesy Long Island Maritime Museum)

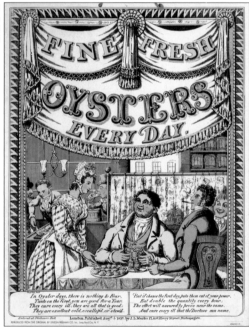

Tonging for oysters in Oxford, Maryland, 1961. (Photo courtesy NOAA)

Skipjacks, traditional Chesapeake oyster boats, drying their sails, 1971.
(Photo courtesy NOAA)

Vats of algae at an oyster hatchery. Each color is a different type of algae with a different nutritional profile.

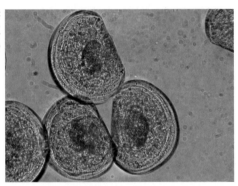

Oyster larvae just a few days old. (Photo courtesy Taylor Shellfish)

Pacific oysters in Willapa Bay. Note the thin, translucent growing edge lit up in the sun. (Photo courtesy NOAA)

The Hama Hama oyster barge on Hood Canal, in the shadows of the Olympic Mountains. (Photo courtesy Hama Hama Oyster Company)

A native Olympia oyster bed in Puget Sound. (Photo by Betsy Peabody)

The Dosewallips River where it empties into Hood Canal, supporting a giant delta of wild oysters. All the natural features of the watershed contribute to the oysters' *terroir*.

Tim Jones, farm manager of Penn Cove Shellfish, with
Penn Cove and Mount Baker behind him.

Oystermen culling oysters from the creek at Oysterponds.

H. C. Terry & Sons, a twentieth-century Greenport oyster producer. (Photo courtesy Long Island Maritime Museum)

tinned oysters. The oyster seed came from Connecticut and the adults were harvested with power dredges. Then the oyster beds disappeared, done in by pollution and a brown tide (see chapter titled "Safety") in 1984–1985 that scorched the life out of Peconic Bay, starting with the phytoplankton and working its way up the food chain.

Now the oysters are back, still sweet, and salty enough to get the mouth watering. The North Fork of Long Island is an eater's paradise, from the porgies and bluefish and steamers to the farmer's markets bursting with tomatoes and peaches to the wines, some of which—such as Lieb Cellars' Pinot Blanc—are a natural match for the local oysters. A supply of supremely good oysters is increasingly flowing out of the East End, all from tiny operations. This time, it's all aquaculture. (Or nearly all; see Mecox Bay.) Most growers use rack-and-bag culture—metal cages submerged in just a few feet of water, just off-shore, accessed by small skiffs.

Remember the distinctive New York license plates of the 1970s and 1980s, burnt-orange with black lettering? That look lives on in Peconic Bay oysters. (If you don't remember the plates, think Cincinnati Bengals instead.) Some orangish local algae may be responsible, or it may be the broodstock. Long Island freshwater is known for its high iron content, so perhaps some of that iron seeps into the bay and affects the look and taste of the oysters. Certainly, once you start imagining the look and smell of a hot, rusty, cast-iron pan, you notice it in the oysters—a metallic touch that enlivens the tongue. Cooks rave about the full and piquant taste cast-iron pans impart to food; perhaps the Peconic Bay does the same thing.

THE NEW YORK, NEW JERSEY, AND CONNECTICUT OYSTERS TO KNOW

BLUEPOINT

Bluepoints have been coasting on their name for nearly two centuries. The Bluepoint rage in New York City began in the early 1800s after delicious, robust wild oysters were found in the waters off the town of Blue Point on Long Island's Great South Bay. As everywhere else, those oysters didn't last long, for New York City quickly devoured every last Bluepoint and called for more. More came. Though already in 1824 the *Gazetteer of the State of New York* was referring to Bluepoints in the past tense, by then a twenty-three-mile-long überbed of oysters had been found in the Great South Bay, baymen were multiplying like fleas, and any oyster from the Great South Bay was being sold as a Bluepoint. That kept up through the entire nineteenth century. Once the bay's wild oysters had been depleted by midcentury, growers replanted the beds with seed oysters from the Chesapeake, let those oysters reach a bare minimum market size of three inches, and sold *those* as Bluepoints. Memories are short; people remembered they were supposed to choose Bluepoints, they just didn't know why. Already in 1881, the U.S. government's report on the oyster industry complained, "The present [Blue Point] is small and round; but the old 'Blue Points,' cherished by the Dutch burghers and peaked-hatted sons of the Hamptons, who toasted the king long before our Revolution was thought of, was of the large, crooked, heavy-shelled, elongated kind with which one becomes familiar all along the coast in examining relics of the natural beds, and which even now are to be found by the thousand in all the mussel-lagoons of the gulf of Saint Lawrence. Now and then, a few years ago, one of these aboriginal oysters, of which two dozen made a sufficient armful, was dragged up and excited the curiosity of every one; but the time has gone by when any more of these monsters may be expected." And by 1910, when the farming of Bluepoints reached its peak in the Great South Bay, the biologist James Kellogg could write of "the popularity of Blue Points and other baby oysters that formerly found no favor in American markets. On account of their very small, thin, rounded shells, these are in great demand. But it is a safe statement that the average American who has experienced the Blue Point flavor in New York, could not sit down in Norfolk to half a dozen large, fat, adult Lynnhavens, which afford not only the finest flavor, but also something to eat, without declaring the superiority of the latter."

Today I could make the same statement, though I would no longer go to Norfolk for my large, fat, superior oysters. You will see Bluepoints on every oyster menu in Manhattan, and quite a few elsewhere, because many people believe they want Bluepoints and nothing but. The oysters themselves could be from anywhere. Ideally they are from Tallmadge Brothers, which maintains a fleet of historic oyster boats in Norwalk, Connecticut, and harvests from the sound. Those are fine, medium-briny shellfish. If your Bluepoints taste like, well, nothing, then they are impostors from farther south. You can do better.

DUCK ISLAND PETITE

Cute, plain brown little oysters from Huntington Bay. These 2½-inch oysters are in the Caraquet category of nonthreatening. The shells are quite thick, the meats pale and plump, the flavor fleeting.

GREAT SOUTH BAY

When last we left the Great South Bay, it was a 1940s cesspool of duck sauce, not fit for oysters or even people. With this in mind, you will no doubt have averted your eyes in horror at the sight of a listing

Tonging for oysters in winter on Great South Bay, late nineteenth century. (Photo courtesy Long Island Maritime Museum)

for Great South Bay oysters. But the bay has improved drastically since those dark duck days, helped by the dying of industry, and it is now pretty clean. The Bluepoints Company, which staggered through the second half of the twentieth century importing frozen lobster, actually tried its hand at oysters again in 1998, and managed to produce fifteen million seed and two million adult oysters as recently as 2002. But, as one grower told me, "Growing oysters is falling-off-a-log easy. Making money at it's the hard part." The business was never profitable and the facility, in West Sayville, may soon be transformed into condos. But *somebody* out there is selling Great South Bay oysters. They are elusive. Keep your eyes, and your taste buds, peeled.

GREAT WHITE

Another of those white, salty, full-bodied, tannic, brittle-shelled Long Island oysters. Great Whites, as you'd expect from the name, are pretty big, and usually a good value.

MECOX BAY

Trace your finger across Long Island, looking for great oyster geography, and east of Great South Bay you suddenly come across a perfect skillet-shaped bay, its handle poking into the Atlantic. This is Mecox

Bay, home to weekend mansions and to a surprisingly robust population of wild oysters, perhaps the last in the region. As such, they are the closest thing alive to the original wild Bluepoints that had New Yorkers all aflutter in 1820. Unlike shallow Great South Bay, Mecox is a deep hole, and its oysters flourish at thirty feet, where they stay cold and crisp. They grow more slowly, too, so a market-sized Mecox Bay is at least three years old, with a Fort Knox shell that makes it easier to shuck than any other Long Island oyster. As a wild oyster, a Mecox Bay can only be harvested in season, which runs from mid-November to the end of April. Its flavor is awfully mild, not salty, and oddly alkaline. Brewster's Seafood, in Hampton Bays, has a saltwater well in Shinnecock where it relays Mecox oysters to get them salted up before selling them, which may add interest.

NEW JERSEY BLUEPOINT

Not a real Bluepoint, of course, but a New Jersey carpetbagger. A gnarly, almost pure-white shell reveals surprisingly plump meat and a distinctive, creamy-yellow nacre. The flavor is mild—some would say boring—which is actually a good approximation of a Bluepoint. My guess is that when most restaurants serve these they are going to call them Bluepoints, not New Jersey Bluepoints, for obvious reasons, so you may have trouble spotting them. Look for the muscular white outer shells (which never break) and the smooth ivory interiors. These feel like wild oysters; they certainly aren't groomed!

What you really want to know is, coming from the land of Newark, are they safe to eat? They come from Delaware Bay, which explains their lack of salt—the Delaware River is no slouch. They are grown near Bivalve, New Jersey—supposedly the clean side of the bay. Ah, yes, Bivalve, New Jersey—it sounds like the caption to some Far Side cartoon, but it's real and, as you might suspect, has been a shellfish center for some time.

Oysterponds

THE OYSTER

Oysterponds are the epitome of East End oysters. They have the classic umber-and-black shells, which in my experience always yield a particularly savory oyster with a refreshingly tannic, cast-iron bite. They have an oceanic salinity of 32 ppt and are always at least four inches—they grow so fast in their creek that any three-inchers are stuck back in the water to grow for a few more months. In fact, Oysterponds grow so fast—note the soft lip on the bill—that they have the thin shells that also seem to characterize East End oysters. Shuck with care. Like most Northeastern oysters, they are good in September, great in November, and stay good through March or April.

THE PLACE

Any card-carrying ostreaphile must greet the appearance of a road sign for a place called *Oysterponds* with a flutter of the heart. Arriving by ferry from Connecticut to this far eastern tip of Long Island, everything seems right for an oyster score. The John Singer Sargent landscape of sea captains' homes, gray bay, and gently stretching salt marshes. The "i"s of osprey nests dotting the distance and the flocks of egrets high-stepping through the ponds. The fact that there are no cities in sight.

Technically, the name of the town is Orient. The town of Oysterponds was founded in 1646, only seven years after Oyster Bay, which is much closer to Manhattan and became a center of the oyster industry. Oyster Bay didn't like people confusing Oysterponds with Oyster Bay, so it convinced the town to change its name to Orient. Today, the name Oysterponds lives on in the historical society, the recreational access, and the oysters, which were harvested in these ponds by Native Americans for centuries before Dutch settlers took over in the 1600s.

Other East End oyster farmers grow their oysters by leasing bottomland in various spots of Peconic and Gardiner's Bays, dropping large metal cages filled with oysters about ten feet deep onto the leases, and later hauling them up with winches attached to boats. That's what you do when you *don't* have particularly good oyster habitat. Oysterponds, however, are different. The ponds themselves are an estuary separated from Gardiner's Bay by grasses and sand dunes. Cutting through the dunes at a five-knot clip is a salt creek that runs with the tides, exchanging all its water every few hours, unlike most estuaries, which can take six months for full turnover. The creek is crystal clear, just a few feet deep, and burgeoning with life. I raked my fingers through the golden sand at the bottom and came up with a handful of clams, then scattered them over the surface and watched them dig their way back under. Oysters that escape the Oysterponds bags do fine on the bottom too, changing from umber to whitish-green and developing strong, ridged shells indicative of life on the bottom. Crabs and fish dart in and out of the grasses and oyster racks.

Most oyster farmers expect 50 percent mortality of their crop from seed to harvest, but when I asked Reg Tutthill about his die-off rate, he looked at me with incomprehension. "Our oysters don't die," he said. "Maybe one now and then." Something about the conditions of the creek makes oysters thrive. Part of that is the growth rate. The disease Dermo (harmless to humans) attacks many Long Island oysters in their third year, but Oysterponds have already reached a generous market size of four inches within eighteen months, so they are well out of the water and in Manhattan bellies before Dermo ever finds them.

THE PRODUCER

Reg Tutthill has the good fortune to *own*, not lease, the prime piece of natural oyster real estate on the East Coast. How do you get such a place? There's a bit of a waiting list: Tutthill's family got theirs in the 1640s as the first Dutch settlers in the area, and they've been lovingly holding it tight ever since. Reg is in his seventies, has had hip and knee replacements, and has every right to enjoy a long retirement. Instead, you'll find him in waders several days a week, knee-deep in his creek, culling oysters with his partners, a few old friends grounded deeply in place. None of them has to be here; they do it because the creek screams out that fat, happy oysters should be raised in it.

The system for doing that is gloriously low-tech. No dredges, no floating trays, no divers, no boats. Just rebar "tables" sitting a foot off the bottom with bags of oysters attached. That's it. Wade out when the weather's nice ("We pick our days," Reg admits), turn the bags to shake off the fouling, move the oysters to the next station in the creek as they grow larger, and pick out the ones that are ready for market. This last step is done in mid-creek on a makeshift table of two sawhorses and a piece of plywood, with a rock to crush the

Reg Tutthill with a few of his friends.

crabs and oyster drills that spill out of each bag with the oysters. Bags of market oysters are stored at a dock on the creek and pulled just a couple of hours before the weekly truck arrives to ship them to K&B Seafoods, the main distributor for Oysterponds. In winter, when ice prevents boat-dependent farmers from reaching their crop, Tutthill and his swift, nonfreezing creek sometimes become the only game in town.

A lot of oyster farmers you meet seem tired. Tired of the years of backbreaking work pulling dredges or four-hundred-pound cages and watching half your crop die before it reaches market size. Not the Oysterponds gang. They seem as if there were no place they'd rather be, taking their rhythm from the creek and each other. "We get to solve the problems of the world while we're out here," they told me as they dumped a new bag of oysters on their table. "Yesterday we solved Social Security. Today we're working on health care."

Standing in that creek, with no company except the egrets and osprey and the golden oysters tumbling onto the table, it's easy to lose track of time. Yet, if anything, these older men seemed to be savoring it, the stream like a water clock marking the passage of the hours.

PIPES COVE

A mainstay at the Grand Central Oyster Bar, at Nick & Toni's in East-hampton, and at other tony places, Pipes Cove oysters are Greenport neighbors to Widow's Hole, the two coves separated by Fanning Point. While Widow's Holes are grown in the backyard of a stately mansion, Pipes Coves live in the back forty of the Silver Sands Motel, growing just beyond the roped-off swimming area. Both Pipes Coves and Widow's Holes have a salted iron flavor note that is the essence of Greenport oysters.

One of the partners in Pipes Cove was quoted in a magazine, saying that when he eats a Pipes Cove, "I like to chew it and let the taste buds explode in my mouth." Which sounds painful, but last time I ate Pipes Coves, all my taste buds survived. That was on the Shelter Island ferry, as I tried to convince my mother that she'd been wrong about oysters all along. Leaning over the rail, I shucked an oyster and handed it to her. She ate it and let the shell drop into the water. "I don't remember them tasting like this," she said. I handed her another. "Have the oysters changed?" she asked. I handed her another. And another. They were all gone by the time we hit Shelter Island.

ROBIN'S ISLAND (EAST END)

Robin's Island is an unblemished 435-acre paradise in Peconic Bay owned by the financier Louis Bacon. The oysters, also known as East Ends, are harvested from waters near the island, and have that recognizably Peconic medium brine and body and iron richness, though not quite the liveliness of a Widow's Hole or Oysterponds, which come from closer to the open sea.

SADDLE ROCK

Saddle Rock is one of New York's famous old oyster names, and another great example of an oyster craze. The original Saddle Rock was a formation in the East River near Norwalk Harbor. There, in 1827, exceptionally large and tasty oysters were discovered. Saddle Rocks quickly became all the rage, known especially for their prodigious size. If you liked large oysters, you looked for Saddle Rocks. By 1832 Saddle Rocks were kaput, but that was no problem for enterprising New Yorkers, who by then sold any large oyster as a Saddle Rock. The name faded away, though memory of it did not, and now it has cleverly been revived—and trademarked. Today, they are no longer from the East River, and you should be happy about that. They are from the Connecticut side of Long Island Sound, and of medium size, with medium brine. Think of them as a larger, saltier Bluepoint.

SHELTER ISLAND

Shelter Island is "sheltered" by the twin forks of Long Island's tail, served by ferries from either fluke. It's a somnolent island of gray-shingled homes and tiny, now-you'll-catch-them-now-you-won't fish markets, with a full quarter of the island devoted to the Mashomack Nature Conservancy Preserve. The Shelter Island Oyster Company was one of the big players in Long Island oysters right up to the 1950s, when the company finally gave up the ghost. Now some clever islanders have revived the name, if not the methods. This iteration of Shelter Island oysters is grown on an eighty-six-acre farm in the clean and salty waters of Gardiner's Bay on the east side of Shelter Island. Like other Peconic Bay oysters, Shelter Islands have the distinctive black-and-rust shells and the black stripe on the top valve. The shells are wafer-thin, so you must be very careful not to shatter them, but once inside you will find a savory three-inch oyster.

WHALE ROCK

Painstakingly grown by Artie Valdez, Whale Rocks are part of the Connecticut cooperative that runs the Noank hatchery and plants oysters in the Mystic River. Whale Rocks are singled out for their perfect shell shapes and generous sizes and sold under that name. Count on a four-inch, deep-cupped, mineral-rich oyster.

WIDOW'S HOLE

Mike Osinski is carrying the torch for all of us dreamers who think, "I'll buy me a house on a stunning piece of waterfront, I'll stick some oysters in my frontyard, and I'll sell them to all the top restaurants!" Somehow he managed to pull it off. Osinski became semi-famous after Bill Buford profiled him in a 2006 *New Yorker* piece. Buford painted him as scattered, which he isn't, yet business-savvy, which he is. He made his fortune writing software and came to oysters a few years ago from a very different angle than most aquaculturists. He bought a wizened, two-story, gray-shingled sea captain's house on a peninsula smack in the

Mike Osinski harvesting Widow's Hole oysters, with Shelter Island in the background.

middle of Greenport, a sizable town, and discovered that he could grow great, bright-tasting oysters just off shore, in cages sitting on shallow bottomland that came with the house. It's a surprising place to grow oysters; stately houses line the shore, and the Shelter Island ferries scoot back and forth within spitting distance of the beds. But Greenport has a state-of-the-art sewer system and its waters are as clean as they were when the Dutch arrived—the state checks every week to make sure.

Even with great oysters, Osinski knew that he still needed to do something to set himself apart from the crowd, so he approached chefs directly, winning over some of the most prestigious New York oyster accounts, including Le Bernardin, the Grand Central Oyster Bar, and Della Famina. Most oysters are shipped to a distributor and then to restaurants, but every Wednesday Osinski loads his van with oysters and delivers them to all his accounts in person. If you dine on Widow's Hole oysters in a restaurant on a Thursday or Friday, you are eating extremely fresh oysters.

Mike and his wife, Isabel, send their two kids off to school each day, then climb aboard their skiff and spend the day hauling up oyster cages. On a good day, they can pull a thousand market-size oysters. The cages come up slippery with bluefish, crabs, and yellow and red seaweed. The red, they've learned, is a sign of good flavor. "We don't yet know why, but if we see a lot of red seaweed on the cages, we know the oysters will be delicious." In fact, the seaweed itself is delicious. I tasted some right on their boat and it was better and fresher than anything in a Japanese restaurant, with a glorious squishy pop to it. Della Famina, in Easthampton, makes a dish with the seaweed and the oysters whenever Osinski can provide it.

The rich, lively Widow's Hole flavor derives from the Peconic itself, and from the hundred-foot-deep channel running between Greenport and Shelter Island, through which most of the bay funnels. In August, that water is opaque with algae, producing plump oysters by September. They are sent to market at about two years of age. During their third year, the shells get marred by sponges, leaving them too unattractive for half-shell presentation. These get grilled for Osinski's "100 Oysters a Day Diet," which he says has suffused him with a bursting health and vitality he's never known.

Where's the widow's hole? It's a miniharbor on the back side of the spit of land Osinski's house sits on. It used to have a freshwater creek spilling into it, though the town redirected that water long ago. Still, the deep hole, protected on all sides, makes the ideal spot for Osinski's dock and for storing the oysters before the Wednesday delivery. The remnants of the creek, now salty, also harbor some wild oysters, which Osinski is in the process of cross-breeding with his oysters to produce an oyster more disease-tolerant and better adapted to the native conditions.

CHESAPEAKE

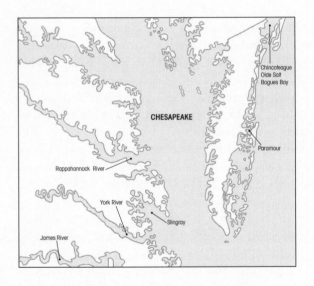

Once upon a time, the Chesapeake Bay was the Napa Valley of oysters. Oysters flourished so thickly along its fractured coasts and warm waters that they presented a shipping hazard, and they grew plump and sweet—famously sweet. A quick glance at a U.S. map makes it obvious that Chesapeake Bay—the nation's largest estuary—is like no other in the country. With the eastern shore of Maryland and Virginia keeping the Atlantic firmly at bay, with a relatively small inlet to the south, and with the rivers of Appalachia—Susquehanna, Potomac, Rappahannock, James—pouring vast quantities of freshwater into the bay (quadruple that of the Connecticut or Hudson Rivers, the next largest), the Chesapeake was an immense basin of the kind of medium-salinity water that could keep billions of oysters very, very happy.

They were safe, too: Neither the *vibrio* parasite of the Gulf of Mexico nor the red tides of the Northeast and Northwest (see the chapter titled "Safety") are found in the Chesapeake. And the huge bay didn't have the pollution problems that plagued New York's oysters. It was a bivalve paradise, all the more so because, as an ancient impact crater and flooded river valley, it is shallow, often less than ten feet deep, so virtually all its hundreds of thousands of acres lie in oysters' preferred depth zone. For two centuries the local oystermen ransacked it with the control and forethought people have always used with "inexhaustible" resources—which is to say, none.

Up to the 1960s, and despite seventy years of dire warnings from scientists, the Chesapeake's oyster grounds remained incredibly productive. Long after New York's fabled oyster grounds ran dry early in the twentieth century, Chesapeake oysters were supplying that market—take a Chesapeake oyster, dip it in Long Island's Great South Bay for a month or three, and presto, it's a Bluepoint! Virginia and Maryland combined to harvest twenty-five million, thirty million, even forty million pounds of oysters annually. Dredging was the method of choice—huge deadrises would scrape the bay floor clean, pulling up oysters and anything else living in that section of the bay, leaving behind nothing but loose mud. Then the crash began. Virginia collapsed first, from twenty-five million pounds in 1960, when the parasite MSX struck its coast, to five million in the 1970s. Maryland, whose fresher waters higher up the bay were less affected by salt-loving MSX, maintained a harvest of fifteen million to twenty million pounds through the 1970s, but in the 1980s it, too, dropped to five million, as the disease Dermo hit. By the mid-1990s, both states had collapsed to one million pounds, and the free fall continued. Today, despite decades of state and federal attempts to revive the fishery, the two states combine for less than 250,000 pounds—not even 1 percent of their historic averages.

It's important to remember that these are wild stocks, harvested primarily from public grounds. Aquaculture has made few inroads in the Chesapeake; when the waters are brimming with fat, wild oysters, making a significant investment in equipment and time to practice aquaculture seems absurd. There was also a strong disincentive toward aquaculture: A frontier mentality held sway, so there was little recognition of the concept of private (leased) grounds. You could lease your bottomland from the state, and buy your seed and plant it, but that wasn't going to stop oystermen—who thought of the whole bay as public—from harvesting your oysters. As one oysterman put it, "If you don't happen to live where your leased bottom is, you can kiss it good-bye. Somebody's going to steal the oysters." This range war between farmers and public dredgers lasted for a good century, and hasn't completely died out; poaching still occurs.

The bayman seems like the clear dunderhead here, but put yourself in his place. You may be a third- or fourth-generation bayman, making your living off the wild as your father and grandfather did before you. The concept of making huge parcels of the bay bottom *private* is anathema. It's the obvious first step in the process of taking a vast public resource out of the hands of the people and giving it to the handful of wealthy industrialists who can afford big aquaculture operations. You will do anything you can to fight this aggression, even if it means ignoring the current laws in favor of an older one: If it's in the bay, it's fair game. Real men don't farm oysters.

There is still great resistance to aquaculture on the Chesapeake. But there are virtually no more wild oysters to harvest. The remaining canneries on the Chesapeake shuck Gulf oysters. The Chesapeake Bay Foundation and the states of Virginia and Maryland are supporting efforts to restock the bay with oysters and rebuild the reefs, but so far those efforts have met with little success. The problem is that the Chesapeake faces a triple whammy: loss of reefs, increased sediment, and rampant disease. Oysters might be able to overcome one or two of these challenges, but not all three. A healthy oyster reef, rising well off the bottom, is safe from the threat of being buried in sediment. But centuries of overharvesting leveled those reefs. Now, when new oysters are planted on the bottom, they can be buried under mud before they ever have the chance to spawn a new generation and begin new reefs. Sedimentation on the Chesapeake, like most other waters in the country, is worse than it used to be, since the wetlands that used to filter rivers, and the vegetation that used to hold riverbanks in place, no longer exist.

The answer to this seems to be artificial reefs: Give oysters a scaffolding to get started, and let them take it from there. People are doing just that, and the oysters would indeed do the rest, but most oysters introduced into the bay are eliminated by predators or by the disease Dermo. Again, if a large natural population were established, it could take some hits from predation and disease and keep going. But the critical mass isn't there to allow enough oysters to reach adulthood, or to allow the natural population to develop resistance to disease. It's a tough question: How do you build the population to the point where it can take care of itself?

One solution is to let aquaculture do its job. A few dozen large-scale farms on the Chesapeake could provide all the same ecological functions as oyster reefs—habitat, nitrogen removal, cleaner water—without consuming millions of dollars annually in taxpayer subsidies, as the current restoration programs do. But this would require the state of Maryland to come to its senses.

Another solution is to breed disease-resistant oysters, to start them in safe havens where they can't be eaten by rays or ravaged by Dermo, and then to plant them on reefs and hope that enough survive to breed and host another generation. That may be working. MSX, which arrived fifty years ago, seems to be taking less of a toll on the oysters. Dermo is not yet solved, but there are a few leads. An experimental colony at the mouth of the Rappahannock River, protected from harvest, now has a thriving population of oysters that are several years old and show little sign of Dermo infection. These oysters could eventually reseed Chesapeake beds with "tougher" oysters.

Except not everyone wants to wait. The majority of Chesapeake baymen, showing the same brilliance they have for the past two centuries, are lobbying hard to be allowed to dredge those oysters instead, eager to trade the bay's future for a few days' profit. They also are pressuring the government to introduce a new oyster to the bay: *Crassostrea ariakensis,* from China. *C. ariakensis* is resistant to MSX and Dermo; tests show that it grows extremely fast in the Chesapeake;

Skipjacks—sail-powered oyster dredgers like these—were still seen in the Annapolis harbor as recently as 1970. (Photo courtesy NOAA)

and it's a prolific breeder. Chesapeake watermen see it doing for the Chesapeake what the Pacific oyster did for the Northwest: revive a dying industry.

But not so fast. Recently *C. ariakensis* was found to be suffering from an unknown disease all its own. More important, anyone with even the slightest sense of history can foresee problems. MSX was likely introduced into the Chesapeake in the 1950s when people tried growing Pacific oysters there. And Dermo hitched a ride from the gulf in the 1980s with some oysters that were relayed from there into the waters of the Chesapeake. Introducing a new critter into an ecosystem has a very, very bad track record. But some argue that that's a moot point as far as Chesapeake oysters are concerned. As one Maryland shellfish specialist said, "We may have an oyster that evolved for a Chesapeake Bay ecosystem that no longer exists." Will *ariakensis* fill this ecological gap? The real question may be, Can it be stopped? Though supposedly confined to a few sterile, experimental populations, *ariakensis* has been turning up in Virginia creeks. Stay tuned.

TASTING CHESAPEAKE OYSTERS

For the half-shell connoisseur, what happens with the Chesapeake's wild oyster population is a distant concern. Those oysters were never of the highest raw-bar standards. The Chesapeake industry has traditionally been for shucked meats.

Even when the Chesapeake was famous for its oysters, this had more to do with the jaw-dropping productivity of the bay than with the essential taste it imparted. Chesapeake oysters were fast-growing, but mild in flavor and soft in texture, midway between a Gulf oyster and, say, a Wellfleet. As you head north up the Chesapeake, farther from the mouth, salinity decreases, until near Baltimore you get water that is virtually fresh. The oysters from this Maryland half of the bay are notably bland. That's why Chesapeake oysters were routinely relayed to New York, Rhode Island, and Massachusetts to be finished off in more savory waters—and then sold as local oysters (a practice still common today with Gulf oysters).

Yet there were always some exceptions to that rule. A handful of places—primarily river mouths on the lower, more saline Virginia side of the bay—have been famous for their oysters since colonial times. And in these places, a few innovative growers are using aquaculture to produce quality oysters. Using off-bottom cages to save the oysters from the silt and the stingrays, they are able to take advantage of the warm, algae-rich waters that always made Chesapeake oysters thrive.

Many individuals with Chesapeake waterfront are also growing oysters using aquaculture methods, but not for profit. As part of a Chesapeake Bay Foundation program to bring back the native oyster, these individuals are raising oysters to boost the population to the critical mass necessary for it to survive on its own. Someday in the future the murky waters we think of when we picture the Chesapeake may be no more than a historical anomaly. When billions of oysters once more filter the entire bay every few days, it may again be as gaspingly clear as when John Smith mapped its waters in 1608.

THE CHESAPEAKE OYSTERS TO KNOW

BARCAT

An affordable oyster and a noble cause rolled into one. Barcats are grown by individuals and small-time aquaculturists throughout the southern Chesapeake, then relayed to a site on the York River—leased by the Croxton cousins of Rappahannock River Oysters—for a month to even out their salinity. Coming from many different farms, the resulting oysters don't exhibit an identifiable *terroir*, but they are consistent in size and shape and are still fine examples of Chesapeake oysters. Priced to make them accessible to consumers and restaurants that might not otherwise take the half-shell plunge, Barcats are intended to get more people eating Chesapeake oysters and more people growing Chesapeake oysters, with the ultimate goal being more oysters in the bay to filter water and improve the ecosystem. A portion of the profits on Barcats even goes to the Chesapeake Bay Foundation for its oyster programs.

The Barcat is named in honor of a type of small oyster boat developed for working the shallows ("bars") around the Chesapeake's Tangier Island, back in the heyday of the baymen—a great symbol for this new breed of independent oyster farmers.

BOGUES BAY

This is the first commercial incarnation of the Suminoe oyster (*C. ariakensis*), coming from a farm out in Chincoteague Inlet. The oyster isn't as bad as Suminoes are advertised to be. It has a pretty, white, wide shell; firm meat; and a mild flavor. Not a showstopper, but a pretty good impersonation of a *virginica*.

CHESAPEAKE

If an oyster is labeled simply a *Chesapeake*, don't expect much. It's like a wine with the basic *Bordeaux* appellation: It covers an immense area, and is the default name for a product that doesn't qualify for anything better. Unless it says otherwise, expect a Chesapeake to be a wild oyster with little flavor that was dredged off the bay floor. Look for more specific appellations—Rappahannock, York, Chincoteague—instead.

CHINCOTEAGUE

Several generations of Americans have associated the name *Chincoteague* with Misty, the Chincoteague pony, but before that *Chincoteague* was an oyster name with a long lineage. Because it's in Virginia, Chincoteague Bay gets lumped in with the Chesapeake, but it's a different beast altogether. Separated from the Chesapeake by a long peninsula and sheltered from the ocean by only the lip of Assateague Island National Seashore, Chincoteague Bay is not fed by any significant sources of freshwater. Oysters from its waters pack the full salt wallop of the Atlantic. For this reason, and because of the easy access, Chincoteague was a popular spot for relaying Gulf oysters on their way to northern markets. Two weeks at Chincoteague gave a little flavor. *Chincoteague Salts* was the classic name many people looked for, and you will still find it in some places. True to the name, it is a very salty oyster, generally skinny and elongated. Also an exceptionally clean one for the mid-Atlantic, as you'd expect from the National Seashore setting. But once you get past the salt, Chincoteagues can be disappointing; there isn't much to back up the brine.

JAMES RIVER

The James River, the southernmost river on the Chesapeake, is a famous old name for oysters. To get to the original Jamestown colony, the colonists had to navigate upriver through twenty miles of oyster shoals. Unusual eddies in the river captured oyster larvae and kept them from being washed downstream, making the James the best spat-producing area on the East Coast. An oyster industry thrived along its shores for centuries, only to die out in the twentieth. The James is again producing oysters, but, alas, the ones I've had have been absent of flavor. Worse, unlike the York and Rappahannock Rivers, the James slides through some major industrial areas, spilling out at Norfolk and Newport News.

LYNNHAVEN

Another well-known Virginia oyster appellation (see biologist James Kellogg's 1910 quote in the New York chapter). Unfortunately, water quality in the Lynnhaven River has been poor for decades. Efforts are under way to restore the Lynnhaven to the point where you can eat the oysters again, and in recent years the Lynnhaven has produced some of the best natural sets of oysters on the entire Chesapeake. A small area of the Lynnhaven was recently opened to harvesting for the first time in many years, which was cause for local celebration, but it will be a few years before we again see Lynnhavens on menus with any regularity.

OLDE SALT

Olde Salts are Travis and Ryan Croxton's take on the famed Chincoteague Salts, grown in the same salty bay. (The Croxtons also produce the Rappahannock River and Stingray oysters.) These carefully farmed, bottom-caged oysters are probably more reliable than Chincoteague Salts, which could come from any number of producers, or from wild stocks, or could be relayed Gulf oysters soaking in the brine for only a couple of weeks.

In any case, Olde Salts *are* very salty. They have a salinity upwards of 30 ppt, as opposed to 15–20 for a true Chesapeake oyster. They taste more like the sea, because more of them *is* the sea. Thanks to that salinity, they grow fast, reaching three-inch size in just six months—a third the time of the Croxton's flagship oyster, the Rappahannock River.

PARAMOUR

Parramore Island is off the Virginia coast, not far south of Chincoteague. There, exposed to the full Atlantic, not a drop of freshwater in sight, it should make a searingly salty oyster. But the oyster that occasionally turns up at a raw bar as *Paramour*—a sexier spelling—is quite mild in my experience, more like a true Chesapeake. Hmmmm.

PROFILE

Rappahannock River

THE OYSTER

The Rappahannock River oyster earned its bona fides long ago. Even back when Chesapeake oysters were considered good, Rappahannocks were deemed a cut above. As Gore Vidal wrote in *Lincoln,* "There were barrels of oysters from the Chesapeake, but none from the Rappahannock, now lost forever to the Union capital . . . the latest Confederate victories had deprived the Yanks of the world's best oysters." If true, the situation must have particularly pleased Robert E. Lee, who was born just a few miles north of the Rappahannock.

The Rapp is unique. It represents a once-preeminent style of oyster, and should be tasted for that reason alone. It is one of the least salty oysters on the East Coast, thanks to its upriver home. You will be hard-pressed to find a *virginica* with the Rapp's sweet and smooth flavor profile. Almost buttery, it is an oyster for people with "no palate or a great palate," as Ryan Croxton says. Picture the sweet and savory qualities of a homemade root-vegetable stock. The low salinity allows an intriguing Blue Ridge minerality to come through, and also makes it a better match for wine than many oysters, and not just the usual high-acid whites like Sauvignon Blanc and Muscadet. You won't find a better oyster for Chardonnay than a Rappahannock River. But consider the oyster and the place: Thomas Jefferson was a known oyster fan and undoubtedly sampled a few Rapps in his lifetime. He may even have savored them with his own Virginia wine. If you are in the area, you would do well to follow his lead and track down a white from one of the many local wineries.

Devotees of briny oysters may be underwhelmed by the Rapp's mildness. But that mildness also gives you carte blanche to play around with condiments. A few drops of lemon juice and the lightest dusting of pepper enliven a Rapp, and caviar can be spectacular as an accompaniment, the butteriness of the oyster keeping the caviar's salt in check. The Washington, D.C., restaurant DC Coast serves them with a shaving of frozen Bloody Mary—a nicely peppery touch. For me, a single drop of ume plum vinegar on each oyster is the way to go, with a glass of sake and maybe a hijiki seaweed salad on the side. Then again, Travis Croxton is a purist and insists on them straight up.

Rappahannocks are a standard Chesapeake *virginica* size, three inches, with a deeper cup than most. The white shells, streaked with ivory and cream, are distinctly lighter than the shells of the Stingrays grown just a few miles south, and pocked with the action of worms that favor the brackish waters (but can't penetrate the shells). They grow relatively quickly in the warm waters of the mid-Atlantic, usually going to market at a year and a half of age. Available September through May, they are probably best in December, when fully fattened for their long winter's nap.

THE PLACE

Topping, Virginia, is a few miles up the Rappahannock River's wide estuary, many miles from the open sea. Not a whole lot of saltwater makes it so far upstream. That gives the Rappahannock River oyster a salt content of just 15 ppt—virtually unheard of on the East Coast. That's still higher than Gulf oysters, which can be as low as 10 ppt, but much lower than oysters grown closer to the open ocean.

The Rappahannock River itself is an anomaly among large Eastern rivers, for it manages to dodge major population centers, threading the needle between D.C. and Richmond on its way to the Chesapeake. It's as clean a river as you'll find in the mid-Atlantic, trickling out of Shenandoah National Park and running 184 miles through forest and farm, widening at the end into a four-mile-wide estuary of sandy shores and piney islands that is a key habitat for many forms of bay wildlife.

THE PRODUCER

Cousins Ryan and Travis Croxton, both in their thirties, have Chesapeake oyster history deep in their veins. It was their great-grandfather, James Arthur Croxton, who first leased five acres of Rappahannock River bottom in 1899. The Baylor Survey was parceling out Chesapeake bottomland for lease for the first time, and Croxton thought it would be wise to get a little while he could. Like many other farmers in the region, he grew crops in the summer and oystered in the winter; a perfect match. His son, William Arthur Croxton, bought up 150 acres of leases and got more serious about oystering. The next generation wasn't interested in oystering, though they paid the leases and threw just enough seed on the grounds to meet the regulations, but their sons took up the cause. Ryan and Travis grew up eating Rappahannock oysters, to the point where they "can't even taste 'em anymore." Some of their earliest memories are of their grandfather shucking oysters into pint jars in his garage, and his oyster stew was their traditional Christmas breakfast. They are fiercely loyal to the Chesapeake and to *Crassostrea virginica*, and are committed to proving, in the face of threats to introduce alien oysters to the bay, that the local oyster and its natural home are a perfect pairing. "There's a reason they call it *virginica*!" they like to say.

William Arthur Croxton, tonging (or posing, perhaps?) on the Rappahannock, mid-twentieth century. (Photo courtesy Rappahannock River Oysters)

The Croxtons raise their oysters from their own broodstock in trays elevated off the river bottom. The cages keep the oysters from being buried on the bottom, and also protect them from the Chesapeake's chief oyster predator: the stingray. Stingrays, which can slurp seed oysters without end and can even crunch up adults, are prolific in the bay. Thanks to the cages, the Croxtons are able to grow oysters that bear little resemblance to the long, skinny oysters fighting for survival amid the silt of the modern Chesapeake—but must bear great resemblance to the Rappahannock River oysters their family has been growing since 1899.

Ironically, Rappahannock River oysters can be easier to find in Hawaii or Denver than around the Chesapeake. Locals still associate Chesapeake oysters with lower-quality shucked meats. In fact, when they began their business, Travis and Ryan didn't even bother with the local market; they went straight to the top. Before they had any accounts, they targeted three high-profile New York restaurants: Le Bernardin, Shaffer City Oyster Bar (because Jay Shaffer had been quoted in *Men's Journal* saying, "I'd never serve an oyster from south of Long Island"), and Jack's Luxury Oyster Bar. They landed all three.

STINGRAY

The Stingray is a quintessential Chesapeake oyster—plump, sweet, and lightly salty. Grown by Travis and Ryan Croxton at Ware Neck in a bay that opens wide to the Chesapeake and has little freshwater river influence, it has 19 ppt salt—a bit more than its cousin, the Rappahannock River oyster, but still less than an Olde Salt or Northern *virginicas*. It's the most balanced of the three Croxton oysters, not too salty, not too sweet, just right. It is harvested at a standard size of three to four inches and about a year of age. Note the interesting shells, white with tiny rods of black, as if iron filings had been mixed in with the calcium carbonate.

If you want to understand the oyster that made the Chesapeake famous, try a Stingray. It isn't a wild oyster, yet for that very reason it has more in common with the oysters that made the Chesapeake's reputation than do the few remaining wild oysters being dredged from the degraded bay bottom. Stingrays, grown in off-bottom cages, benefit from superior water quality and food supply—conditions much closer to the pristine bay of two centuries ago and the high oyster reefs that dominated it.

YORK RIVER

The York River bleeds history. Here, within spitting distance of the oyster beds, the battle of Yorktown decisively settled the course of American and world history. George Washington, born a few miles north, would have sampled the oysters in this neck of the woods, perhaps with a mug of ale in celebration of Cornwallis's surrender in 1781.

The York is ideally situated for oysters. It's low in the Chesapeake, with a direct line east to the open Atlantic. The salinity is higher than other Chesapeake river mouths, ranging from 19 to 24 ppt, depending on rainfall and how much of that Atlantic water can push its way up-river, yet the oysters always balance the salt with that buttery Virginia mountain quality. York River oysters have an ideal shepherd in Tommy Leggett, the scientist who helped bring oyster aquaculture to Virginia and who heads the Oyster Recovery Project for the Chesapeake Bay Foundation. Leggett's day job involves working with volunteers to grow millions of healthy seed oysters and introduce them to the bay in places where they are likely to survive and reproduce. To keep himself grounded, he also farms oysters near his home on the York River. He sells only about a thousand a week, so York Rivers are a rare treat. They can be ordered through Rappahannock River Oysters (see Growers Who Ship Direct).

GULF COAST

The Oyster industry on the Gulf of Mexico produces more oysters than any other region of the country. Oysters grow everywhere in the gulf's tepid waters. In fact, Europeans were amazed by early accounts of the region, which claimed that the oysters grew on trees there. Technically, they did. The trees were salt-tolerant mangroves, whose lower branches were underwater at high tide. At low tide, oysters attached to them would hang above the water.

Louisiana leads the way in the gulf, producing a full 40 percent of the country's oysters—three times as many as Washington State, its nearest competitor. (Hurricane Katrina temporarily cut production by half.) But you wouldn't know it to look at the menu of any raw bar north of the Mason-Dixon Line. Most oyster bars from New York to San Francisco have a "No Gulf" policy. The primary reason is a little malefactor called *Vibrio vulnificus*.

Vulnificus. Even the name sounds like a villain of ancient Rome. "Et tu, Vulnificus?" And this vibrio is a brute. Found primarily in the Gulf of Mexico, it is active only in warm waters. At its heyday in the eighties and nineties, it killed thirty or so people a year via oysters, a full 50 percent of the people who contracted it, making it the most virulent food-borne illness in America. Now that number is down to about ten to fifteen people a year, thanks in part to new processing techniques and in part to a 2003 California law that banned the sale of raw Gulf oysters between April and October after several people died from them in the LA area.

Vulnificus also kills without its oyster intermediary. If you happen to swim in the warm Gulf of Mexico in the summer and have open cuts, or swallow some seawater, or give *vulnificus* some other way of entering you, that's all it needs. *Vulnificus* likes to live in the muck at the bottom of shallow coastal areas, so it's particularly active when that muck gets stirred up by very warm water or by storms. Hurricane Katrina generated a brief surge of *vulnificus* infections, unconnected to oysters.

Fortunately, *vulnificus*, like its milder Northwest cousin *Vibrio parahaemolyticus*, is destroyed by cooking. A cooked Gulf oyster is a safe Gulf oyster. And Louisiana, serendipitously, has the greatest tradition of oyster cookery in America. It only makes sense. Oysters proliferate in the warm gulf. The Mississippi keeps the salinity down to a level ideal for young oysters, but such warm, brackish water makes for a mild oyster that is uninteresting on its own. When you have an abundant resource that needs a cook's helping hand, you tend to get a great cuisine. Gulf oysters are cheaper than others, meaning they are the one remaining oyster you can afford to use in quantity, which many dishes require. So when in New Orleans, or Terrebone Parrish, or even Apalachicola, that is your chance to go crazy with oyster dishes, unburdened by the guilt that you are ruining a pricey food by putting it to the fire.

Don't forgo raw Gulf oysters entirely. Ten deaths a year, among all the millions of eaters of those oysters, isn't that many. The Centers for Disease Control (CDC) estimate that food-borne illness kills *five thousand* people a year. Your odds are better with oysters than they are with rare hamburger. Virtually all those who have been done in by vibrio had weakened immune systems. If your white blood cells are at the top of their game, they'll rout *vulnificus* from your body after a couple of days of mild illness. Still, any risk of death is likely more than you want to take, and there are a couple of easy ways to reduce your risk to zero.

Almost all the deaths that have occurred have been in the warmer months of April to October, when *vulnificus* is active. November through March seems safe. But if you want to be really safe, make sure your Gulf oysters have gone through a procedure known as HPP, for Hydrostatic Pressure Process. This method, developed by the Voisin family, who have been in the oyster business in Louisiana since before it was part of the United States, involves running the live oysters through intense pressure chambers where they are subjected to pressures of 37,500 pounds per square inch for up to 180 seconds. This destroys bacteria lurking in the oyster, as well as killing the oyster. It also has an effect that the Voisins didn't originally anticipate: It shucks the oysters. The pressure causes the adductor muscle to detach from the top and bottom shells. What comes out of the HPP machine is an oyster whose top shell easily twists off and which slides right off its bottom shell. The oysters are immediately refrigerated for fresh half-shell service or flash-frozen for casinos, cruise ships, hotel buffets, Costco, and other clients looking to move large numbers of raw oysters without having to deal with the shucking.

You, the oyster gourmet, may well be recoiling in horror. *He's been singing the praises of terroir, and now he wants us to eat flash-frozen Gulf oysters? Yuck!* I hear you, I do. But not everybody can pay $3 for a pampered Kumamoto, flown in by private jet from Humboldt Bay, and I think the safe Gulf oyster has its place. God knows, faced with the choice between a hydrostatically shucked oyster and writhing death by *vulnificus*, I'll take the hydro. Besides, the idea of an oyster that was shucked without being touched by a knife is intriguing. Certainly many respectable oysters are ruined by shell shrapnel or by an errant knife through the heart (the heart being, alas, right next to the lower adductor muscle). With HPP, there are no burst oysters, no shell fragments. Of course, the oyster is no longer alive, either, which may be a pro or a con, depending on your carnivorous inclinations. And it's unclear how the quality of an HPP oyster compares to a traditionally shucked one. Some people who experimented with the machines found that the texture of the meat deteriorated more quickly.

HPP does open up new possibilities. The Voisins are experimenting with "popcorn oysters"—tiny raw oysters to be eaten as casino bar food, dozens at a time. When shuckers are involved, the cost of opening very small oysters is prohibitive. But an HPP machine can do thousands in a minute. It's the steam shovel versus John Henry all over again—and we know how that one ends. But for now, at least, John Henry is holding his own in the oyster business.

The Voisin family sells its HPP oysters under the Gold Band label, though likely you won't see them listed as anything other than *oysters* on a menu. Still, those bands do draw attention. One Northwest restaurateur told me the story of a woman who visited his oyster bar and asked for some of "those Las Vegas oysters with the bands." He explained that they didn't have any such oysters, but they did have many different oysters from local waters that she could try on the half-shell. No, she wanted only Las Vegas oysters. He explained to her that those oysters probably weren't *from* Las Vegas. Eventually he convinced the woman to try a few local oysters, which, she allowed, were acceptable but not quite as good as the Las Vegas oysters.

In truth, Vegas is fast becoming an oyster powerhouse. The restaurant scene in Vegas rivals that of any metropolis, and now many leading French chefs are choosing to open their signature U.S. restaurants in Vegas rather than New York. Even the casinos and their buffets play an important role. Many people try their first raw oyster in a casino. Call it the "gambling mind-set." You're living large, letting it all ride, Lady Luck is with you—and then you see that raw oyster beckoning to you. What's one more infinitesimal risk? You are, after all, a gambler. Pop, down it goes: delicious. Another oyster convert. Your interest piqued, you may even start to explore the wider world of oyster geography.

Entry-level Gulf oysters sure worked for me. In college, in Sarasota, late on a Friday afternoon, we would buy a bushel of oysters, several cases of horrendously cheap beer, packs of saltines, and a few jars of Tabasco, and set up amid the royal palms in the dorm courtyard. We would shuck, slurp, drink, and dare passersby to try their first oyster. It was a people magnet, and a party always emerged, Frisbees floating through the palms as the warm night settled. Those were great evenings, and we certainly couldn't have pulled them off with expensive oysters.

Thank the maligned Gulf oyster for keeping oysters from being an exclusive treat. Oysters grow like weeds down in the gulf. They are still natural-set, still wild, more or less. The lower salinity levels of the gulf have protected wild oysters from certain diseases in a way that hasn't happened in the Chesapeake. Nearly half the oysters in Louisiana still come from the public fishery. Even the leased lands tend to be natural-set; the primary task of the farmers is to move spat from areas of lower salinity to areas of higher salinity as they mature.

Not that the salinity ever gets truly high. Gulf salinity ranges from 5 to 15 ppt. And because the water never cools down much, the oysters never go dormant. They have no need to store up much of a glycogen food supply. They're like the people who live next to the grocery store and shop every day—no larder. They also don't have to save up their sperm or eggs for one summer blast into waters warm enough for larvae to survive; in fact, they sometimes do the reverse, spawning in spurts over an extended period, then shutting down for the peak of the summer heat.

What this means is that Gulf oysters don't change in flavor throughout the year as much as Northern oysters. They are a little fatter in winter, a little thinner in summer, but always mild and somewhat soft—they relax on the half-shell in a way cold-water oysters don't. Gulf oysters are usually sold as generic oysters—indicative of a region that pays less attention to the nuances of different raw oysters than to their culinary possibilities. After all, this is the land that invented Oysters Rockefeller, Po' Boys, Barbecued Oysters, and myriad other oyster concoctions.

APALACHICOLA

The primary exception to the no-appellation rule is Apalachicola. Apalachicola Bay—thirty miles of shallow oyster paradise on the Florida panhandle—produces 90 percent of Florida's oysters. The best may come from Big Bayou, a remote and pristine area on the saltier western part of the bay, near Saint Vincent Island, a National Wildlife Refuge. But, in general, all oysters from Apalachicola Bay go by the Apalachicola name. They are surprisingly old for warm-water oysters.

Tonging for oysters on
Apalachicola Bay. (Photo
courtesy NOAA)

Without the head start of a floating nursery, it takes the oysters about
three years to reach three inches.

Apalachicola is the last place in the United States where wild oysters are still harvested by tongs from small boats. It's an astonishing and
atavistic sight in a state not known for embracing the past. (No, the locals aren't preservationists. Large boats simply run aground on the
mudflats.) Old men with trucking hats and flat-bottomed, twenty-
three-foot boats scoop oysters up onto the culling board, where a second man tosses back everything that isn't a three-inch oyster. The men
generally work in five to ten feet of water, which describes most of
Apalachicola Bay. A good oysterman can feel through his tongs the
difference between oysters and empty shells.

If you want to see those oystermen at work, go soon, because most
of them aren't getting any younger. Few kids want to enter a low-
paying trade that requires backbreaking days in hundred-degree summer heat. Worse, the bay has been closed to shellfishing in recent years
about a third of the time, due to stormwater runoff and red tide, both
of which are on the increase. (Hurricanes call regularly on Apalachicola.)
The number of baymen has declined from 1,600 in the 1970s to just
300 today, many of those working part-time.

Picking up the slack for the declining wild fishery is aquaculture.
Tommy Ward, whose family received some of the only leases ever
granted on the bay, has been farming large areas of the western bay, out
toward an area called 13 Mile that has always been an oyster company

town—though *town* is a stretch. Ward cultivates his bottomland with cultch to catch the spat, and harvests with a mechanical dredge—one of the few in these parts. His Apalachicola oysters tend to be plumper and saltier than most Gulf oysters. Sitting on an outside deck at 13 Mile, the heat hanging on your shoulders like a wet blanket, with nothing to do but order another round of "Apalach" oysters and another frosty pitcher of beer, you might wonder why anyone would bother wanting anything else.

CALIFORNIA AND OREGON

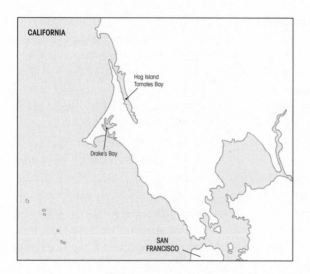

For a big state, California's oyster industry is confined to a small area. Tomales Bay is the center of the action, with several small growers, including Hog Island. Coast Seafoods, the largest oyster company in the country, has major Kumamoto farms to the north in Humboldt Bay. Other than that, there are a couple of crazy outriders growing oysters in suspension culture in the open ocean of Southern California, one farm in Drake's Estero, and that's it.

It's all in the geography. California isn't blessed with many bays. It has one world-class bay (San Francisco), and one dinky one (Humboldt). San Francisco Bay held billions of Olympia oysters in the 1850s, zero in the 1860s. By the time Pacific oyster seed was available from Japan, San Francisco Bay was far too polluted to grow oysters. A heavy-metal sink, it was officially closed to shellfishing in 1939, and has only gotten worse since. Humboldt Bay is much cleaner and produces more Kumamoto oysters than any other bay on earth.

Tomales Bay, the other workable body of water, is a geological freak. When Point Reyes, the tomahawk-shaped wedge of land that is the tip of the Pacific Continental Plate, slammed into the rest of California, which edges the North American Continental Plate, it didn't make a perfect fit. Tomales Bay is the imperfection, more a crevice than a typical bay. That imperfection is sliding northward at a rate of two inches per year as the plates continue to grind together. Every now and then they come unstuck and jump—twenty feet at once in 1906, leveling much of San Francisco in the process. In geological terms, Tomales Bay is living on borrowed time.

As far as human time frames go, however, the bay has grown good oysters for quite a while. Olympias used to thrive along its sparkling shores, and a few may still be hiding out there. Pacifics is what you'll find today. All around the bay are the floating trays and buoys marking lease sites. *Floating* is the operative verb—bottom culture is nonexistent in California. True, the Johnson Oyster Company did can oysters for decades in Drake's Estero, but today the industry is devoted to half-shell oysters and favors suspending them. The San Francisco/Oakland city-state gobbles up almost everything the Point Reyes area can grow. California oysters are getting rarer outside the state.

Oregon oysters still get around. Like its wine industry, Oregon's oyster business is centered on boutique operations, making up in interest what they lack in quantity. Often they are strong flavored, more like earthy Puget Sound oysters than the crisp brine of California or the light lettuce of Willapa Bay and Hood Canal.

Both Oregon and California owe their incredibly productive coastal waters to the prevailing ocean and wind currents. Normally, a lot of the nutrients that wash out to sea quickly sink to the sea bottom before phytoplankton, which exist only near the surface where the light is, can make use of them. This is particularly true for iron, which is essential

Tomales Bay. (Photo by Peter Perkins)

for phytoplankton growth. But the North Pacific Gyre, which flows north to south, combines with the winds to create an upwelling effect. Cold, nutrient-laden water is brought up from the bottom to the surface, feeding phytoplankton and the rest of the food chain that depends on the phytoplankton. Despite the cold temperature, the seawater that enters the Pacific Northwest's estuaries is as productive as any in the world.

THE CALIFORNIA AND OREGON OYSTERS TO KNOW

CARLSBAD BLOND

Carlsbad was a sleepy beach town midway between San Diego and LA before Lego decided to build a theme park there in the late 1990s. The oyster, the only one I know of from this stretch of coast, has a bit of a theme park look to it: glassy shells with jagged fans of white and purple stripes reminiscent of a South Beach hotel light fixture. It is grown offshore in suspended culture—the only way to grow oysters in these bayless parts—and has the weak adductor muscle and reduced shelf life one expects as a result. The flavor is quite salty for a Pacific, metallic and alkaline at the end—an unusual taste imparted by Southern California's waters.

The swirling patterns of
Carlsbad Blonds.

DRAKE'S BAY

Drake's Estero is a shallow blue bow tie nestled into Northern California's Point Reyes National Seashore. The oyster farm, operated by special arrangement with the National Park Service, was the historic Johnson Oyster Company from 1957 until 2005, when it was bought by the Lunny family of organic beef fame. The Lunnys graze their cattle on the dry, windswept grasslands of Point Reyes; they seem to be treating their oysters with equal care. They are fanatical about water quality in the Estero and have even switched their boats from two-stroke motors to cleaner-burning four-strokes.

The oysters are cultivated by a method that was highly progressive when Charlie Johnson borrowed it from the Japanese in the 1950s, but now is fully retro. Metal wires are threaded through cultch on which spat have set, then hung from racks built in the bay. The resulting oysters are tender and delicate, quite briny, as you'd expect from an area that sees virtually no rain, and sweet with a touch of bitter herb. They benefit enormously from the backing mountains and the surrounding, 71,000-acre National Seashore, which wall them off from all population sources, orient them toward the empty Pacific, and provide impeccable water quality. Alas, the National Park Service, in all its wisdom, is planning to close the oyster farm in 2012. Apparently it's inappropriate to grow food in a national park. Visit while you can, buy some oysters, and fill out a postcard telling the park service to go shuck themselves.

The Drake's Bay Oyster Company (formerly the Johnson Oyster Company), for decades the only enterprise of any kind on Drake's Estero, is about as low-key as it gets. (Photo by Peter Perkins)

FRENCH HOG

French Hog was Hog Island's cheeky name for its European Flat oysters. Grown in suspended culture, they had a reputation for being strong and metallic, as you would expect in Flats, but bearable. Thanks to the worldwide dearth of *edulis* seed, French Hogs are not currently being grown. Whether this is a temporary or permanent situation remains to be seen.

HOG ISLAND KUMAMOTO

A very sweet and fruity Kumo, coming from the same Tomales Bay waters and rack-and-bag system as Hog Island's Sweetwater. It's three years old at harvest.

HOG ISLAND SWEETWATER

Hog Island Oyster Company was founded on California's Tomales Bay by three marine biologists in 1982. They now raise three different oysters on 160 leased acres in the bay, all in rack-and-bag systems. The Sweetwater is their Pacific oyster and their most popular. It is indeed deliciously sweet, pleasantly briny, black shelled, and always beautifully shaped, thanks to regular tumbling that keeps it from reaching harvest size until at least two years of age. Hog Island is the only company I know that holds its oysters in a tank after harvest, where they are purified with saltwater that has been sterilized with ultraviolet light.

Hog Island has become a huge success story, selling many of their three million oysters a year to the San Francisco area alone, many through their own oyster bar at the Ferry Building Marketplace. The farm is also a very popular destination, with oysters for sale and grills for rent overlooking Tomales Bay.

HOG ISLAND VIRGINICA

Hog Island was the first company on the West Coast to revive the farming of *virginicas*. The flavors in the Hog Island Virginica are not as happy a marriage as those in Washington State's Totten Virginica, which tends to be larger, plumper, and richer. Somehow, that sweetness one tastes in California oysters clashes with the steely minerality one expects in a *virginica*. It's not a bad oyster—and certainly just as good as most three-inch East Coast *virginicas*—but that rare Tomales sweetness finds a much purer expression in Hog Island's Kumamotos and Sweetwaters.

HOPE RANCH (BERNIE'S OPEN OCEAN OYSTERS)

Bernard Friedman, of Santa Barbara Mariculture, grows his very unusual oysters a mile offshore, making them the most oceanic oysters in America. The Southern California coastline isn't blessed with natural bays or inlets, so oysters must be grown in suspended culture. Friedman's oysters grow in lantern nets twenty to fifty feet deep in water that can be one hundred feet deep. Friedman needs that deep water; if the water is shallower than fifty feet on that coast, the oysters and equipment get beaten up in storms by the powerful Pacific waves.

Growing in the clean, clear, warm ocean, Friedman's oysters are remarkable in several ways. The yellow and black stripes on the shells look a lot like the Carlsbad Blonds grown farther south. Many Pacific oysters have these stripes as babies, but usually the stripes disappear as the oysters get scoured by sediment close to shore. Lantern-net oysters keep their stripes.

The oysters also grow very quickly in this high-energy ocean environment. Reaching market size in a little over a year, they have the easy, mellow flavor you'd expect in a Southern California oyster, lots of brine, and a thin shell—so thin, in fact, that Friedman claims you don't even need an oyster knife to open one. Just snap off the tip of the shell with your hand and reach in with a kitchen knife to cut the adductor muscle.

The seasonal flavor of Friedman's oysters is not driven so much by water temperature as by the spring and fall algae blooms. After the blooms, the oysters get particularly fat and sweet, meaning they are at their peak in June and July and again in October and November. The oysters are all triploids, so spawning is not a consideration, and that far offshore his lease area is free from pollution, vibrio, or any of the other problems that can haunt oysters. He has never been closed by regulatory agencies for any reason. He sells his oysters in restaurants and bars under the Hope Ranch brand, and at the Santa Barbara Farmer's Market as Bernie's Open Ocean Oysters.

KUMAMOTO

California and Oregon grow a lot of Kumamotos. Hog Island Shellfish grows them. Coast Seafoods, a large operation with oysters in both California and Washington State, grows massive "plantations" of Kumamotos on long lines in Humboldt Bay, suspended about a foot off the bottom. Kumamotos aren't always identified by provenance, so it's hard to specify distinctions. Oregon is blessed with sandy beaches, and many Oregon Kumos are beach-cultured on those firm bottoms; they are rougher looking, stronger flavored, and harder shelled than the Humboldt longline Kumos. They can also taste watery after a hard rain. But in general, both California and Oregon Kumos have the classic attributes: small size, deep cup, wonderfully plump meat, and sweet, fruity flavor.

NETARTS BAY

The gunmetal gray waters of Netarts Bay and Tillamook Bay, in northern Oregon, are alive with charter fishing boats. Numerous rivers empty into the bays, making them salmon paradises. Tucked out of the way of all this action, Netarts Bay oysters are beach-cultured and taste like it: strong, tongue-coating, slightly metallic in flavor. The meats have a softness and a distinctive black line through the mantle.

TOMALES BAY

The Tomales Bay Oyster Company is California's dean of oyster operations, in business continuously since 1909. It concentrates on Pacifics. While the waters are the same shallow, relatively warm environment so helpful to Hog Island's oysters (the southern end of Tomales Bay is one of the only spots in Northern California where the water ever gets swimmable), everything else is different. Tomales Bay Oyster Company is scruffy and low-key, and its oysters are bottom-grown and hand-picked. Not as pretty or deep-cupped as Hog Islands, they are stronger flavored.

YAQUINA BAY

Deep-cupped, sweet, and melony, this is a Pacific masquerading as a Kumamoto. The thin shell and mild flavor clearly mark this oyster as a product of suspension culture. The Wachsmuth family, who founded the Dan & Louis Oyster Bar in Portland in 1907, later founded the Oregon Oyster Company in Yaquina Bay to ensure a supply of oysters for their restaurant. But the history of oystering in Yaquina Bay is even older than the Wachsmuths. Yaquina was the next bay up from San Francisco with a sizable supply of Olympias, as reported by a stranded boat captain who discovered them in 1852. But the size of the estuary was minuscule compared to the big bays, and, in terms of slowing down the hunt for new oyster supplies, it proved little more than a speed bump on the way to Shoalwater (Willapa) Bay in Washington State. The Olys were cleaned out almost immediately, and the industry foundered until being picked up by the Pacific oyster in the 1920s.

WASHINGTON STATE

SAY YOU WERE the god of oyster eaters, charged with the task of designing oyster nirvana. You'd create an ocean current (like the North Pacific Gyre) that crosses thousands of miles of open water and stops right at your door, bringing an eternal supply of pristine cold water to keep temperatures low. You'd design a fractalized coast of fissures and inlets, all folded in on itself to make myriad pockets of calm, sheltered water (like Puget Sound). For variety, you'd throw in a genuine glacial fjord (a Hood Canal) whose icy waters produce a distinctively firm and clean-flavored oyster, plus a shallow seaside bay (such as Willapa) for briny oysters. You'd build an immense mountain range up on the coast (like the Olympics) to rake incoming clouds and create a climate of generous rain, feeding mountain rivers that sweep sweet nutrients and freshwater into the estuaries. And you'd add a culture of appreciative restaurateurs, seafood shops, and consumers, ensuring that every stunning waterfront had an eatery serving fresh local oysters.

Welcome to oyster nirvana.

Washington State has dominated the oyster industry on the West Coast since the 1850s and the half-shell business nationwide since the 1980s. Nowhere else possesses such an amazing jumble of landscapes, of oyster species, and of nuanced oysters. Nowhere else, except the Gulf of Mexico, do oysters still grow wild with such abundance. No state has so many parks where anyone can harvest shellfish. No city is as oyster-mad as Seattle.

Virtually all this culture is built on the Pacific oyster, a Japanese transplant never seen in the state until the 1920s. Olympias, the native

West Coast oyster, were virtually extinct by then, done in by overharvesting and pollution from pulp mills. Eastern oysters, after a brief flirtation, hadn't worked out either. Like the cavalry thundering over the hill in a Hollywood Western, the Pacific oyster arrived just in time to save a dying industry, the first four hundred cases landing from Japan in 1919 after an eighteen-day sea voyage. Unlike said Hollywood cavalry, the oysters promptly expired upon arrival. Unceremoniously dumped into Samish Bay, they harbored a surprise, for caking their shells were millions of infinitesimal—and alive—spat. Two years later, the floor of Samish Bay was thick with six-inch Pacific oysters.

For the growers of Washington State, the Pacific oyster seemed too good to be true. It abided pollution like a pigeon. It grew astonishingly fast and astoundingly large. A yearling Pacific oyster would have ten times the meat of a mature Olympia.

For the original importers of Pacific oysters, J. Emi Tsukimoto and Joe Miyagi, it *was* too good to be true. They were innovative, yes; they were hard-working, yes; but they were also Japanese. When the Anti-Alien Land Act of 1921 was passed, prohibiting noncitizens from owning anything in the United States, the writing was on the wall. Tsukimoto and Miyagi sold their land and company and returned to Japan while they still could.

Meanwhile, Washington's oystermen discovered that the elfin Olympia oyster had been holding them back. Bolstered by the new überoyster, their production numbers exploded, from 6,500 gallons of meat in 1929 to 1.1 million gallons in 1941. They continued to import seed from Japan for all those oysters, until World War II put a stop to that practice. A blessing in disguise, the cutoff forced growers to tackle the challenge of seed production. By the 1940s, they had mastered catching naturally spawned larvae. This, combined with renewed seed sales from Japan, got them through until hatcheries became adept at generating millions of larvae in tanks in the 1980s. The Pacific oyster—and oysterman—was safe.

How much of the opposite mind-sets of the Eastern and Western oyster industries can be traced back to this imported oyster savior? Easterners hitched their wagons to the native *Crassostrea virginica* and have stuck with it ever since. Westerners had to find a new oyster and have continued to experiment with other species. They brought in *virginicas* and European Flats. They tried out the Suminoe and the Tasmanian oyster. In the 1940s, they brought in the Kumamoto when Pacifics were hard to get. It grew slowly and stayed small, so for decades it was an afterthought. In the 1990s, as the half-shell market took off, everyone realized that the do-no-wrong Kumo had approval ratings that would be the envy of any president. It is now among the most popular of oysters. Undoubtedly, Northwest growers will continue to try out new species and culture methods in their ongoing hunt for the Next New Oyster.

NORTH PUGET SOUND

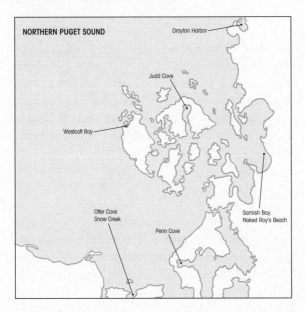

South Puget Sound, with its gentle beaches, is ready-made for oyster farming. North Puget Sound is not. The island coves to the north are deep and rocky, so it's no surprise that most of Washington's suspended-culture operations are concentrated in this area. With fewer land influences, the oysters from North Puget Sound tend to be brinier than those of the South Sound and lighter flavored—more cucumber than smoke.

BAKER

An oyster that, like the Rainier, is named for one of western Washington's dominant mountains. Bakers are big—close to five inches—and at the upper limit of the half-shell size. Grown on Samish Bay's windswept beaches, they are like oversized Penn Cove Selects, which they may indeed be. Great, but rare, oysters.

JUDD COVE

A Pacific oyster grown in the immaculate waters of Orcas Island, between Washington and British Columbia. Out there, they are practically immune to the vibrio and red tide attacks that affect mainland Washington oysters. Grown in bags on long lines, Judd Coves have pretty shells with purple and green swirls, and creamy white flesh contrasting with a precise black mantle. They are mild and vegetal in flavor, only slightly salty, and easy to eat.

NAKED ROY'S BEACH

A terrific oyster, fruity and rich, with a nose that mixes rhubarb, spinach, and river humus. The shell has a deep, pearly interior and frills so extreme you wonder how the thing closes. The resemblance to a Penn Cove Select is strong, and since both oysters come from Samish Bay, it's tempting to believe that something about Samish Bay's sandy shores and windward orientation produces oysters with amazing, wavy shells. But forget the oyster; what about Naked Roy? He was a character known for staking out a particular section of sand on Samish Bay and working on his full-body tan. He has been immortalized in the unofficial name of the beach and now the oyster. And that makes *three* great oysters—the others being

Rhode Island's Moonstones and Martha's Vineyard's Tomahawks, from near Gay Head—associated with nude beaches.

OTTER COVE

Many oysters in Washington State are started as seed in suspension and then scattered on intertidal beaches to harden for the second half of their lives. Otter Cove oysters are just the reverse, making them unique. They are wild oysters harvested from mid–Hood Canal beaches and brought to Snow Creek Seafarms. There, the oysters are transferred to rack and bag and dipped into the briny waters of Discovery Bay for a few months. Free from the disruptions of tidal exposure and predation, the oysters feed continuously and fatten up. They take on a touch of the tang of Discovery Bay, but maintain the thick shells developed from a few years on the rough-and-ready beaches of Hood Canal. That, in fact, was why Tom Madsen started doing Otter Coves—to satisfy the requests of chefs who had asked for an oyster with the flavor of his Snow Creeks but without the brittle shells. *Otter Cove* is the old-timers' name for Madsen's corner of Discovery Bay, where people used to go to hunt otters. The hunters are gone but the otters remain. They delight in tangling Madsen's oyster equipment every chance they get. He says they make up in entertainment value what they cost him in time.

PENN COVE SELECT

Each fall Elliott's Oyster Bar on Pier 56 in Seattle hosts its "Oyster New Year," a frenzy of oyster consumption, and part of the festivities is the Most Beautiful Oyster contest. Growers submit what they consider their prettiest oyster, then the anonymous nominees spend their evening on a multitiered pedestal being judged by a panel of experts. Here's the catch: The first round of judging involves closed shells, but then a chef shucks all the oysters and a second round of judging focuses on the half-shell presentation. The growers have no idea what their oysters will look like once shucked—unless they are so in touch with their oysters that they can sense it from the outside. That must be the case for Penn Coves, because they have something of a stranglehold on the

The floating oyster and mussel rafts of Penn Cove, with Mount Baker on the horizon.

Most Beautiful Oyster competition. Three times in the past several years they have won. The 2006 competition was such a slam-dunk that it was almost embarrassing for the other oysters. One plump contestant sat there in its perfect filigreed shell, simply vibrating with class and vitality. It mopped the stage with the other fourteen entrants and received a perfect score from many judges.

That oyster was a Penn Cove Select, and though not every Penn Cove will get a perfect score, a lot come pretty close. Beach-cultured in Samish Bay, then hung in the deep waters of Whidbey Island's Penn Cove to purge, they are one of the quintessential Northwest oysters, eternally popular. They always have a nice size—four inches or so—gray-green shells, and the crunchy freshness of a salted cucumber. *Select* is the key word here—oysters that don't make the cut are mercilessly culled.

It's impossible to say how much of a Penn Cove Select's flavor is due to Samish Bay and how much to its time at Penn Cove. Both have an influence. Samish creates a lovely, hard-shelled oyster. Penn Cove, which is shaped like a catcher's mitt, receives the nutrient-rich waters pitched out of the Skagit River, directly across the passage from Whidbey Island, possibly brightening the flavor a little, as well as contributing a 28-ppt salinity to the oyster. Penn Cove sells twenty-six different oysters from its floating rafts in Penn Cove, all from different West Coast growers, as well as millions of mussels, but it would be hard to top its own.

SAMISH BAY

Samish Bay was where the first Pacific oysters grew in 1919 after being tossed from their cargo ship. It has been chock-full of them ever since. Its shallow, firm-bottomed shores are ideal for beach culture, and that's what you see in Samish. Numerous oyster growers, including some of the biggest, have farms in Samish Bay. Whoever is producing a Samish Bay, expect a less cleaned-up version of a Penn Cove Select—rough, lichen-green shells, medium salt, and plump, sweet, mild meats.

SNOW CREEK

"You're the guys with the shack on the beach," is how Tom and Marie Madsen often get identified by oyster buyers. True, the Madsens have kept things very simple in the twenty years they've been farming oysters. They were the second farm to focus on the half-shell trade, after Westcott Bay, and they had to learn through trial and error. "You don't know a thing about oysters until you've killed a couple million of 'em," Tom says.

Like Westcott Bay, Snow Creek uses suspended culture, because Discovery Bay is deep, with no natural beaches. Snow Creeks are grown in water ninety feet deep, and out near the mouth of Discovery Bay the bottom drops to three hundred feet. They are started in suspended trays and then transferred to bags attached to rebar racks and dropped just off the bottom, where they can fatten up and develop full flavor. They are both sweet and salty, with a distinctive Disco Bay iron tang. The delicate shells have an orange-brown tint to them and a black stripe reminiscent of Long Island's Peconic Bay oysters (such as Widow's Holes and Oysterponds). One is tempted to peg that iron quality on the upweller effect of the North Pacific Gyre, sweeping iron-rich bottom waters straight into Discovery Bay as it turns down the coast. Think of Snow Creeks as the Pacific analogs to those East End *virginicas*.

Discovery Bay is big and deep and opens wide onto the Straits of Juan de Fuca. The nearly unpopulated bay is pristine—and marine. No significant rivers feed into it, just tiny, icy Snow Creek, so it maintains a salinity of around 30 ppt. Its cliffs are lined with nothing but Douglas fir, hemlock, madrona, and big-leaf maple, its waters filled with otters and loons. Hokusai would have felt right at home making his woodcuts here.

SNOW CREEK FLAT

The strongest, most terrifying oyster in Washington State lurks in the crystal depths of Discovery Bay, waiting to ambush unsuspecting eaters. It goes by the name of Snow Creek Flat. It has been grown in Discovery Bay since the 1980s, but it keeps a low profile, and if you find it you are a lucky duck. Or not. I've seen people contort their faces upon trying one and start spitting out words like "creosote." Or, "I feel like I just licked a piling!" I wouldn't go that far. Broth and hazelnut and fish sauce, sure. Scared yet?

The seed for Snow Creek Flats comes from the same hatchery as Westcott Bay's Flats, and the growing technique (suspended culture) is virtually identical, yet the flavors of the two oysters are worlds apart. Snow Creek Flats have that mouth-filling umami twang and corrupt meatiness, while Westcotts have just a hint of metal. "It's the water," you say, yet the Straits of Juan de Fuca, which pour into Discovery Bay, also fill Westcott Bay, just fifteen miles north, a few hours later. The shells don't even look alike: Snow Creeks are mottled with rust and gold, while Westcotts are almost pure white. What gives? I can't say for sure, but I know oysters that grow in crowded conditions and can't get quite enough food tend to have pale shells. Perhaps Westcott crowds their Flats to lighten the flavor and make it more palatable to most consumers. If you've never had a Flat, start with a Westcott. If you like it, and are ready for adventure, tackle a Snow Creek.

Westcott Bay Flat

THE OYSTER

Westcott Bay became famous in the 1980s for its European Flats—the first commercially produced in America. Though the Flats now play a smaller role than the Westcott Bay Petites, they are still the Flat you are most likely to encounter. They are also the easiest to confront: Because of the growing techniques and the nature of Westcott Bay, out in pristine San Juan Island, they have a milder flavor than any other American Flat—more in keeping with the French Flats they are modeled on. You still get the copper at the back corners of your tongue, but not the full burst of nutty caviar you get with some Flats. The small, round shell is almost uniformly white, just flecks of pink coloring it, and the meat is pale with a distinctive orange tinge to the mantle. A unique, if austere, oyster. Flats in Washington State usually spawn in May, then recover and get fat in late August or early September, when they are at their sweet and crunchy best.

THE PLACE

Westcott Bay gets lumped in with other Washington State oysters, but its geographical reality is so different that it should be thought of separately. Unlike the mountainous, drenched Olympic Peninsula, the San Juan Islands are low-lying and get little rain. Westcott Bay has little freshwater and thus stays saltier than the mountain-fed inlets of Hood Canal and Puget Sound. Well-protected but open to the southwest, Westcott Bay points right at the Straits of Juan de Fuca, whose waters swirl around the southern end of Vancouver Island and move aggressively toward Vancouver. These extreme currents produce a fifteen-foot tidal flush in Westcott Bay, guaranteeing all the algae-packed water an oyster can drink. Fresh from the cold North Pacific, it's squeaky clean, contributing to that famous, spotless Westcott flavor. Another perk: Westcott manages to dodge many of the red tides and vibrio alerts that shut down shallower growing areas.

THE PRODUCER

Bill Webb changed the Pacific oyster industry forever when he embraced lantern nets in the 1970s. He had been running a summer camp on his property on Westcott Bay for years, but never gave any thought to oysters, despite the productive algae blooms in the bay, because the bay bottom was steep and rocky and impossible for shellfish to get a perch on. Then Kenneth Chew, an oyster scientist at the University of Washington, asked Webb for permission to use his land to experiment with suspension culture in the bay. Webb watched the experiments, liked what he saw, and decided to turn it into a business. Chew introduced Webb to lantern nets, which the Japanese had been using for some time, and the first lantern-net shellfish operation in America began. The year was 1976, half-shell oysters were barely an afterthought, and Webb knew he wouldn't be able to charge enough for Pacific oysters to pay for the lantern nets and other costs. But he also knew of France's famous Belon and of the high esteem people had for it, and figured U.S. connoisseurs might be willing to pay enough for a European Flat oyster to make the whole thing work. Because Flats like to grow underwater all the time, and don't take well to silt or to exposure at low tide, they seemed a perfect match for his lantern nets. He named his oyster a Westcott Belon (now called a Westcott Flat), and oyster fanatics on both coasts have been thanking him ever since.

But things change. America's oyster culture has caught up with the gourmets, and today many more people are willing to appreciate—and pay for—Pacific oysters on the half-shell than dare brave the coppery Flat seas. And Flats, always finicky with their slow growth rates, long summer spawn, and poor shelf life, have become an even tougher business with the recent spread of Bonamia, a disease that wipes them out. To avoid contamination, no hatchery in the United States is currently producing Flat seed. Westcott Bay recently made the decision to concentrate on its Westcott Bay Petites.

WESTCOTT BAY PETITE

A Westcott Bay Petite is delicacy itself: fine, filigreed shells; three-inch size, sweet, mild meat that is just salty enough to keep things interesting. Westcott Bays are the original astronaut oysters, floating all their lives high above the bottom, so they never touch mud or grit of any kind, never develop significant (read: chewy) muscles, and maintain a particularly light flavor and creamy texture that many appreciate. From infancy, Westcott Bay Petites get the royal treatment: a couple of weeks in floating upwellers, then six months of childhood in nursery trays near the surface, then six months in lantern nets hanging in eight to ten feet of water. Suspended near the surface with a superior food supply, no jostling at the bottom, no predators, and no sex (they are all triploids), Westcotts have no "downtime." They feed 24/7 and mature quickly, stuffed with sweet glycogen and ready for market at a year of age or a little more. This also keeps their flavor exceptionally mild, and makes them a great starter oyster. But the fast growth and easy livin' means their shells never thicken; they fracture easily, so order Westcotts at an oyster bar where somebody else gets to shuck. (At Grand Central Oyster Bar, you will find Westcott Bay Sweets. This is the old name for Westcott Bay Petites, from an era when they differentiated between their triploids [Sweets] and diploids [Petites]. Today, the oysters are all triploids and all called Petites, but Grand Central likes the old name and continues to use it.)

SOUTH PUGET SOUND

Puget Sound reaches into Washington State like an arm dipping into a barrel. Its upper arm abuts Seattle, its elbow bends at Tacoma, and at Olympia it spreads five fingers into the land. Those five long, narrow inlets—Hammersley, Little Skookum, Totten, Eld, and Budd—comprise some of the most famous oyster appellations in the Northwest. Budd reaches directly into downtown Olympia and is closed to shellfishing, but the other four are thick with amazingly fast-growing oysters and clams. Each inlet has its distinctions, but they all contribute that characteristic South Sound flavor—full, rich, intense, more sweet than salty, a hint of cooked greens or seaweed, bordering on musky. It's like a sea version of collards with pork fat.

An extraordinary two hundred miles from the open sea, the South Sound has relatively low salinity; the sea is less of a factor. After navigating all that coastline, the water that reaches the South Sound has experienced countless land influences. It's also nutrient-rich, thus algae-rich. Rivers, tidal zones, and mudflats each add their own algae-mineral cocktail to the mix. Salmon push up those inlets in fall, flooding them with nutrients when they die. If Eastern oysters smell like wet rocks at low tide, South Sound oysters smell like wet earth at low tide. It's an acquired taste. In fact, one longtime South Sound grower confessed to me that he prefers the delicate, salty taste of Willapa Bay oysters to his own. But those who acquire it consider milder oysters too boring. They toast each other's arch taste with a musky Pinot Gris and never look back.

South Sound is blessed with a geography of miles of gentle, intertidal beaches. In the twentieth century, most farmers used rack-and-bag systems to protect their oysters from predators and to facilitate ease of harvesting. But oysters that never reach the beach never develop strong shells, so in the past few years most growers have adopted a hybrid system: Grow the seed in bags until it is big enough to resist most predators, then turn it loose on the beach to toughen up. You can even modulate the beach conditions: Spread them high on the beach, about a million per acre, where many predators can't go because of the long exposures at low tide, then, once they're larger and tougher, move them lower on the beach to the "fattening grounds" where they can feed almost all the time for the final few months. Oysters grow to market size in southern Puget Sound in a mere year—far faster than in Willapa Bay or Hood Canal.

In addition to being a prolific producer of Pacific oysters, South Sound produces virtually all the Olympia oysters on the planet. The oysters, in fact, are named for the city at the head of the bay.

BARRON POINT

A typical Little Skookum oyster, begun in bags and then spread on beaches to mature, soft-textured, sweet, not salty, and musky flavored.

CHELSEA GEM

A great oyster from Eld Inlet, a paragon of oyster appellations. Oysters in Eld grow fast, fat, and creamy-sweet, and Chelsea Gems are no exception. Unlike most Eld oysters, however, Chelsea Gems are not beach-cultured. Instead, they spend their lives in rack and bag, which maintains their black and tan coloration. You'd think this would produce brittle shells—especially since Eld Inlet is known for that—but the racks are staked low on the beach, where the oysters get beat up in every tide, and even exposed four or five times each month, which makes them strengthen their shells just enough. They come to market at the extraordinarily tender age of five months, by which time they are petite three-inchers with very deep cups, due to all the natural tumbling. Inside is a little fella with all the sweetness and low salinity of other South Sound oysters but none of the low-tide flavors common to the beach-cultured varieties.

EAGLE ROCK

Yes, there is an actual Eagle Rock in Totten Inlet. And yes, bald eagles like to perch on it. That is about all the connection they have with the oysters, which they haughtily ignore. The oysters themselves are classic Totten oysters, grown in mesh bags for eight months, then scattered on the beach to fatten and harden. They are creamy and sweet, with that distinctive Totten nori flavor. More salty than Skookums and many other South Sound oysters.

ELD INLET

If you want to plumb the mysteries of oysters, Eld Inlet would make a good subject. Since the beginning of the oyster industry in Puget Sound, Eld has been recognized for growing the richest oysters. A century ago, bags of oysters from Eld and Totten Inlets commanded two dollars more than bags from neighboring Oakland Bay. Something about the algae content of Eld gives the oyster meats a creamy yellow color, as if they were rich in butter. They may be higher in fat, but mostly it's glycogen they're rich in. The mystery of Eld is that the same conditions that grow the sweetest of oysters for some reason grow thin shells, even though they are beach-cultured. A lack of calcium in the water might be suspected, but why would Eld be any different from its neighboring inlets in calcium? Whatever the reason, most Elds get "topped" and frozen on the half-shell by Taylor Shellfish, the primary grower in Eld, then sent to the appreciative Hong Kong market. If you do see Elds at an oyster bar, enjoy the sweet meats and buttery, grassy finish, and pity the poor shucker.

HAMMERSLEY INLET

"People from Montana go crazy for this oyster," my server said as he plunked my first Hammersley Inlet in front of me. I'm not sure what to make of this, but it's hard to argue. The Hammer is big, plump, creamy-white, strong, deeply fluted, and unsubtle—everything I'd want in an oyster if I were from Montana. Hammersley Inlet is one of the South Sound inlets known for fat, funky, full-flavored oysters. Hammers have a strong cucumber finish with a metal chaser. They tend to be unusually deep-cupped, too. They are "bag-to-beach" oysters, grown in off-bottom bags until they are large enough to deter most predators, then scattered in the intertidal section of the beach to develop full size, shell strength, and flavor. That they do. When you tilt the shell up, a surprising amount of oyster slides into your maw. An excellent choice for aficionados of powerful and rangy oysters.

KUMAMOTO

If Kumamotos were grown by hundreds of different growers in different areas, we'd undoubtedly be talking about the subtle variations in each Kumo. But not that many people produce Kumos, and oyster bars always list them as simply *Kumamoto*. In Washington State, most Kumos are produced by Taylor Shellfish in Oakland Bay, part of the South Sound labyrinth of inlets and passages. Oakland Bay is an anomaly. Unlike the rich bottomland of much of the South Sound, it has gravelly, glacial soils. It grows good shell, probably due to the presence of limestone or some other source of calcium, but not good meat. Its oysters stay thin—except for the Kumos. For whatever reason, Kumamotos often do better in thinner waters like that of Oakland Bay. Taylor's Kumamotos have all the classic characteristics: two-inch size, ultradeep cups filled so fully with green-tinged, ivory meat that the oysters have a supple, pillowy look. That look belies one of Kumos' most pleasing but overlooked qualities: a wonderful denseness that makes them great fun to chew. They are sweet as can be, devoid of bitterness or fishiness, and they have an unmistakable honeydew finish. Sometimes all you want from the world is sweetness and light; at such times, the Kumo is your oyster.

MAPLE POINT

Another alias for Eld Inlet oysters. See "Eld Inlet" for the full scoop.

OLYMPIA

When an entire species of oyster is named for a single place on earth, you can expect something unique. You get it with Olys, which are no longer cultivated anywhere but the Olympia area—primarily Totten and Little Skookum inlets. This was the only spot the native oysters were able to escape the pollution and overharvesting that wiped them out elsewhere on the West Coast. Around Olympia, they are farmed as they always have been: natural-set, bottom-grown on hard shell–and–gravel substrate, harvested by hand at low tide. No machinery, no hatchery seed, no imported species. Dikes, originally built in the late 1800s, keep enough water in the inlets at low tide to protect the oysters from extreme heat or cold.

The growers still working with Olys are the ones too committed to give up, whatever the economics. These include Taylor Shellfish, which has been farming Olys for "only" a century, the Olympia Oyster Company, which has been at it in Totten Inlet since 1878, and Little Skookum Shellfish, where Brett Bishop's family started farming Olys on the inlet in 1883. His teenage son will be the sixth generation to take up the business. Olys all share an unmistakable sweet, metallic, celery-salt flavor. Those from Totten are said to be more coppery, while those from Little Skookum are nutty and musky.

It's difficult to overemphasize how tiny these oysters are. It takes 250 shucked meats to fill a pint. Olys also grow slowly—about four years to harvest, as opposed to one for a Pacific—which makes them expensive, and many people balk at paying so much for a pixie. Yet it would be a mistake to skip them in favor of a larger oyster, thinking that you were getting more for your money. An Oly is small, but it packs more flavor and interest than a full-sized Pacific or Eastern oyster. And isn't it flavor you're after? If you're looking to fill your belly, I suggest the potatoes.

RAINIER

A big oyster, named for the behemoth that dominates most views of southern Puget Sound. Rainiers are usually four inches but can be up to six inches in length, more suitable for the barbecue than the raw bar. The predominant taste is salt, without much sweetness.

SKOOKUM

Little Skookum Inlet marks the farthest capillary of Puget Sound. Fed by Lynch Creek, which is stuffed with salmon each fall, it counts the

Little Skookum Shellfish on tiny Little Skookum Inlet.

surrounding land as a much stronger influence than the sea. That is one key to understanding Little Skookum oysters; the other is the inlet's shape. Little Skookum's basin is a wide, shallow U. It empties completely into Totten Inlet at low tide and is one continuous shellfish bed from shore to shore. Its exposed upstream mudflats, warmed and moist, are a finer algae incubator than any hatchery. When the tide returns, a carpet of green and brown is lifted off the mudflats and puréed in the currents, creating a thick, funky soup that grows fat, buttery clams and oysters. It grows them fast, too: Oysters reach three-inch market size in as little as six months, and generally have the raised "coonfoot" ridges on their shells indicative of an oyster bottom-grown in swift currents (which in Little Skookum can reach several miles per hour). As you might expect from an inlet so shallow and far from the sea, Little Skookum oysters are not salty.

I once ate Little Skookums with a leggy blonde who proposed that *Skookum* should be a verb, as in "Let's skookum." I think it's more of an adjective, and it's the perfect word to describe the taste of those oysters: skooky. If you don't know what *skooky* is, I'm not sure I can make you understand, but eat a Little Skookum oyster and you'll get it right away: rich, musky, soft-fleshed, and bursting with vegetal bayou intrigue.

STEAMBOAT

Steamboat Island is a small, supposedly steamboat-shaped knob of hemlock and madrona trees, wild berries and gravelly beaches, rising right where Totten Inlet joins the other fingers of southern Puget Sound. Isolated yet well positioned, it makes extraordinary oyster habitat. It's a Totten by any other name, deep-cupped and fluted, gray-green, fast-growing, with a mild, earthy flavor and a cucumbery crispness as you chew.

TOTTEN INLET

The two most famous appellations in south Puget Sound are Totten Inlet and Little Skookum Inlet, and since Little Skookum is actually a tributary of Totten, the two often are thought of interchangeably. Both have seriously algae-thick waters, leading to market-sized oysters in a year or less. But differences do exist. While Little Skookum is basically a creek bed that fills at high tide, Totten is ninety feet deep in places and much more a creature of the sea. It produces oysters with the rich seaweedy flavor South Sound is famous for, but a bit saltier and less earthy than Little Skookum. Little Skookum oysters get first crack at the intense brown and green mudflat algae that develop at the head of Little Skookum, while Totten oysters get a mix of those mudflat algae and ones that grow in deeper water. Many believe the resulting oyster to be the perfect combination of flavors—strong, but still sea. Most oysters raised in Totten Inlet are beach-grown, giving them nice hard shells. Taylor Shellfish and Little Skookum Shellfish are the largest and oldest oyster farms in Totten Inlet and the likely source of your Tottens. That's a good thing, since both are known for meticulous quality and safety standards.

TOTTEN VIRGINICA

There was a time when the Eastern oyster, *Crassostrea virginica*, dominated the Northwest industry. Starting in the 1890s, once railroads made it possible to transport live Eastern seed oysters to California and Washington, many growers switched from the fast-disappearing native Olympia oysters to Easterns. Easterns were larger and commanded higher prices. They also grew to a marketable size more quickly. They were less fragile and had better survival rates during both harvest and shipment. Grown in Willapa Bay and Puget Sound, they tasted deliciously sweet. Financially, they made much more sense. There was only one problem: They didn't reproduce. A few did, and to this day a far-flung colony exists in Boundary Bay, British Columbia, and a handful turn up in Willapa, but the great majority of Eastern oysters never got warm enough in the cool Northwest to even think about sex. Northwest growers had to buy seed from the East Coast every year, which cut into their profits and their independence. When the vigorous Pacific oyster came along, which grew twice as fast as a *virginica* and grew anywhere, growers didn't think twice before jumping ship. The Eastern oyster disappeared from the Northwest.

Taylor Shellfish was a part of those early days, and apparently had been thinking about *virginicas* ever since. Bill Taylor's great-grandfather had an area in Totten Inlet a century ago called the "Eastern Bed" where *virginicas* were planted in the spring and harvested in the fall, once they were fat with Totten sweetness. Today, with local hatcheries now providing oyster seed, the primary obstacle to raising Eastern oysters is gone. Recently, Taylor brought the Eastern oyster back to Puget Sound, and Totten Virginicas were an instant hit. With the incomparable, springy texture of an Eastern oyster and the ripeness imparted by Totten Inlet, they leaped to many people's must-have lists. Demand has outpaced supply ever since, mostly due to seed issues. *Virginicas* still don't reproduce reliably in Pacific waters, even in hatcheries. When you find one, try it, if only to explore whether nature or nurture makes the oyster. How does a Totten Virginica differ from its distant East Coast siblings? How does it compare to its *gigas* neighbors in Totten Inlet? These are the things that keep us oyster geeks up at night.

WILDCAT COVE

A great name, and a good oyster. Wildcat Cove is a tiny alcove of water just where Little Skookum Inlet feeds into Totten Inlet. If I were the first oyster farmer on earth and had my pick of spots, I'd probably start right here—rich plankton, great water exchange, no boat traffic. The oyster is fat and meaty, strong flavored, tough shelled, as you'd expect from a bag-to-beach South Sound oyster. The rich environment imparts a very sweet collard-greens flavor with a melon-rind finish. The shells tend to be fluted and horned.

HOOD CANAL

Just a few miles of fir forest separate Hood Canal from Puget Sound, but geologically they are worlds apart. South Puget Sound is a land of gentle terrain and shallow inlets. Hood Canal, on the other hand, is steep and deep: steep mountains above, deep waters below. It is not a canal; no human is responsible for it, other than the typographer who mistyped

"Hood Channel," the original name chosen by the mariner George Vancouver when he first spied it in 1792. But forget "channel" and "canal"; it's a genuine fjord, the only one in the continental United States.

What's a fjord? Take a glacier, use it to gouge a steep and narrow valley, fill that valley with saltwater, and you've got a fjord. Because sea levels were lower during the ice age, glaciers sometimes carved their valleys in areas that are now well below sea level. When global temperatures warmed, ice caps melted, the seas rose again, and these glacial channels were filled with seawater. Fjords tend to have steep mountains on their sides, equally steep sides underwater (Hood Canal averages five hundred feet in depth), and an underwater sill near the sea entrance, which is the rock and soil bulldozed into a wall by the front of the glacier.

For Hood Canal, that sill looms large. It acts like a baffle, preventing most water in the canal from exchanging with the sea. While many inlets in Puget Sound change all their water daily, it takes many years for a complete turnover in Hood Canal. This situation, combined with Hood Canal's steep sides and extreme depth, means that the water in the fjord is stratified. It tends to settle into layers, with the saltier, colder, denser water on the bottom and the fresher, warmer, lighter water on top. This is not so good if you live in the southern end of the fjord, sixty-plus miles from the sea, which also happens to be the well-populated end. Not able to flush out the nutrients that flow into it from land, southern Hood Canal has in recent years experienced major algae blooms. When the algae dies and decays, it takes the oxygen with it, and the water goes hypoxic—devoid of oxygen. No animals can live in this "dead zone." Major efforts are currently under way to reduce nutrient-loading into the southern canal.

Fortunately, the mid- and upper canal are in much better shape, especially for shellfish. The eight-thousand-foot Olympic Mountains basically fall off into Hood Canal. River after river—Skokomish, Hamma Hamma, Duckabush, Dosewallips, Quilcene—comes surging down those mountain slopes and barrels into the canal at breakneck speed, filling it with sweet, oxygen-rich water. The steepness of the land prevents towns from getting much of a foothold; populations are sparse.

Oysters adore Hood Canal. Sure, there may be oxygen problems a hundred feet down, but up in the intertidal zone, things are just right. The water is kept brackish, cold, and oxygenated by the Olympic rivers. Even more important, the glacier left behind a gravelly till, quite unlike the muddy substrate that dominates Puget Sound. Firm river deltas line the canal, every one of them laced with brackish sloughs and thick with oysters. (It's no coincidence that almost all the river names above also name an oyster.) Slow-growing oysters, to be sure. Thank the ever-frigid waters, which stay in the 40s most of the year. In winter, there isn't much sunlight, either; almost no algae grows in Hood Canal, and the oysters go into a holding pattern, living off their glycogen reserves. In spring, Hood Canal experiences a significant diatom bloom, an algae that the oysters seem to adore; they become sweetest then. Another algae bloom occurs in the fall, but it involves different plankton, not diatoms, and the oysters stay more salty than sweet.

You can see the difference in food supply between Hood Canal and southern Puget Sound at a simple glance. Stick your arm all the way in South Sound and you won't be able to see your hand. But on Hood Canal, with polarized sunglasses, you can count the oysters on the bottom. Those slow-growing oysters are tough for an oyster farmer looking for a quick return on his seed investment, but they're the real deal for oyster eaters: A five-year-old oyster has a satisfying tooth to it that a watery two-year-old of the same size doesn't. The classic Hood Canal flavor is very different from that of southern Puget Sound; more lettuce and lemon zest, saltier, less sweet, and very firm for a Pacific.

Route 101 hugs the west side of Hood Canal along most of its length, treating you to jaw-dropping views at every curve: hemlocks tumbling into the sea, eagles perched above rocky crags, golden big-leaf maple leaves pinwheeling along the roadsides in the wake of every passing car in fall. Many people sell oysters along the canal. Look for the hand-drawn signs, as well as that singular Washington phenomenon, the kiosk-sized espresso drive-thru that also sells local oysters. Most restaurants on the canal offer several oyster dishes.

But why pay anything for your oysters when you can harvest them yourself? One of the great pleasures of Hood Canal is picking your own

The Dosewallips River Delta, Hood Canal.

oysters from its beaches and deltas. Wild oysters grow everywhere, maintaining a vigorous natural set that is rare on either coast. Public tidelands and state parks line the canal, most allowing recreational shellfishing. Dosewallips State Park is the crown jewel, with more than three million harvest-sized oysters studding its beaches. Dosewallips has stood the test of time—Native Americans gathered oysters there centuries ago. Watch for harbor seals as you harvest; they love to haul themselves out on the flats to bask in the sun. Seal Rock Campground, Shine Tidelands State Park, and Whitney Point, next to the Washington State Shellfish Lab, are also excellent shellfishing locations. Get a fishing license before harvesting, and check signs at the parks to make sure oyster season is open and that there are no closings for health reasons.

BAYWATER SWEET

A triploid Pacific oyster farmed by Joth Davis, one of the smart guys in oysterdom. There's something about marine scientists, such as Bob Rheault of Moonstone Oysters, John Finger of Hog Island, and Tommy Leggett of York Rivers, that compels them to farm oysters. Davis, who is in charge of hatchery research for Taylor Shellfish, grows his in Thorndyke Bay, near the top of Hood Canal, not far from the famous floating bridge. The oysters, farmed using a rack-and-bag system, are one of the few Hood Canal oysters I know that aren't beach-cultured, though they are still exposed at low tides. Davis also tumbles them quite a bit, which explains their deep cups and strong shells. They are a bit milder than most Hood Canal oysters, no doubt because they are off the bottom, and as sweet an oyster as you will ever taste. Since they are in the upper Hood Canal, not far from the sea, they are also quite salty. This combination of strong salt and strong sweet makes them a perennial favorite at Seattle oyster bars. Interestingly, Joth Davis was raised in Cape Cod eating *virginicas*, but now prefers *gigas*, making him one of the few people to switch teams. His brother, Chris Davis, is part of Maine's Pemaquid Oyster Company and is firmly devoted to *virginicas*. Davis family reunions involve a good-natured contest for bivalve supremacy.

DABOB BAY

Whitecap-whipped Dabob Bay forms the hood in Hood Canal's cobra shape. Hundreds of feet deep, surrounded by steep, dark, unbroken evergreen forest, it grows good oysters. It was the spot chosen by Taylor Shellfish for its hatchery, due to the clean, clear waters. Those waters are not algae-rich—the bay is too cold and too far from any substantial source of nutrients—which is what you want in a hatchery. You don't want wild algae competing with the select strains you introduce to the water you draw from the bay. With limited food, Dabob oysters grow slowly, staying light and crisp and salty. Quilcene Bay, which opens off Dabob, grows virtually the same oysters but more prolifically (more nutrients, shallower shoreline), and that's the name you're more likely to see, though Dabobs taste a bit purer.

GOLD CREEK

A mild oyster from the southern half of Hood Canal, cultivated on the beach in the standard Hood Canal practice. Clean, but with less of the bright lettucey freshness notable in Hama Hamas or the salty sweetness of Baywater Sweets.

Hama Hama

THE OYSTER

Back in the 1970s, when an oyster was an oyster was an oyster, Hama Hamas were one of the few West Coast names sought by connoisseurs. They were famed for their size, shell strength, firmness, cucumber flavor, and light finish. Nothing has changed. When you see a Hama Hama, you know it is a well-weathered oyster. The knobby, heavy, sand-green shells speak to life on the beach—not just for a few months, but from infancy.

Are Hama Hamas really more robust than other oysters? It's tempting to think so. After all, every one of those larvae did it the old-fashioned way, conceiving in the wild and icy reaches of Hood Canal, navigating its way to the perfect beach, then grabbing onto a piece of shell and holding tight. No two weeks in a warm hatchery bath for these guys.

No one knows whether this makes any difference to the quality of the grown oyster, but I do know that when you bite into a five-year-old Hama Hama, you're into something substantial. It's a full-contact experience, your taste buds popping with salt and citrus, your teeth working, your nasal passage filled with aromas of lettuce and lovage.

THE PLACE

Hamma Hamma means "stinky, stinky" in the parlance of the local Skokomish tribe, which named the river for its propensity to reek with the carcasses of decaying salmon each fall. It was said that a healthy salmon river could be smelled a mile away during spawning. Stinky salmon become nitrogen for algae growth, which feeds oyster growth, so those dying salmon were reincarnated as fat oysters down on the river delta each winter. Today, the salmon run on the Hamma Hamma occurs at a fraction of its historical plenitude, and Hama Hama oysters have to get by on leaner winter fare. (Sharp-eyed readers will have noticed that the river name has four *M*s while the oyster company has two. That bifurcation happened decades ago, when the official spelling was still up in the air, and no one is willing to budge. If you are stumped on pronunciation, all you need to know is that matriarch Helena James used to refer to herself as the "Hama Hama Oyster Mamma.") Like trees, oyster shells show rings of growth, and you can see the spurt in the shells from each spring's plankton bloom, as well as a smaller one for each fall's bloom.

It's hard to imagine a more covetable oyster ground than the delta of the Hamma Hamma. The shortest major river on Hood Canal, it comes pouring out of the Fortress of Solitude that is Olympic National Forest, eighteen miles from its headwaters in Mildred Lake, draining a tight and contained watershed of snowfields, old-growth trees, canyons, waterfalls, and pools where mountain lions drink (one chased company manager Adam James a few years ago). Roosevelt Elk bugle from the high ground and graze the lower grasslands. Green-furred maple trees hug the riverbanks. Gravel from the mountains washes downstream in the spring runoff and packs the oysterbeds with hard substrate. To the east, across the canal, electricity hasn't yet arrived.

A major challenge for most oyster farmers is maintaining water quality for the watershed that feeds their bay or estuary. The houses or industry or timberlands upstream aren't necessarily managed with shellfish health in mind. But Hama Hama owns the timberland along the river that bathes its oysters, and, as you might expect, manages it with their oysters' future in mind. No fertilizer, no aerial spraying, no cutting near the river. It's a wonderfully symbiotic business. The rest of the watershed is all national forest, meaning there are more elk than people populating the Hamma Hamma valley.

THE PRODUCER

"People visit us to see how oyster companies worked thirty years ago," says Lissa James, a fourth-generation part of the Hama Hama Oyster Company family. Hama Hama does things as they have always been done, which is what you do when you happen to own some of the best oyster *terroir* in the world. All their oysters are natural-set. I examined one palm-sized piece of cultch that had sixty spat growing on it from the June spawn.

Hama Hama does give nature a hand by relocating oysters to prevent overcrowding and to take advantage of the best spots. Amid its vast beach are networks of freshwater sloughs, brackish bays, low beaches, and high ones. Some spots get great natural sets, some cradle young oysters, some are best at growing out big ones.

The diverse Hama Hama Company.

Adam James maps the beach as if preparing for a D-Day landing, marking the strategic advantages of each area and planning his deployments.

To harvest Hama Hama oysters, pickers simply high-grade the beach at low tide, filling tubs with everything large. At high tide, the oysters purge any grit, then a barge comes through, finds the tubs by the buoys attached, hauls them up, and brings them directly to the culling house at the shore, where they are immediately shucked or packed for shipping.

Hama Hama has an unusual problem in this era of dwindling natural resources. Its oysters are growing and reproducing faster than they can be harvested. The company sells mostly extra-smalls (two to three inches) and smalls (three to four inches), because that's what U.S. customers want. Once a natural-set Pacific oyster makes it beyond five inches, it is home free; no market! Hama Hama is currently burdened by a phalanx of nine-year-old monsters from 1998, date of the last superprolific natural set. But watch out, you monsters. China is coming knocking. For the Chinese, connoisseurs of "oyster steaks," hearing that someone is harvesting their juvenile oysters but sitting on the big boys is kind of like us hearing from a diamond mine that "We're selling these little ones, but we don't know what to do with the big ones." Well, China knows what to do with them. As a distributor recently told Adam James, "There are two billion people in the Far East and three hundred million of them want your oysters." Stop by the Hama Hama store while you can still get a dozen glorious six-inchers for six bucks.

PEBBLE COVE

Pebble Coves were the oysters I saw doing the oyster luge at Elliott's, in which otherwise sensible people wait, mouths agape, at the bottom of an ice sculpture for oysters to be dumped at the top and sluice their way down a twisting trough to the bottom. I guess Pebble Cove gets the award for the Fastest Oyster. It also happens to be tasty—nicely chewy for a Pacific, with clean, lettucelike flavors and moderate salt. It's bag-grown on the gravelly shores of southern Hood Canal, so avoid it in late summer and early fall when vibrio gets frisky.

Canterbury Oyster Farm on Quilcene Bay was a main producer of Quilcene oysters until it ceased operation in 1991.

QUILCENE

Oystering has always been central to the life of Quilcene Bay and the eponymous town. The local saloon is called The Whistling Oyster. Many people cultivate oysters in Quilcene—or harvest wild ones—so it's hard to generalize about a Quilcene oyster. You'll see two-inch shrimps and six-inch grillers and everything in between. Whatever they look like on the outside, all have that clean, mild Hood Canal flavor inside. If you're in Quilcene, follow the too-good-to-be-true Linger Longer Road along the shore to the Public Tidelands area. At low tide, in season, you can harvest your own oysters to your heart's content.

SISTER POINT

An oyster from southern Hood Canal, right at the "Great Bend," an area I generally avoid because the water sloshing around in that end of the canal takes *years* to flush out. Bag-started, beach-finished, and thick-shelled in the standard Hood Canal fashion, Sister Points taste mostly of salt with a bit of cucumber at the finish.

WILLAPA BAY AND GRAY'S HARBOR

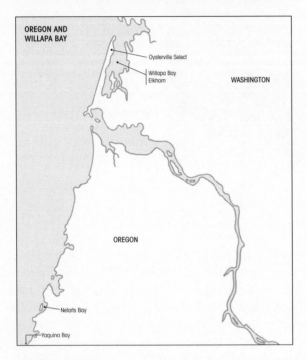

Willapa Bay was where it began, and where it almost ended. The Washington State oyster industry got its start back in 1850, when Willapa was known as Shoalwater Bay. The market was San Francisco forty-niners, and Willapa was the next great estuary up the coast from California, whose oysters were exhausted almost as soon as they were discovered. Willapa opened directly onto the Pacific, giving it much faster access to San Francisco than Puget Sound had, yet it was well protected by a barrier beach twenty miles long that left only a small exit to the ocean. What's more, its shallow flats—a full half of the bay is exposed every low tide—made for the easiest oyster harvesting imaginable. Settlers quickly muscled out the local Native Americans and established a hugely lucrative industry.

By 1900 the native oyster was wiped out in Willapa—which is why it got officially named for Olympia, where it still existed. Oystermen did not yet grasp that, by removing the shell substrate from the bay, they were removing the surface the larvae needed to set on. With all those millions of shells being shipped to San Francisco, and the bottom muddied and shell-less, the natural conditions of the bay that had made it favorable for oyster growth for thousands of years suddenly changed.

Lacking a native resource, Willapa growers looked east, importing their first load of *virginicas* in 1894. The *virginicas* didn't spawn well in the local waters, but they did grow well, and the Willapa industry carried on until 1919 by bringing in *virginica* seed by railroad each year. A catastrophic and unexplained die-off in that year wiped out the *virginica* industry just as the Pacific oyster was establishing a beachhead in Washington, and Willapa growers didn't miss a beat, switching species for the second time and somehow convincing consumers to do the same. Today, Willapa Bay and Gray's Harbor, a smaller but similar bay to the north, continue to produce a lot of oysters—over forty million pounds a year, almost 10 percent of the U.S. total. Virtually all of this has been for the shucked-meat market, but with that market in decline, some Willapa growers are changing to in-shell. Still, this is old-school, large-scale oystering, involving dumping cultch and either hand-picking or dredging the flats.

Although Willapa Bay is still prolific in its oyster production, it faces an ongoing problem in the form of spartina, a gnarly and unkillable grass common to the New England coast. Spartina arrived in Willapa along with one of those early shipments of *virginicas*. Unlike the native eelgrass, which has evolved to coexist with oysters, spartina makes poor habitat for many native species, and it grows so thick that seeding the bottom with oysters becomes impossible. So far, the spartina has more than held its own against efforts to eradicate it.

ELKHORN

The Elkhorn Oyster Company is one of the few in Willapa Bay concentrating on half-shell oysters. Speckled white and black shells, tinged with green and bumpy with barnacles, make Elkhorns among the more rustic-looking oysters. They're not prettified or citified. They are, however, meaty and briny, even mineral and musky, the strongest flavored of Willapa oysters. Impressive and worth a try.

OYSTERVILLE SELECT

Hand-picked from the tidal flats—often in the dead of night, time of
the best winter low tides—these beauties from Oysterville Sea Farms
are the pick of the Willapa litter, natural-set and carefully culled to impeccable standards for shell shape and meat quality. Dan Driscoll

Two ends of the harvesting-
method spectrum on Willapa
Bay: hand-picking and dredging. (Photos courtesy NOAA)

seemed like an iconoclast when he inherited a cannery building from his father in the early 1990s and focused on select oysters for half-shell service; now he just seems ahead of his time—an odd quality for the moldering ghost town of Oysterville. The gray-shingled Oysterville Sea Farms building, which is on the National Register of Historic Places and looks like it, teeters on the windswept edge of the bay. There's nowhere I'd rather drive four hours out of my way to buy a dozen oysters.

WILLAPA BAY

Not many oysters from Willapa Bay make it to half-shell service. Few Willapa oysters develop the perfect form that most restaurants seek, which is a shame, because the classic Willapa flavor—lightly salty, sweetly cucumber, and delicate; as pure sea as you get in a Pacific oyster—is quite nice and markedly different from most Washington oysters. The name you are most likely to encounter is that of Willapa Bay itself. It could be from many producers, could be dredged or hand-picked, could be natural-set or hatchery seed. What you can count on is that it will be from the cleanest estuary in the United States. Look for a small, khaki shell with deep ridges and a clean white interior.

BRITISH COLUMBIA AND ALASKA

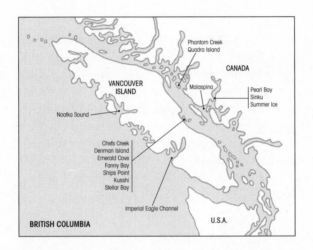

Any contest for Most Photogenic Oyster Region would go to British Columbia in a cakewalk. Every oyster farm seems to be framed by soaring sitka spruce, palatial white peaks, and maybe the fin of an orca cutting the water surface. Most of the BC coast is fjords, cut by glaciers, which makes for a landscape that is awe-inspiring—yet homogeneous. Coastal British Columbia doesn't have the varied geography of Washington State—no Puget Sound inlets working deep into the land, no gentle Willapa Bay mudflats—and its oysters don't vary greatly in flavor. Most of BC's oyster farms are clustered in the Strait of Georgia, the hundred-mile-long inland sea stretching north of Vancouver. Sheltered by the massive bulk of Vancouver Island, the strait offers endless calm hideaways for oysters. The landscape is wild

British Columbia oysters being cleaned and packed. (Photo courtesy British Columbia Shellfish Growers Association)

and unpolluted, the water very cold, and the oysters clean and mild. That smoothness is what many people want in a Pacific oyster. You won't get overwhelming or strange flavors from many BC oysters, just a little salt, a little sweetness, and, if you pay close attention, often a green apple candy note.

With so many oysters coming from a similar area, the biggest distinction to make in BC is growing method: tray-raised, beach-grown, or a mix of the two? Some BC oyster farmers have become very creative, trying out techniques not used elsewhere. This has made certain BC oysters extremely popular.

BC oysters are almost always fragile. This makes sense for the tray-grown oysters, but even the beach oysters have blown-glass shells that bear little resemblance to the green concrete slabs of Washington State beach oysters. Perhaps this comes from a calcium deficiency;

perhaps something else in the environment is responsible. Whatever the cause, it gives BC oysters a waifish quality that is incongruous with the frontier landscape from which they come.

Occasionally, Alaska oysters appear at oyster bars in the Lower 48. No, oysters did not conquer Alaska on their own. An oyster wouldn't spawn in Alaska if its life depended on it, which I suppose it does. The tiny Alaska oyster industry depends on hatchery-raised seed that is dunked in the briny depths—30 to 120 feet down, where it won't freeze—where it slowly, oh so slowly, grows. A market-sized Alaska oyster is a triumph of patience and hope in the face of economic realism. The taste and appearance is similar to BC oysters, although often saltier. The price usually reflects the expense of lengthy air shipping.

THE BC AND ALASKA OYSTERS TO KNOW

CANOE LAGOON

The best of the Alaska oysters I've tasted—and one of the best Pacifics, period—these are among the all-time favorites of Aquagrill's Jeremy Marshall. Canoe Lagoons look like Nootkas on steroids. They have the same beautiful black, auburn, and pink swirls on their shells, but these shells have the thick, layered look of oysters that have been around a while. At five inches in length, they are a rewarding mouthful. The deep, focused cups make me suspect the oysters were well tumbled in their youth. The flavor is strongly briny with a powerful cucumber finish that almost coats the tongue. This is a big oyster, from a big place. That place is Tongass National Forest, the largest in the United States. Canoe Lagoons come from Coffman Cove on Prince of Wales Island, part of the Alexander Archipelago, right on the Inside Passage cruise ships take to Alaska. It's a world of brown bears, sitka spruce, and buckets and buckets of rain.

CHEFS CREEK

One of the Baynes Sound floating-tray oysters, Chefs Creeks have the classic look: three-inch, skinny shells, not deep in cup, indicating fast growth in a suspended environment with good food supply; pure ivory meats with dark black mantles; and a big, creamy flavor. A solid oyster, probably getting more attention from chefs because of the name.

DENMAN ISLAND

Denman Island shelters Baynes Sound and many BC oyster appellations—Chefs Creek, Fanny Bay, Deep Bay, Emerald Cove, Ships Point—from the open and wild Strait of Georgia. As you might expect, these oysters are virtually identical to Fanny Bays: three inches, elongated, rough-shelled, with medium salt, a very clean flavor, and the familiar cucumber finish.

EMERALD COVE

An oyster with a wonderfully pearlescent *exterior* shell. Turn these lichen-green beauties in your hand and watch the luster play across the surface. Emerald Coves are grown off Denman Island. Inside you get the mild, creamed-cucumber flavor common to this area.

FANNY BAY

Fanny Bays were one of the first BC oysters to become widely available, and they're still considered the archetypal BC oyster—smooth, but with a pronounced cucumber finish. The town of Fanny Bay sits on Baynes Sound, but faced with a choice on an oyster list between a Baynes Sound and a Fanny Bay, which would you go for? The shells are beautifully fluted, as we expect for a tray-raised oyster. You never get a bad Fanny Bay. Somebody is practicing rigorous quality control in the Fanny Bay culling house.

IMPERIAL EAGLE CHANNEL

At East Coast oyster bars, the Imperial Eagle Channel is sometimes listed as a Washington oyster, possibly because of confusion with Eagle Rock, a Puget Sound oyster. But the Imperial Eagle is pure BC—West Vancouver Island, in fact, one of only a few from that far-flung coast (Nootka Sound is another). Imperial Eagle Channel is part of Barkley Sound in Pacific Rim National Park—*pristine* hardly does it justice. The bag-to-beach oysters have unusual shells, thin and narrow but extremely deep-cupped, like the bucket of an excavator (with the frills serving as the teeth), with otherworldly pink, purple, and orange swirls. The taste is strong on salt (pure ocean water comes right through the channel) but light on follow-through.

KUSSHI

The oyster that looks and sounds like a Pokémon character, the Kusshi is muscling in on the Kumamoto's territory. Still a rarity on East Coast menus, Kusshis are all the rage out West. Grown by Keith Reid, a highly innovative grower in Deep Bay, Kusshis are a triumph of human ingenuity. Deep Bay, as you might guess, is deep, and thus lends itself to suspended-culture oyster growing. Oysters grow quickly in such equipment and they tend to have thin, brittle shells that lose their liquid during transport or shatter during shucking. Smart growers address this problem by tumbling the oysters periodically. Bring the trays of oysters to land, dump them into long, spinning metal cylinders, tumble them, then put them back in the plastic trays and resuspend them. This breaks off the thin growing edge and forces them to thicken their shells. But it's extremely labor-intensive and oyster mortality rates can be high.

Reid took the tumbling idea to the next level. He designed round, plastic oyster trays that fit directly into a tumbler. The tumbler can live on a boat and visit the oyster floats directly. The process is very quick and efficient, and the oysters are out of the water for much less time, so they can be tumbled more frequently. That forces them to cup up. The resulting oyster, called a Kusshi, Japanese for "precious," is almost as deep as it is long—just over two inches. The unusual cornucopia shape and stunning, smooth, purple-black shell are due to the tumbling, which smooths off any frills. The depth and pillowy softness inside make the Kusshi resemble a Kumamoto, but it's a plain-old Pacific that's been tumbled into bonsai form. Fair-weather oyster eaters love the Kusshi's small size and ultraclean flavor—more delicate than a Kumo. Restaurants love the cookie-cutter nature of the oyster. Thrill-seeking oyster eaters may move on after an early Kusshi infatuation.

MALASPINA

A sweet, if mild, oyster with a distinct watermelon-rind aroma. Malaspinas tend to have creamy-white flesh and simple, narrow, khaki shells, toughened by intertidal life on the beaches of Malaspina Inlet, 150 miles north of Vancouver in an area known as the Sunshine Coast because it gets so little rain (at least, compared with the mist factory of most of coastal BC). The road network is virtually nonexistent in these parts, and few people are around except for the oyster growers. Malaspinas come out of some clean, clean water, and travel a long, long way to get to your plate.

NOOTKA SOUND

The finest of BC oysters, grown in the remote, oceanside fjords of West Vancouver Island, where the wolves and sea lions and passing gray whales rarely see a person. No roads run to Nootka Sound; only a few intrepid kayakers manage to explore it. What they find is a paradise of lush coastal rain forest, sandy beaches, and incredibly diverse life, both in and out of the water. Captain James Cook found all that, too, when he became the first European to set foot on the soil of British Columbia in 1778. The natives who already lived there knew they had a paradise on their hands and didn't particularly want to share it. They shouted "itchme nutka, itchme nutka" at his ship, which meant "go around"—to the next bay, please, not here. Cook, ever the optimist, interpreted it as "Welcome to Nootka," and the name stuck.

Nootkas are advertised as intertidal beach oysters, but the shells have all the markings of suspension culture: a pulled teardrop shape, and fluted, striped shells that look as though a watercolor artist streaked them in purple and dusty rose. Nootkas have very white meats and very black mantles. Their flavor takes you on a roller coaster, with brine up front, then the nutty sweetness of nori, and finally a finish hinting at anise.

It's tempting to make a lot out of the fact that Nootkas offer the most delicious and complex taste of any BC oyster, and come from one of the most diverse, complex, and pure ecosystems. Is it the strong salmon runs in the fall, decaying far upstream and feeding glorious algae blooms? Is it the dense thatch of salmonberries and huckleberries tingeing the rivers that run into the sound? Is it the concentration of sea otters (supposedly one of the most numerous in the world) that somehow affect the shellfish? Impossible to say, but a mystery that gets to the heart of why good food is sacred.

PEARL BAY

Pearl Bay grows three brands of oysters in suspended trays in Jervis Inlet, part of British Columbia's Sunshine Coast. This oasis amid the rain forest stays shockingly dry for the Pacific Northwest—storms exhaust themselves over Vancouver Island before reaching the Sunshine Coast. The oysters from such waters are on the salty side, which makes sense. Pearl Bay's three oysters—Pearl Bay, Sinku, and Summer Ice—are from the same seed, but grow at different depths: three depths, three marine communities, three *terroirs*. The Pearl Bays are grown on the surface and have the most typical BC flavor: sweet, smooth, and cucumbery.

PHANTOM CREEK

One of the few BC oysters grown bag-to-beach, as so many are in Washington State. Phantom Creeks start off in suspension near Cortes Island, at the very top of the Strait of Georgia, and after a couple of years are turned loose on the beaches of the island for a few months of intertidal toughening. The result is not as gnarly as beach-grown BC oysters, but better shells and shelf life than the suspension oysters.

QUADRA ISLAND

Nice little cocktail-sized Pacific oysters from the very northern end of the Strait of Georgia, in Desolation Sound. Quadra Islands have the cuteness of a Kusshi, with more flavor but less meat. Tray-grown from start to finish, and harvested at about two years of age, they have artsy, delicate white shells, flecked with pink and brown, and lots of baroque, ridged horns. In both coloration and ornamentation they remind me of those spiked caterpillars that turn up in the spring. The flavor hints at green apple candy, with a slight tarragon finish, but is lighter than most Pacific oysters, as you'd expect from a suspended oyster grown this far north. The cups have surprising variation for a tray-grown oyster; sometimes they are shallow and harbor almost no oyster at all.

SHIPS POINT

Brownish, barnacle-encrusted three-inch Pacifics, gritty and no-nonsense from beach life. Grown in Baynes Sound, these are Fanny Bay doppelgangers. The flavor is moderately salty with a bitter cucumber finish. The oyster is marketed as having a smaller stomach, thus less green algae in the gut and a milder flavor. But I haven't seen any hatchery marketing small-bellied oysters, or heard of anyone doing gastric bypass operations on shellfish, so I remain skeptical.

SINKU

Sinkus are identical oysters to Pearl Bays, but suspended in trays fifteen feet deep instead of on the surface. Not much phytoplankton thrives that far down, so the oysters' diet consists of more zooplankton (microscopic animals). This gives them less of a vegetal flavor—no cucumber or seaweed here—and more of a mild, cold milk taste. The cold, deep water keeps them nicely crisp—though not as crisp as Summer Ices, their deep-sea-diving siblings.

STELLAR BAY

A Stellar Bay is a larger Kusshi. Same grower (Keith Reid), same spot (Deep Bay), same species (Pacific), same process (aggressive tumbling), but a Stellar Bay is allowed to get a little larger. Not huge, mind you, just big enough to fill the mouth. Open a Stellar Bay and what immediately strikes you is the bountiful amplitude of its white flesh, which practically spills out of the shell. It doesn't exactly look natural, but it's compelling all the same. It's due to all that tumbling, which retards shell growth but doesn't stop the oyster from growing and pushing against the inside of the shell. What you get in a Stellar Bay or a Kusshi is more meat than you expect, a terrifically deep cup, and very little liquor (no room!). A top choice for those who prefer mild oysters.

SUMMER ICE

The third of the Pearl Bay Oyster brands, Summer Ices are a brilliant solution to the R month problem (see the chapter on "Safety"). From May to September, when most oysters are spawning, Summer Ices are suspended *sixty* feet deep in Jervis Inlet. That deep, in eternal winter, no warming or spawning occurs. Sure, you can achieve the same thing by growing triploid oysters, but you can't get the firmness that only comes with cold waters. Summer Ices, in fact, are the firmest Pacific oysters I've ever tasted, and one of my first choices in July or August. The flavor is very mild, so they benefit from a little lime or mignonette.

INTERNATIONAL WATERS

IN THE UNITED States, the pickings are slim for international oysters. Other than Canada, only Mexico, Chile, and New Zealand have live shellfish trade agreements with the United States. No farmer in Chile currently has the economic muscle to fly oysters north. With any luck, that will change soon, because Chile has some unusual oysters that would be greeted with gusto in America. Meanwhile, Mexico and New Zealand are both shipping a growing supply of excellent oysters to our shores.

Of course, zealous ostreaphiles won't settle for waiting to see what oysters come to America. They will go to the oysters. While such explorations are beyond the scope of this book, it's worth noting that the current oystermania is not just a North American phenomenon. In addition to the countries mentioned above, Brazil, Ireland, France, Spain, China, Japan, Thailand, and Australia all have healthy oyster industries.

Oyster aquaculture in Japan.
(Photo courtesy NOAA)

THE INTERNATIONAL OYSTERS TO KNOW

BAHIA FALSA

Who would have thought Mexico could grow such pretty little oysters? Striped with purple and green, these cuties resemble Kumamotos in their petite size and deep cups. Not in flavor, though. Bahia Falsas start with supreme, almost overwhelming salt, as can come only from an oyster living where it virtually never rains and the water is higher in salinity than the open ocean. The salt then gives over to sweetness and an unmistakable finish of watermelon rind. This is a surprisingly powerful oyster in a little package, and it screams out for a Corona and lime.

Mexico's regulatory standards do not exactly inspire confidence in most American oyster eaters—if you can't drink the water, why the hell would you eat the oysters?—but fear not, these babies aren't coming from a Mexico City sewer. They are raised off the coast of San Quintin, in Baja California, an undeveloped area of vacation homes and sportfishing tourism. An oyster industry has thrived here for twenty-five years, taking advantage of clean waters carpeted with eelgrass—a good sign of water quality. *Bahia Falsa* means "false bay," but it sure looks like a real bay, and a pretty good one. The original name, bestowed by wishful-thinking Portuguese explorers in the 1600s, was *Bay of Eleven Thousand Virgins*. It was meant to honor Saint Ursula, a sixth-century Roman martyr, and her eleven thousand handmaidens. (If the thought of eleven thousand virgin handmaidens sounds unlikely, give yourself points for paying attention. The original Latin inscription read: "XI M. V." For centuries this was read as "11 mille virgos." By the time somebody realized the *M* stood for "martyred," not "mille," it was too late. Christopher Columbus named the Virgin Islands in the Caribbean after the same story.)

COROMANDEL

It's a little demoralizing when a *foreign* oyster beats all your home team oysters, but that's what happened to me one day at the Grand Central

Oyster Bar. After tasting perhaps fifteen different Pacific oysters, I identified a clear winner—the Coromandel. It was brinier than most Pacifics, crisper than any of the others except the Summer Ice, and bright with citrus aromas. And that's *after* being flown ten thousand miles from New Zealand! One can only imagine how good they are in Coromandel, a spur off New Zealand's North Island once known for its hippie enclave and now for its oysters and mussels. It's well worth sampling a Coromandel to take note of what flavors a whole different hemisphere can impart in an oyster.

EL CARDON

Another Mexican oyster from Bahia Falsa. El Cardons come a bit bigger than Bahia Falsas, with viridian outer shells and stunning mother-of-pearl interiors shimmering with green and purple. Like Bahia Falsas, the salt is extreme and the finish clearly watermelon rind. The adductor muscles can be unpleasantly chewy, which may be an argument for keeping Baja oysters small.

KUMAMOTO (BAJA)

Kumos from Baja are appearing more and more frequently at raw bars, and they're always good, as well as being more affordable than your California and Washington State Kumos. Sweet and melonlike, they are grown by Mark Reynolds, a "disillusioned banker" now trying his hand at oysters in the pristine waters of Laguna Manuela, near Ensenada. Baja, with its sparse populace and total lack of industry, makes for great shellfish farming; a Baja Kumo grows to market size in a year, instead of the four years it takes a northwest Kumo. In addition to oysters, Reynolds is playing around with abalone and a scallop known as *mana de lyon*. Reynolds has a funny challenge: The Baja region produces high-quality oysters and has high labor costs (due to the lack of local workers). Yet, because it's Mexico, the perception is just the opposite. Thus far, Baja Kumos are a bit lower priced than most, making them a steal.

EVERYTHING YOU WANTED TO KNOW ABOUT OYSTERS BUT WERE AFRAID TO ASK

SHIPPING, SELECTING, STORING, SHUCKING, SERVING, AND SAVORING YOUR OYSTERS

SHIPPING

"You live in Vermont and you're writing a book about oysters—that's so funny." If I had a dime for every time someone has said that to me . . . well, I could buy a few oysters and have them shipped to my door. That's what I do, and whether you live in Denver or Duluth or Dallas, that's what you can do, too. Live oysters ship miraculously well—a fact not lost on oyster purveyors, who as early as 1869 were already shipping live oysters from the East Coast to San Francisco by rail. Remember, this was before refrigeration, and the trip could take three weeks, the oysters packed in damp straw so they wouldn't dry out. Only about one in four oysters made it, but it *was* possible. Today, with UPS trucks zipping to any outpost of the empire in two days, it's a piece of cake.

In fact, I'd argue that my Vermont oysters are some of the freshest oysters being consumed anywhere in the country—considerably fresher than the typical oysters being downed in some oyster bars, even those on the coast. Say I order a box of Moonstones straight from the Rhode Island grower. I know Bob Rheault harvests to order and is going to pull my oysters out of Point Judith Pond that day and put them on a truck. A day later, by UPS Ground, they reach me way out here in the sticks, packed in Styrofoam and icepacks and still redolent of the deep. They were in the sea two days before. If I order a plate of oysters at Joe Blow's Oyster Bar, however, it's a different story. Joe Blow can't deal with every oyster grower directly, so he gets all his oysters from a wholesaler once a week. How many days

Widow's Hole oysters in wet
storage, awaiting delivery.

were those oysters out of the water by the time they reached the
wholesaler? With good growers, only a couple of days; otherwise,
you never know. Then they sit around the walk-in for a few days before being trucked off to restaurants. So those oysters are at least
a week out of the water by the time they hit your mignonette, possibly more.

There are three points about this worth stressing. The first is that,
no matter where you live in the country, you have access to ultrafresh
oysters. Order them from a reputable producer and you, too, can kiss
the sea on the lips, even in Omaha.

The second point is that not all oyster bars are created equal. It
pays to frequent restaurants that specialize in oysters and sell thousands a week. They move through their inventory constantly and generally get several shipments throughout the week. They may even get
deliveries straight from growers. And they work with distributors
that are fanatical about freshness. A supplier like Penn Cove Shellfish, for example, keeps the oysters from many small growers hanging
four feet deep in the cool waters of Penn Cove until they are ordered,
and then delivers those oysters to Washington-area restaurants
within twelve hours and even New York, via air, in a day. Top restaurants that don't specialize in oysters, but whose reputations are based
on the superb quality of their ingredients, are also going to make sure

their oysters are very fresh. Clam shacks that run an oyster appetizer as an afterthought are a different story. At any restaurant, it's perfectly acceptable to ask what day the oysters came in, or which oysters are the freshest.

The third point is that those week-old oysters at Joe Blow's are not heinous. They lose that fresh flavor over time, but they aren't *bad* the way a slab of beef that's been slowly rotting in the walk-in for a week is bad. They are still alive (or should be). Food starts to decompose the instant it dies—hence our fanaticism about freshness. But a live oyster isn't decomposing, no matter how long it's been out of the water. If Joe Blow is your only neighborhood option, don't hesitate to enjoy those oysters.

SELECTING

If you're buying your oysters from a retail shop or a grower, or if you're harvesting your own, you get the bonus of picking through the selection. But what to look for? Choose your oysters, those "fruits of the sea," the same way you choose your fruit: You want individuals that are heavy for their size. Pick an oyster that fills its shell completely. Not all do, and none does all the time: After spawning, they shrink quite a bit. So unlike a fruit, whose quality steadily rises until it finally rots, an oyster yo-yos. You can get some sense of fatness by shaking the shells; you don't want a lot of sloshing inside. Weight is the best indicator of quality; an oyster that grew slowly, got fat, and created a thick shell in the process will be denser and weightier than its similar-sized brethren. If the oyster makes a hollow sound when you tap on the shell, it has lost its liquor and should be avoided.

Ease of shucking is almost as important to a pleasurable oyster experience as taste of the meat. Again, density is the thing to look for. You can also tell visually. You want an oyster that looks robust and muscular, even gnarly. If you will be putting your knife in through the hinge end, look for a nice clear notch there.

Freshness is also vital. Merchants should display the tag showing where and when the oysters were harvested. You'll find it sticking out of the ice in which the oysters are displayed, or stapled to the back of the display sign. If you don't see it, ask for it.

STORING

Once you get your oysters, you want to keep them COLD—around 40 degrees. The refrigerator is perfect. You will have instructions from your grower *not* to store them in plastic, so they can breathe. I have yet to reconcile this with the fact that they have just been shipped to me in plastic. Maybe it matters if you are going to store them for weeks, but that would be a minor tragedy. Besides, at fridge temperatures, these oysters aren't breathing much. I have stored dozens of oysters in loose plastic grocery bags in the fruit bin of my fridge for days with no casualties.

Still, you paid a lot for your oysters, you have already invested more than a little love in them, and you want them to be perfect, so treat them perfectly. Put them in a large bowl—cup side down, so they retain their liquor—and cover them with a wet cloth to keep them from drying out. (Refrigerators are good dehydrators.) Re-wet the cloth every couple of days.

SHUCKING

Away from the coddling of your favorite raw bar, you are going to be forced to shuck your own oysters. This is a good thing. Like changing a tire, it's one of those basic tasks every fully realized human being should master. It's liberating. It will save you a boatload of money and impress your guests. It's even a great icebreaker—knives, towels, and Band-Aids all around, then let the shells fly!

You'd think that after several thousand years of experimentation humanity would have settled on the best way to shuck an oyster, yet methods are surprisingly diverse. The simplified explanation goes like this: Northeasterners go in through the hinge (pointed) end, while West Coasters and Southerners go in through the bill (rounded) end. All industrial shuckers go in through the bill because it is much faster. You punch your knife in at a downward angle, quickly cut the bottom muscle first, lift the oyster up by its top shell, from which it dangles, and cut it off into a bucket. But this method invariably leaves both oyster and shell looking a little worse for wear, so "table" shuckers on both coasts go in through the hinge, the method most likely to yield an unmarred oyster ready for its fifteen seconds of fame.

Many competition-level shuckers go in through the side on their oysters—a method that takes more skill but can be much faster: The knife can go in and sweep across the top shell, severing the adductor muscle, practically in one motion. But it takes a lot of experience to be able to find the right spot on the side of the shell and to work the knife in.

Assuming you are concerned with presentation, and have no pressing need to shuck a hundred oysters in a minute, you'll want to stick to the prettiest and most foolproof method: the hinge. First you'll need some equipment. Choice of knife is essential, but so is your armor: towels, gloves, gauntlets, whatever. Don't skip this part of your prep work. You are going to be taking a sharp knife in one hand, directing it toward the flesh of your other palm, and shoving, with just a crumbly shell in between. Accidents can and will happen. Take a look at the hands of a pro shucker at a raw bar. We amateurs have even higher rates of mishap.

A good pair of gloves protects your hands really well. The downside is that once you have the oyster open and need to switch to the dainty work of prepping the oyster for presentation—severing the bottom muscle, flicking bits of shell out, dressing it with condiments, nestling it in the ice, or even slurping it (gloves take away all the sexiness)—you tend to make a mess of it in gloves, and it's inconvenient to keep removing your gloves for each oyster.

Towels don't provide full hand protection—they don't help your knife-wielding hand at all—but they do everything else better, including catch loose juices. I recommend them. If you are brand new to shucking, place a towel over your table or counter as well. It will protect the table, soak up juice, and give you a wide canvas to wipe your knife clean. (You are about to make a mess.) Oyster shells often come still caked with *terroir*. That's a nice sign of authenticity. Before beginning, you can, and should, rinse them briefly to get any loose dirt off, but don't wash them severely or you may taint their precious liquor with tap water. Besides, there's no way to remove the mud lurking in the very crannies your knife is going to explore. Fear not; once you pry the top shell up, simply wipe your knife clean on the handy towel before cutting the adductor muscle.

Fold the kitchen towel several times so it's thick enough to stop the knife when it slips and comes hurtling at you. If you are right-handed, hold the kitchen towel in your left hand. Hold the bill end of the oyster, cupped shell down, between the folds of the towel in your left hand, so the hinge end is sticking out, and press it firmly against the table. With the knife in your right hand, find a spot in the hinge along the line where the two shells meet, and begin to work your knife in.

Step 1. Hold the oyster in a folded kitchen towel and wriggle the knife into the hinge.

Novice shuckers' biggest mistake is forcing the knife in, which causes shattered shells, mangled meats, and bleeding hands. If you choose your spot well and are patient, you need to exert surprisingly little force. Try a few spots, pressing slightly, until you feel or see the knife make a little progress. I press the heel of my right hand against the butt of the knife, providing gradual but steady pressure, and wriggle the handle with my fingers. Rotate your wrist in a slight rocking motion to try to wedge your way in. You need to penetrate only a quarter-inch or so before you can pry the shells apart by fully rotating the knife blade. You can also open the shell by pushing straight down on the knife handle, as you would pry open the top of a can of paint. This method works best if you have a Nantucket-style knife (see below) and if your oysters have thick shells—though it's also a good way to snap the tip off your blade.

Once you've wedged the shells apart, you're on easy street. If the knife has mud or shell fragments on it, wipe it off on the towel before proceeding. If the knife is clean, just slide it around from the hinge to the side and continue. Your goal in this next operation is not to cut the oyster meat, so keep the knife as tight against the inside of the top shell as you can. For leverage, I usually keep my thumb pressed against the bill of the shell. It's a bit like the handhold for peeling an apple: knife in the fingers, following the thumb's lead. (This is where I sometimes get cut. I'm pretty good about not stabbing my palm with the knife, but oyster shells are sharp, and sometimes, after I've opened a few dozen, I notice that my thumb is finely filleted.)

Step 2. Keep the knife pressed against the top shell and pull it toward you.

Keeping the knife tight against the inside of the upper shell, sweep it toward you to cut the top muscle as close to where it connects to the shell as possible. You'll feel the resistance of the muscle and the pop when it's cut. Then, you can easily lift off the upper shell.

Step 3. After cutting the upper adductor muscle, remove the top shell.

If all has gone well, you will be left with a perfect, clean oyster sitting in its cup. Sometimes shell fragments will slip in during shucking; if so, flick them away using the clean tip of the knife. Other times, you will have hewed so closely to the upper shell that, instead of severing the adductor muscle, you'll have sliced a wafer of shell instead, which will still be attached to the muscle. Not a disaster: Simply cut away the muscle beneath the wafer of shell and flick them both out.

Your last step is to cut the bottom muscle so that the oyster can be smoothly slurped in one quick motion. Don't ignore this all-important step; your guests are relying on you not to make them look like idiots. The sexy carnality of tossing a raw oyster into your mouth can instantly turn into the disgusting pathos of being caught, head tilted back, oyster dangling from its still-attached shell while you use your lips in a desperate attempt to free it before anyone notices.

A common misconception is that the adductor muscle attaches directly underneath the oyster, at the center of the bottom cup. It doesn't. It's actually over on the inside curve, where the shell rises. (Many oysters are shaped more like half of a yin-yang symbol than like a disk or teardrop.) Examine an old oyster shell and you will see the blackish-purple "scar" where the muscle was attached. That's the area you want to go for, and it means you don't need to dig underneath the oyster and thrash around, which will leave you with an oyster that looks molested. Instead, reach in along the slope, again making sure to stick tight against the shell, and cut in one small motion. (It's acceptable to flip the mantle of the meat back in order to facilitate this, just make sure to flip it back before serving.)

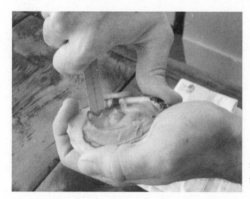

Step 4. Cut the bottom adductor muscle.

Presto. You have an oyster ready for slurping, looking as natural as when it was alive (which it may barely be).

Very rarely, along with your oyster, you will expose a tiny, living, soft-shell crab. Lucky you. This is *Pinnotheres ostreum*, the oyster crab, which coexists quite naturally with the oyster. It is an exceedingly uncommon delicacy. Fry it in butter (a few seconds per side) and enjoy it, then walk around all day with an extra bounce in your step, knowing that the oyster gods have touched your brow.

Grilling, steaming, and roasting are three alternatives to shucking. Obviously, this makes for a different experience than eating the cold, raw oyster, but it is certainly traditional. Until the advent of strong metal tools, in fact, roasting in coals was probably the primary method of oyster opening. The only other option for early cultures would have been to smash off the tip of the bill with a rock and cut the muscle from there—a method still popular in twentieth-century shucking houses. But in middens, we find plenty of nice, whole shells.

A nifty emergency shucking method is the microwave. A few seconds in one will leave oysters gapping, warm, and ready for sauce. You can also freeze them just until they start to gap (for the very good reason that they are dead). This avoids cooking them, though you run the risk of forgetting about them and having oyster ice cubes on your hands—which probably have their place.

KNIVES

Just as different geographical areas have produced different shucking methods, a surprising assortment of oyster knives have evolved, with each area claiming theirs is hands down the best and expressing bewilderment that the other types are capable of breaching an oyster at all.

The Chesapeake style of knife has a fairly long, skinny blade—about four inches—and an egg-shaped handle for grip and leverage. Many professional shuckers I've observed have been using some version of this as they go in through the bill end.

I prefer the New Haven design, whose shorter blade (under three inches) and longer, contoured handle allow for more finesse. Some versions have straight blades; others curve at the tip for extra leverage.

The West Coast style features a very short, stubby blade—less than two inches—and a handle guard. The guard is a nice idea, but I find this knife useless. Maybe it evolved to shuck Olympias and is ideal for them; with larger oysters, the short blade can't reach the adductor muscle. A West Coast knife with an immense black rubber handle is the oyster knife most common in contemporary kitchen stores. It would give you great confidence in a bar fight, but should otherwise be avoided.

Whatever oyster knife you choose, get a strong, thin blade. There's

Four oyster knives. The white-handled New Haven style (third from the top) is the only one that works.

always a trade-off: the thinner the blade, the weaker it is, but the more easily it slides between the shells. It's shocking how many cheap oyster knives bend on their first try. Other blades are made thick, for strength, and are thus incapable of penetrating an oyster shell without breaking it.

Handles can be either wood, black rubber, or hard polypropylene plastic. I favor the plastic, which is virtually indestructible, and which can be molded to a better hand shape. Shucking houses are required to use plastic. For individuals, there's no denying that wood provides a rustic appeal.

If you plan on shucking a lot of oysters in your future, you might want to follow the lead of Patrick McMurray, the world's top competitive oyster shucker, who holds the world record for having shucked thirty-three oysters in one minute. He designed his own knife, taking a steel blade that seems to be a New Haven design and wedding it to a yellow epoxy grip custom-molded to fit his right hand. Picture a banana sitting too long on the counter with a stiletto emerging from one end.

Even the best and strongest oyster knife is going to break eventually. Short of tungsten, no material can be both thin and tough enough to withstand repeated attacks on limestone. It's a good idea to have a spare knife in waiting. In a pinch, however, a flathead screwdriver—combined with a paring knife for cutting the muscle—works surprisingly well.

SERVING

Raw oysters should be served cold. In addition to tasting better that way, they will also keep your conscience free. A 55-degree oyster may show signs of stirring, like a regular heartbeat. A 40-degree oyster is about as conscious as a spruce tree in December—and you know what we do to *them*. A cold oyster is flatlining; its ignorance is your bliss.

True, cold that extreme will blunt the full oyster flavor a little—a plus for some. But even if you prefer the fuller flavor of a warmer oyster, you then face texture issues. As with sushi, you want to keep the flesh firm and crisp—the same qualities you'd want in your sake or white wine accompaniment. All have more freshness and zing when cool. When both raw oysters and white wine get warm, they can seem tired and flabby.

Now, having said all that, I confess to having fished plenty of oysters out of 60-degree water and eaten them there on the spot. They tasted divine—not cold, but fresh and seaweedy and still vibrating with the life of their creek, the energy of the waves and tides. They were of a continuum with their environment. You can taste the whole estuary in oysters still the same temperature as their habitat—maybe not what you want all the time, but it's an experience you'll go back to in your mind again and again.

In most cases, crushed ice is an oyster server's best friend. Not only will it keep the oysters the perfect temperature, but it also solves the dilemma of how to keep the half-shells and their watery contents upright. They need a medium that will adjust to their contours. Rock salt was common in the days when crushed ice was not. If you are in the right place at the right time, wide bowls of packed snow can be elegance itself. It disappears fast, but so do trays of oysters, so that's usually not a problem. (One solution: Skip the containers, nestle the oysters *outside* in the snow, jab some bottles of beer around them, and call the J. Crew photographers.) Martha Stewart might use wooden trays of chilled river pebbles for a Zen-like touch, preferably with fronds of seaweed draped just so.

All this assumes that you are serving the oysters on their shells. The shell completes the experience. It is a record of that oyster's life, a

color printout of the changing seasons and the mineral and algae concentrations in a patch of sea over time. It has a smell all its own, different from the oysters. And the contrast of rock-hard shell and fleshy
oyster is part of the appeal.

Plates with half-shell-shaped cutouts were common in the mid-
twentieth century, signaling a cultural nadir to which, with any luck, we
shall not return. Shot glasses are the new and dubious rage: Dump a
shucked oyster in one, along with its liquor and whatever sauces or al-
cohols you'd like, then slam it. This may not be elegant, but it has a certain appeal, and it helps newbies get that first oyster down. Of course,
you need a lot of shot glasses to pull this off at home; reusing dirty shot
glasses destroys the mood.

How many oysters per person? Know your guests. If Casanova is
coming, you need fifty for him alone. As a general rule, if oysters are
simply the hors d'oeuvre, plan on three oysters per person (assuming a
standard three-inch oyster). Some people will eat many more, some
will eat none. But if oysters are a theme for the evening, you need a lot.
Plan on at least six per person; many people have no trouble downing a
dozen.

SAVORING

Short of Twister, few things get a party rolling like a bar lined with
fresh oysters and chilled bottles of beer and Champagne. The primal
act of shucking and devouring live shellfish, paired with the instant
buzz delivered by bubbly alcohol, gets people in an anything-goes
mind-set. Your main goal should be to make people comfortable so
they have an unforgettable evening and are oyster converts forevermore. Does your crowd prefer things relaxed (the hoedown style of pic-
nic tables, piles of oysters, metal shucking pails, and crates of beer) or
elegant (white napkins, cocktail forks, Champagne flutes)?

But what's best for the oysters? In addition to making the setting
fit the crowd, the environment should present the oysters at their best. If
the goal is to savor the differences between oysters from distinct places,
go for the white tablecloth. Keep the focus on the oysters: colors,

shapes, sizes, flavors. Provide a range of white wines and other drinks. (See "Oyster Wines and Other Libations" for details.) Encourage people to try at least one oyster naked (the oyster, that is), but supply a full array of condiments. Most guests will want at least a squeeze of lemon. Provide, at minimum, wedges of lemons *and* limes. Better still, serve an array of citrus wedges—grapefruit, orange, lemon, lime, blood orange—for the stunning colors as much as anything else. Meyer lemons are my favorite citrus with oysters.

Mignonette always interests people, and you can make some fascinating ones. (See the recipe chapter for a full range of condiments.) With either mignonette or citrus juice, use much less than you think you need. The goal is for the acid to counteract the salt and to make the oyster taste fresh and clean. Four drops is usually enough. One wedge of lemon can get you through an entire plate of oysters. Umeboshi vinegar, made from Japanese pickled plums, has a wondrous flavor but is intensely salty. I like using a single drop of it to enliven very mild oysters.

Then there is the dilemma of cocktail sauce, James Beard's "red menace." It is a horrendous thing to do to a nice oyster, or even a decent shrimp. No, *you* don't want to use it, but you'll be surprised how many otherwise sensible people like that crutch. Unless your guests are all seasoned oyster veterans, keep it nearby. You want everyone to have a good time. Encourage the milquetoasts to try a drop of hot sauce instead. It gives them a familiar taste to cling to, yet doesn't drown the oyster.

Forks or no forks? There's something irresistible about the direct assault of human on oyster, no metal intermediary. But maybe your guests don't know each other that well. Maybe the president is coming for dinner. That calls for cocktail forks. Forks guarantee a full separation of oyster from shell and clean entry into the mouth.

Forks give the option of slurping the liquor after eating the meat. If you eat oysters straight out of the shell, you must slurp beforehand, or eat everything at once. No one agrees on what's best. Should the liquor be an aperitif? A chaser? Should you avoid it altogether so you can eat more oysters and less salt? I like going forkless and decisively gulping everything at once, like a shark.

Oysters have a split personality. Their flavor and texture are complex enough to be the center of attention at a high-class affair. As one of the great process foods, however, they also make a nifty rhythm section for a party, punctuating the chatter with the steady clack of shells being opened. This hoedown persona requires a whole different approach. The oysters should fade into the background, keeping people stimulated and occupied without them even realizing it. White tablecloths and mignonette would be too fussy. Wine pairings would draw too much attention. Keep things simple—lots of beer, some lime wedges and pepper grinders, hot sauce, tubs for the empty shells, and an atmosphere casual enough that people won't worry about making a mess.

An old European tradition, still common in France but already considered antique in the United States when M. F. K. Fisher reminisced about it in the 1940s, is to accompany oysters with thin black bread and sweet butter—an elaborate, and more satisfying, version of the saltines that accompany some oysters nowadays. The bread makes a good foil for the saltiness of the oyster, and may even, as Fisher recommends, be the better place to squeeze your lemon. To me it's a strange collision—the earthy weight of black bread with the liquid lightness of oysters—but I know some otherwise highly intelligent people who love the combination. Admittedly, it will whisk you back to a golden, nostalgic time, which isn't always a bad thing.

OYSTER WINES AND
OTHER LIBATIONS

IN *A MOVEABLE* Feast, his posthumously published slam of Gertrude
Stein and the rest of Paris's expats, Ernest Hemingway wrote what
would become a hallowed passage for the oyster community: "As I ate
the oysters with their strong taste of the sea and their faint metallic
taste that the cold white wine washed away, leaving only the sea taste
and the succulent texture, and as I drank their liquid from each shell
and washed it down with the crisp taste of the wine, I lost the empty
feeling and began to be happy and to make plans."

Never mind that this oft-quoted passage reads like a first draft (it
was published posthumously for a reason), it has helped make oysters'
wine-friendly reputation. The marriage of the two is sanctified. But
should it be?

HERESY, PART I

Oyster and wine tastings have become trendy on both coasts of America, with judges pursuing that moment when the flavors produce syner-
gistic bliss in the brain. Food and wine magazines devote features to the
subject. You'd think that oysters and wine were the most natural pairing
since Tracy and Hepburn.

Don't believe it.

Spectacular oyster-wine combos do exist, and when the two click,
your soul throbs with pleasure. It's a reminder of why we love food and
art in the first place. But such moments are few and far between. Most
oysters slay most wines. Their strong salt flattens wine's flavor, while

their umami twists it into metallic or bitter new forms. I do think oyster and wine tastings are great fun, not because they are orgies of gustatory bliss but because they are such challenges. Finding the excellent match amid all the failures is a thrill—and a relief.

Sauvignon Blanc wines dominate virtually every oyster-wine competition. Seventy to 80 percent of the gold medal winners of the Pacific Coast Wine Competition have been Sauvignon Blancs. That event is limited to Pacific Coast wines, but Washington D.C.'s Old Ebbitt Grill holds a competition for wines from around the world, and New Zealand Sauvignon Blancs rule the roost, with Sancerres (French Sauvignon Blancs) and Champagnes dueling for a distant second place, and American wines barely registering.

What's so special about New Zealand? It has a climate that combines qualities of the Old World and the New. California's long sunny days and hot summers allow its Sauvignon Blanc grapes to get very ripe and produce melon and peach aromas. Sancerre, in France's cool and cloudy Loire Valley, doesn't produce such ripe grapes and instead has leaner, grassy wines with a ringing tartness. New Zealand has all the sun of California, accounting for the tropical fruit aromas of its Sauvignon Blanc, but it is cooler, more on a par with Sancerre, so its wines maintain all their acidity. The result is an amazing balance of exotic fruit and refreshing zippiness—a bit like a kiwi, which is mnemonically convenient, considering the source.

Sauvignon Blanc is one of the only grapes to mix fruitiness with strong acidity, which is why it is the standard choice with oysters—but not just any oysters. Kumamotos display the same melon flavors and can make a dazzling partner for American and especially New Zealand Sauvignon Blancs. They aren't too salty and aren't metallic in the least—two qualities that can kill wines. Kumos are the only oyster used to judge the Pacific Coast wine winners, and they are the only oyster that always works.

Burdened by conventional wisdom, I used to always drink Sauvignon Blanc with my oysters. I would eat my Malpeques, sip my wine, grimace at the sour twang it left on my tongue, and wonder what I was missing.

What I was missing, of course, was that I was eating the wrong oysters. I wasn't alone. Up and down the East Coast, we've been eating our *virginicas,* dutifully knocking back our Sauvignon Blanc, and all the while wondering if we were the crazy ones.

You can't blame us. We were getting it from both sides. In California, they loved their Sauvignon Blanc. In France, they trumpeted Sancerre with oysters, or Muscadet or Chablis, two other full-pucker options. But they were both eating Pacific oysters. Sauvignon Blanc's acidity is a great counterpoint to the sweetness of Pacifics and the closely related Kumamoto. (True, a few of the French drinkers were probably eating Flats, in which case God help the wine.) The sweet and sour enhance each other, as in lemonade, and the fruitiness in both the wine and the oysters gets to shine.

This doesn't work with Eastern oysters. With little sweetness or fruitiness, but strong salt and mineral flavors, Eastern oysters combined with Sauvignon Blanc produce a mouthful of sour metal. Yuck. (It's worth mentioning that I'm discussing the naked Eastern oyster. Sprinkle some mignonette, or a good shot of citrus, on an Eastern oyster and you will taste a lot less oyster, due to the acids and sugars, but it will pair well with Sauvignon Blancs and most other white wines.)

In general, quieter wines are better for Eastern oysters. For instance, the surprise winner of the Grand Central Oyster Bar's 2006 oyster wine competition, where the majority of oysters were Eastern, was a Grüner Veltliner. Grüner, Austria's national grape, is bone dry, a prerequisite for complementing oysters. Even a hint of sweetness in the wine will obliterate any sense of sweetness or body in the oyster. In place of Sauvignon Blanc's fruitiness or grassiness, Grüner has a peppery mix of minerals: stone, flint, chalk. It's sometimes described as salty. That mix of minerals, light body, and medium acidity makes it potentially spectacular with Eastern oysters.

Champagne is another winner—the drier the better. A *blanc de blanc* Champagne, which is made from all Chardonnay grapes, has the light body to perfectly complement light-bodied Eastern oysters— those from Canada with medium salinity, such as Beausoleils or Malpeques, are best. The combination can be brilliant. The bubbles run interference and prevent the umami in the oysters from twanging the wine. This is the same reason that Champagne is the recommended foil to caviar, another umami powerhouse.

Umami, as described earlier, is a fifth type of taste generally described as savory. Caviar, oysters, anchovies, smoked fish, and blue cheese all have it in abundance, and all make difficult wine matches. Umami enhances any bitterness in wine, which is why all red wines (which have more bitter tannins in them) are disasters with such foods. It also can transform rich wine flavors into metallic ones, which is why full-bodied Chardonnays fail. Eastern oysters may have more umami than their Pacific counterparts, since this phenomenon is more noticeable with them.

With that umami waiting to assault your wine, the goal of choosing a bottle to go with your oysters is not so much about achieving brilliant synergy—though lightning does strike every now and then—but about finding wine that, like a fencer turned sideways, doesn't give the attacker too much of a target.

Chablis, a classic Gallic pick for oysters, has the proper focused sharpness. This far northern island of Burgundy grows only Chardonnay grapes, but makes them into a lean-and-mean style of wine unrecognizable to people used to the fat, vanilla Chardonnays of Australia and California. Chablis wines aren't aged in oak, so they don't develop buttery flavors. They do develop a steely pointedness, thanks to their cool northern climate and unique chalky soil. That soil, rich in limestone, was once seabed. It is the remains of trillions of tiny shellfish. Scoop up a handful of whitish soil in a Chablis vineyard and you'll find fossilized oyster shells. *Chablis derives its unique flavor from ancient oysters.* That seems as good a reason as any to drink it with oysters. Other versions of Chardonnay aged in stainless steel instead of oak can be good, too.

Dry Riesling, Chenin Blanc, and Pinot Blanc are gambles that sometimes pay off—Rieslings, in particular, can have a summer-rain aroma that is potentially brilliant with oysters. Spain's Albariño is an up-and-coming grape famed for its seafood affinity and marketed as a Chardonnay substitute, but it's still a bit rich for oysters and is better with the sweetness of scallops.

The alternative to reaching for unlikely greatness in your oyster wine is to play it safe. You could do worse than to serve something very light, very cheap, and very cold. One-dimensional Italian whites such as Pinot Grigio and Gavi are reliably refreshing. Portugal's Vinho Verde, which combines flyweight body, slight acidity, and a prickle of CO_2, is one of the best bets.

A wine that should work with oysters, but doesn't, is *fino* sherry, the classic, fortified Spanish tapa wine. In the United States people are more familiar with sweet versions of sherry, but the Spanish prefer bone-dry fino sherry with seafood, particularly an uncommon style called Manzanilla that is aged on the seashore, where it takes on the salty tang of the sea. Sounds perfect for oysters, right? Unfortunately, the tang becomes way too tangy when paired with oysters.

With Olympia and European Flat oysters, all wine matches fly out the window. The oysters are just too intense, too metallic, too umami. Sparkling wine or Vinho Verde might survive. Retsina, already bitter and resiny and unruinable, couldn't hurt. At least you wouldn't be sullying a great wine. But why fight the metal? Instead, embrace it. The soft drink Tab, which also tastes like metal, makes the most unique pairing of all. A cooler of Maine Belons, a six-pack of Tab, a Boston Whaler, and a fishing pole is a recipe for a strange and magnificent afternoon as your tongue slowly surrenders to the abuse and even begins to take pleasure in it.

To summarize, here are seven rules for oyster wines:

1. Pacific and Kumamoto oysters work better than Eastern oysters with almost all wines.

2. Easterns work better than Olympias or Flats.

3. Lighter, less briny oysters work best.

4. With Easterns, try Grüner Veltliner or Champagne first, then Chablis, Vinho Verde, Riesling, Chenin Blanc, Pinot Blanc, or even Pinot Grigio.

5. With Pacifics and Kumamotos, try Sauvignon Blanc first, then Champagne, Chablis, or Muscadet, then any of the other wines listed for Eastern oysters.

6. Sprinkle some mignonette on your oysters, and suddenly most white wines work, particularly Sauvignon Blanc.

7. Whatever wine you choose, keep it cold and refreshing. Although we generally serve white wines too cold for full aroma development, this is one occasion where you want to keep the aromatic chemistry damped down.

HERESY, PART II

While I'm turning sacred cows into corned beef hash, I may as well keep going. Even the best oyster wines are not necessarily the best libations to have with oysters. A martini, with its mineral bite, works better all around. Far too formidable to be pushed around by the umami in the oyster, the gin holds its own and even adds a cool clarity to the oyster. Diving into the crystal stillness of a table of oysters and martinis can have the feel of a 1960s Jacques Cousteau fantasy. An olive in the martini would be salt overkill, but a twist of lemon peel is superb.

Campari and soda makes a surprising and festive option, a way of turning bitterness into a positive. The slice of orange is essential. Any sparkling aperitif can be a refreshing contrast to an oyster's saltiness.

The best refresher, of course, is beer. With the saltiest oysters, nothing's better. As with wine, quality is not necessarily a plus. The goal is to have something light and fizzy to wipe the palate clean. Rich microbrews are too thick for oysters. Very hoppy beers, such as India Pale Ale, are too fruity and bitter. A clean lager is good, a wheat hefeweizen, with a wedge of lemon, even better. But in truth an icy cold Budweiser in a frosty mug works surprisingly well.

Sake—Japanese rice wine—is superb with salty oysters. Served ice cold in a wineglass, sake has a clarity and refined flavor that help bring out the elegance in the oysters. Most sakes have a whiff of sweet and abstract fruitiness that is enhanced by salt and umami (which is why they work with soy sauce). I once made a memorable lunch of ultra-briny Pemaquid oysters and sake. All good sake labels list where they fall on the sweet-dry scale, and often on the crispness scale, too. Paired with oysters, the drier and crisper the better.

HERESY, PART III

Is it absolutely essential that you catch a buzz while consuming your oysters? If not, I have one more suggestion. Forget the wine, the beer, the sake, and the gin. The most transcendent libation with oysters is nonalcoholic. It works equally well with Pacifics or Easterns. It's even great with Olympias and Flats. It's good with sweet oysters and incredibly refreshing with briny ones. It's widely available and amazingly affordable.

It's water. Don't laugh until you've tried it. Nothing complements the sea nature of oysters as well as cold, fresh water. Still water is fine, but Perrier, with its funky minerality and gentle effervescence, is divine. Sometimes I think it's the only taste light enough to remind us that oysters are concentrated sea. You taste the oyster, wet rocks at low tide, then the Perrier, a stream burbling over river stones. You're back in the tidepools where life began.

RECIPES

MOST OYSTER COOKERY is misguided. Why take a delicate, fleeting flavor and disrupt it with heat? True, a few minutes of cooking can firm up their flesh and make them more palatable to oyster skeptics, but the makeup of oysters is such that, if they are cooked for any significant amount of time, the proteins link up into a tough, chewy little mass. Sure, if you cook them for several *hours* they will start to soften up again, but the same could be said about tennis balls. A common thread through most successful oyster recipes I've tried is that the oysters are handled incredibly gently—warmed more than cooked.

I believe that any oyster recipe should face two screening processes before it makes it into your kitchen. First: Would the oysters be preferable raw? If so, toss the recipe. Second: Would the dish be better with something other than oysters? If clams, scallops, or even shrimp would be as good, or better, why not save the oysters for one of the roles for which they are uniquely suited? The following recipes are a few that I think do capture the gestalt of oysters, in very different ways. In all of them, the quality of the oysters is crucial. It may be tempting to use those pop-top tins of preshucked oysters sold in every supermarket, but they will ruin any dish with their tinny flavor and rubbery texture.

MIGNONETTE QUARTET

I was thirty-four years old when I discovered I'd been using the wrong part of the lemon my whole life. Lemon juice is fine to brighten a drink or a piece of fish with a shot of acidity, but everything that is floral and piquant about lemons is found in the zest—the grated peel, which contains the aromatic oil.

Virtually any dish that calls for lemon juice can be made better by adding lemon juice *and* zest. It's easy to do: First grate the colored peel using a very fine grater, being careful not to grate the bitter white pith that lies just underneath, then cut the wedge of peel-less lemon from the rest of the fruit and juice it. Many types of citrus can be used this way, though lemons, Meyer lemons, tangerines, oranges, and yuzu (a Japanese fruit with a lemon-line flavor) are best. Lime zest is not as fragrant as lemon. (If you will be using the zest, buy organic citrus, because conventional citrus is often dipped in wax.)

Mignonette—red-wine vinegar spiced with shallots and pepper—is the classic French sauce for oysters, but I find citrus superior. Because it has only half the acidity of vinegar, it is less overpowering, and it has sweet and floral touches that mingle with oyster flavors better than harsh vinegar does. A simple trickle of citrus juice on an oyster is good, but creating a mignonette of juice, zest, shallots, and pepper is superb.

Any acid will counteract saltiness (think malt vinegar on french fries), so citrus and mignonettes help to balance overly briny oysters. They also enliven a dull oyster. They do obliterate a certain amount of the fresh oyster flavor, so I prefer nothing on the best oysters. On the other hand, they alter full-bodied, high-umami oysters in a way that makes them much more successful with wine, particularly floral wines like Sauvignon Blanc. Providing a range of mignonettes, such as the following quartet, excites people to explore—always the sign of a good party.

Blood Orange Mignonette

Roger Tory Peterson describes a purple finch as "like a sparrow dipped in raspberry juice." Well, a blood orange is like a tangerine dipped in raspberry juice. The color and the flavor are clearly and distinctly raspberry. That makes for a delightful mignonette. You could purée actual raspberries with tangerine juice to achieve somewhat the same effect, but you wouldn't have the sharpness provided by blood oranges.

Juice of 2 blood oranges
1 shallot, peeled and minced
1 teaspoon (3 g) ground pepper

Mix all ingredients in a nonreactive bowl. Serve immediately.

Makes about $^{1}/_{2}$ cup (125 ml)

Meyer Lemon Mignonette

Meyer lemons are crosses of mandarins (tangerines) and lemons, but somehow the cross created an herbal perfume missing from either parent. You can smell it right through the thin, orange-yellow skin—a scent like wandering thyme-carpeted paths in an orange grove—and it drives me wild. As you'd expect, it makes a spectacular mignonette.

Juice and zest of 2 Meyer lemons
1 shallot, peeled and minced
1 teaspoon (3 g) ground pepper

Mix all ingredients in a nonreactive bowl. Serve immediately.

Makes about $^{1}/_{2}$ cup (125 ml)

Tarragon Vinegar Mignonette

The woodsy liquorish flavor of tarragon is terrific with oysters, and tarragon vinegar is widely available, making this mignonette a snap. You can reduce the harshness of the vinegar, and increase the complexity of the flavor, by cutting it with a tart white wine such as Sauvignon Blanc, Chablis, or Muscadet.

1/2 cup (125 ml) tarragon vinegar
1/2 cup (125 ml) dry white wine

1 shallot, peeled and minced
2 teaspoons (6 g) fresh ground pepper

Mix all ingredients in a nonreactive bowl. Serve immediately.

Makes 1 cup (250 ml)

Japanese Mignonette

The Japanese are serious oyster fans. I've combined some typical Japanese ingredients to create a mignonette that screams out to be paired with oysters and a glass of ice-cold sake. Virtually all the wasabi in the world is actually horseradish with green food coloring. Real wasabi is incredibly rare but vastly superior. It has less kick than faux wasabi, but a fascinating suite of fresh, green, peppery flavors. Outside of Japanese mountain streams, it is grown only in New Zealand and British Columbia. If you can find the fresh root, and pair it with equally fresh British Columbia oysters, you are in for a real treat.

½ cup (125 ml) rice wine vinegar or sake
A small dab of fresh ground wasabi root (optional)
1 tablespoon (15 g) ginger root, peeled and grated (optional)
Juice and zest of 2 yuzus, or 1 lemon and 1 lime

Mix all ingredients in a nonreactive bowl. Serve immediately.

Makes about 1 cup (250 ml)

Elliott's Iced Champagne Mignonette

When you plunk yourself down at the bar at Elliott's, on the Seattle waterfront, and order some oysters, you will be presented with a single sauce: their signature Iced Champagne Mignonette. Nothing else compares. By transforming a mignonette into a granita by carefully freezing it, you get a sauce that obediently stays atop its oyster. And the ice crystals serve as tiny flavor capsules, bursting in your mouth with lemony tartness.

1 ounce (30 g) shallots, peeled and finely minced
2/3 cup (150 ml) red wine vinegar
2/3 cup (150 ml) rice wine vinegar
1¹/₂ cups (350 ml) Mumm's Champagne
1¹/₂ teaspoons (8 g) minced lemon zest
1 teaspoon (3 g) finely ground black pepper
1 teaspoon (3 g) finely ground mixed peppercorns

1. Combine all ingredients in a bowl and place the mixture in a shallow pan so it is only 1 inch (2.5 cm) deep.
2. Place the pan in the freezer. Every half-hour, until it is completely frozen, agitate it by scraping with a fork to break up the ice crystals. The final product should look like shaved ice. Keep covered until serving.

Makes 2 cups (500 ml)

Oyster Stew for Dummies

The best oyster recipes are usually the simplest. For the goodness of the oysters to come through intact, it's best to cook gently and to keep gratuitous ingredients to a minimum. Nowhere is that philosophy more evident than in basic oyster stew, a dish unchanged for centuries. Cooks sometimes resist the simplicity of the recipe; it seems too easy, and they feel they should be doing more somehow. But nothing more is necessary to make this dish completely successful. With so little involved, the quality of the ingredients is critical: good oysters and good cream. If you can get cream that isn't ultrapasteurized, bravo. The fact that this soup can be thrown together in five minutes (assuming you have shucked oysters on hand) makes it ideal dinner-party fare.

24 shucked oysters (about a pint [500 ml]), liquor reserved
1 pint (500 ml) heavy cream
2 tablespoons (30 g) butter
Salt and pepper
Optional garnishes: paprika, minced parsley, hot sauce, Worcestershire

sauce, and oyster crackers are all acceptable. A pat of butter on top is glorious, if decadent.

1. Warm the cream and oyster liquor in a pot or saucepan.
2. In a soup pot, melt the butter over medium heat. Add the oysters and cook just until their edges begin to curl. (If using the paprika, it can be added with the oysters or sprinkled at the end.)
3. Add the cream, stir, and heat to the edge of boiling. When the oysters have plumped, turn off the heat. Boiled oysters turn tough.
4. Adjust the seasoning, garnish as you please (or let your guests do their own), and serve.

Serves 4 to 6 as a first course

Oyster Stew for Foodies

Great on Christmas Eve or New Year's Eve. That's the traditional time for oyster stew, though this version breaks with tradition. Many oyster stews call for bacon. The smoky aspect is nice, but to me the bacon overwhelms the oysters. Instead, I like bonito flakes (katsuobushi)—a standard Japanese pantry item, available at any hippy-dippy market—which give miso soup its smokiness. The flakes are made by drying chunks of bonito (a mackerel relative) until rock-hard and then shaving them. They add an addictive umami kick to any dish. Here, unlike bacon, they keep the flavor fully sea—as does the fish sauce, another umami standby. (A lifetime's supply costs $3 at any good supermarket.) Artichoke hearts always do well with oysters and cream. If you're going all out, a dollop of crème fraîche and caviar on top could do no wrong.

1 pint (500 ml) heavy cream
½ cup (125 ml) bonito flakes
2 tablespoons (30 g) butter
2 shallots, peeled and minced
1 cup (250 ml) artichoke hearts (canned, frozen, or fresh cooked),
    chopped
24 shucked oysters (about a pint [500 ml]), liquor reserved

Pepper, fish sauce, Pernod (optional)
Minced parsley or chives to garnish (optional)

1. Heat the cream and oyster liquor in a saucepan until it begins to boil. Turn off the heat, add the bonito flakes, and let sit.
2. Heat the butter in a large pot over medium heat. Add the shallots and sauté until soft, about 3 minutes. Add the artichoke hearts, stir, and cook another minute.
3. Pour the cream through a strainer into the pot (discarding the strained bonito flakes) and cook, stirring, until piping hot. Add the oysters and cook until they are plump and heated through, about five minutes. Do not allow the soup to boil.
4. Taste the soup and add pepper, a dash of fish sauce, and a dash of Pernod to taste. You could skip all of these and just add salt, but you won't achieve the same depth of flavor.
5. Ladle into soup bowls and garnish as you like.

Serves 4

Coconut Oyster Stew

Thailand has many oyster farms and many recipes for oysters. Raw ones are served with a traditional Thai dipping sauce of garlic, lime juice, fish sauce, and chilies. Cooked ones turn up in coconut milk stews. Any kind of oyster works in the previous two stew recipes, but here, with the sweetness of the coconut milk, Pacifics or Kumamotos are clearly superior. Don't try to eat lemongrass; the stalks are incredibly tough. Think of them as Thai bay leaves, added to dishes for fragrance.

2 lemongrass stalks
2 tablespoons (30 g) canola or peanut oil
1 tablespoon (15 g) fresh ginger, peeled and minced
4 shallots, peeled and chopped
2 garlic cloves, peeled and minced
1/2 teaspoon (1 g) red pepper flakes
1 red bell pepper, stemmed, seeded, and chopped

1 zucchini, chopped

1 14-ounce (420 ml) can unsweetened coconut milk

24 shucked oysters (about a pint [500 ml]), liquor reserved

Juice of ½ lime

Dash of fish sauce

Cilantro to garnish

1. Chop the ends off the lemongrass stalks and smash the stalks with a heavy kitchen implement. Set aside.

2. Heat the oil in a large pot over medium heat. Add the ginger, shallots, and garlic and sauté until softened, about 3 minutes.

3. Add the red pepper flakes, the bell pepper, and the zucchini and sauté an additional 3 minutes.

4. Add the coconut milk and oyster liquor and simmer until the vegetables are tender, about 15 minutes.

5. Add the oysters and cook until they are heated through and plump, about 3 minutes. Do not boil. Turn off the heat.

6. Add the lime juice and fish sauce, stir, and taste. Add more if desired.

7. Ladle into soup bowls, garnish with minced cilantro, and serve.

Serves 4

Chestnut and Oyster Soup

At Thanksgiving I like to start everyone off with a plate of raw oysters, then transition to a course of chestnut soup. The salty, savory oysters play off the creamy and nutty soup wonderfully, and both evoke old-fashioned falls on the Eastern Seaboard, pre–chestnut blight, when the crown of a single chestnut tree could shade a quarter acre and uncountable billions of nuts littered the ground, mirroring the multitude of fat oysters in the water. The two foods were fall staples for many Native Americans. I've always been tempted to combine them. Now I have. The result is elegance itself.

Fresh chestnuts yield the best results, though they are a pain to prepare. You can skip steps 1 and 2 in this recipe by using frozen chestnut meats (pretty good) or canned (not so good), and still end up with something fairly tasty. It's up to you whether convenience or flavor is at the top of your list today.

1 pound (500 g) fresh chestnuts, or 8 ounces (250 g) canned or frozen
2 tablespoons (30 g) butter
2 shallots, peeled and chopped
3 cups (750 ml) chicken stock
24 shucked oysters (about a pint [500 ml]), liquor reserved
1 cup (250 ml) heavy cream
Black pepper to taste
Optional garnishes: minced parsley, crème fraîche

1. Bring a pot of salted water to a boil. With a paring knife, carve a ring around each chestnut and add them all to the pot. Boil for 5 minutes.

2. Remove a few nuts at a time and peel the outer shell and inner skin. This is easiest when the nuts are hot, which is why you remove only a few at a time.

3. In a large pot, melt the butter over medium heat. Add the shallots and sauté until soft, about 3 minutes.

4. Add the chestnuts and stock and simmer until the chestnuts are fully soft, about 30 minutes.

5. Purée the soup in a food processor and return it to the pot.

6. Add the cream, oysters, oyster liquor, and pepper and reheat until piping hot. Do not boil. Serve immediately, with whatever garnishes you prefer.

Serves 4 to 6

Poached Oysters with Caviar Cream

Really a variation on oyster stew, with the proportion of oysters to liquid altered to make it a sauce and not a soup. Poaching oysters is the gentlest way to cook them and probably the best at preserving their essence.

24 shucked oysters, liquor and bottom shells reserved
1/4 cup (60 ml) dry white wine, such as Chablis
1/2 cup (125 ml) heavy cream
Zest of 1/4 Meyer lemon, mandarin (tangerine), or regular lemon

Salt and pepper to taste
2 ounces (60 g) caviar

1. Arrange the bottom shells on 4 to 6 small plates, using salt or pebbles, if necessary, to keep the shells upright.
2. In a medium saucepan, poach the oysters, oyster liquor, wine, and heavy cream at the barest simmer until the oysters have plumped, about 3 minutes. Using a slotted spoon, remove the oysters, place them in a bowl, and keep warm.
3. Turn the heat to medium and reduce the liquid until it makes a thick sauce, about 10–20 minutes. Turn off the heat, add the zest, stir, and let sit for a minute or two. Taste and add salt or pepper if needed. (But remember that salty caviar is still to come.)
4. Spoon an oyster onto each shell, cover with a spoonful or two of sauce, and top with a sprinkling of caviar. Serve immediately.

Serves 4 to 6

Oysters in Black Bean Sauce

The Chinese like to steam large oysters and serve them with black bean sauce. I think it's simpler to stir-fry medium oysters in the sauce. Chinese black beans are actually soybeans that have been fermented to a shriveled black deliciousness. They are, along with miso and soy sauce, a way to release the umami in soybeans. You can buy fermented black beans in any Asian grocery, and they are easy to use, but if you want the easy way out, you can buy perfectly good jars of black bean sauce at the supermarket, stir-fry the oysters and vegetables in this recipe, and just add the jarred sauce at the end. Either way, serve over rice.

1/2 cup (125 ml) fermented black beans
1/4 cup (60 ml) sherry
2 teaspoons (15 g) sugar
2 tablespoons (30 ml) soy sauce
2 tablespoons (30 ml) peanut or canola oil

2 ounces (60 g) ginger root, peeled and minced
4 garlic cloves, peeled and minced
A dash of red pepper flakes (optional)
36 medium oysters, shucked and drained
1 tablespoon (15 g) cornstarch, dissolved in ¼ cup (60 ml) water or
  oyster liquor
Scallions to garnish

1. Mix the black beans, sherry, sugar, and soy sauce in a bowl and set aside.
2. In a wok or large skillet, heat the oil over high heat.
3. When very hot, add the ginger, garlic, and red pepper flakes and cook, stirring constantly, for about 15 seconds. Add the oysters and cook an additional 15 seconds.
4. Add the black bean mixture and cook, stirring, until hot and bubbling, about 1 to 2 minutes.
5. Add the cornstarch mixture and cook, stirring, until the sauce is thick and glossy, about 1 minute. Serve immediately, garnished with chopped scallions.

Serves 4

Variation: You can increase the veggie content of this dish by throwing in thinly sliced red bell peppers, bok choy, or baby Chinese corn with the ginger and garlic.

Oyster Roast

An obvious attraction of roasting oysters is that it allows you to shuck unlimited quantities in 5 minutes. You don't even need an oyster knife—which is why this was the preferred shucking method of Native Americans. The goal is not to overcook the oysters, so check them frequently. As soon as the shells start to gap, get 'em out. Serve with a variety of mignonettes and other sauces, especially the Fishy Aïoli. You can also roast oysters outdoors on a grill over hot coals. It takes a few minutes longer, depending on the intensity of the coals, but adds a memorable smoky touch (which can be enhanced by tossing something damp, like wet wood or seaweed, onto the coals). Indoors or out, oven mitts and tongs will preserve the skin on your fingertips.

48 medium to large oysters in their shells

1. Preheat oven to 450 degrees (230°C).
2. Arrange the oysters, cup side down, in a baking pan. You can line the pan with rock salt to help keep the oysters level, so they don't spill their liquor, or you can pack the oysters tight enough that they all support one another.
3. Bake until the oysters gap, about 7 to 10 minutes. Any that don't gap can be pried open with a knife. Serve immediately.

Serves 4 to 8

Fishy Aïoli

In his wonderful book The Big Oyster, *Mark Kurlansky listed an ancient Roman recipe for a raw-oyster accompaniment: mayonnaise made with garum. Garum was a black liquid made by fermenting fish guts in the sun for longer than you want to know. Its nearest modern-day analog is fish sauce, a staple of Southeast Asian cuisine. I created this recipe as a lark after reading Kurlansky's book, but the resulting sauce was so howlingly good that I now make all my aïoli this way (and I make a lot of aïoli). It's good with raw oysters, better with roasted oysters, great with vegetable crudités (especially radishes), and at its very best topping a bowl of bouillabaisse.*

1 egg
2 teaspoons (10 ml) lemon juice
2 teaspoons (10 ml) fish sauce
Pepper to taste
2 cloves garlic, peeled and minced
1¹/₂ cups (350 ml) extra-virgin olive oil

1. In the bowl of a food processor, combine all the ingredients except the olive oil. Blend until smooth.
2. With the motor running, drizzle the olive oil through the feed tube in a slow, steady stream. The mixture should become the consistency of mayonnaise. Taste and add more lemon juice, fish sauce, or pepper to taste.

Makes about 2 cups (500 ml)

Baked Oysters in Tarragon Butter

Oysters have an affinity for any sort of anise flavor. Fennel and basil both complement them, but tarragon, with its dark intrigue, is especially good. Baking oysters in a very hot oven, for a very brief time, preserves their oysterness, and the butter cap keeps them from drying out. If your oysters are salty, use unsalted butter. If they are mild, use salted butter.

1 clove garlic, peeled and minced
1 ounce (30 g) fresh tarragon leaves, minced
A few grinds fresh pepper
1 stick butter (250 g), softened
24 oysters on the half-shell
Lemon wedges for serving

1. In a bowl, mix the garlic, tarragon, and pepper into the butter. Let sit while you preheat the oven, so the flavors will meld.
2. Preheat oven to 450 degrees (230°C).
3. Place the oysters on a baking tray. Rock salt on the tray will help keep the shells upright.
4. Spoon 1 teaspoon (5 g) of the butter onto each oyster, then bake for 3 to 5 minutes until the butter is hot and bubbling. Serve on individual plates with lemon wedges.

Serves 4 to 6 as a first course

Oyster Sea Salad

More than other recipes in this book, this one accentuates oysters' sea nature. It also calls the bluff of all those restaurants and caterers that like to display their oysters atop beds of seaweed, but won't get real and serve the two together. It is idyllic in hot weather with iced green tea. Seaweeds, as well as being among the most nutritious of foods, have a wonderful popping texture that improves many dishes. Dried seaweeds, panko, and bonito flakes can be found at any good natural foods store. Pacific oysters, indigenous to Japan, are the obvious choice here.

1 ounce (30 g) dried wakame

1 ounce (30 g) dried hijiki

1 large carrot, peeled and julienned

4 red radishes, julienned

¼ cup (60 ml) rice wine vinegar

1 tablespoon (15 g) sugar

½ cup (125 ml) loosely packed bonito flakes

1 tablespoon (15 ml) soy sauce

1 teaspoon (5 ml) toasted sesame oil

Juice of ½ lime

¼ cup (60 ml) peanut or canola oil

24 oysters, shucked, drained, and patted dry

1 cup (250 ml) panko (Japanese bread crumbs)

1. Soak the dried seaweeds in a large bowl of water for 10 minutes. (They will expand greatly.) Drain and press any excess water out. The central rib of wakame can be tough; taste one and decide whether you want to remove it or not. Cut the seaweeds into bite-sized pieces.
2. Combine the seaweeds, carrot, and radishes in a large bowl.
3. Combine the vinegar and sugar in a small saucepan. Bring to a simmer and stir until the sugar dissolves. Turn off the heat, then scatter the bonito flakes over the top and let sit for 5 minutes so the flavor of the bonito flakes is absorbed by the vinegar.
4. Strain the vinegar into a small bowl, pressing on the solids and

then discarding them. Mix in the soy sauce, sesame oil, and lime juice. Taste and adjust the sweet/sour/salty ratio as you like. Pour half this dressing over the salad and toss.

5. Heat the oil in a large skillet over medium heat. Dredge the oysters in the panko, then fry them until golden on the bottom, $1\,^1\!/_2$ to 2 minutes. Turn and fry them on the other side until golden, another minute or so.

6. Divide the salad onto four individual salad plates, top each with six oysters, and drizzle the remaining dressing over the top. Serve immediately.

Serves 4

Jay Shaffer's Fried Oysters over Creamed Spinach with Chipotle Aïoli

---

Shaffer City Oyster Bar is one of the great oyster spots in Manhattan, and this dish is one of proprietor Jay Shaffer's favorites. It twists Oysters Rockefeller into a much smarter dish, and Jay says that the chipotle aïoli, which has a beautiful smoky-spicy flavor, makes the bivalves really pop. You can use regular breadcrumbs if you can't find panko, but panko are more jagged than other breadcrumbs and produce more crunch. For the home cook, it's easiest to use canned chipotle peppers.

20 oysters, shucked, with bottom shells reserved
1 teaspoon (5 g) cumin
$^1\!/_4$ teaspoon (1 g) cayenne pepper
$^1\!/_4$ cup (60 ml) paprika
$^1\!/_4$ cup (60 ml) cornmeal
$^1\!/_4$ cup (60 ml) panko (Japanese breadcrumbs)
$^3\!/_4$ cup (180 ml) all purpose flour
1 teaspoon (6 g) salt
$^1\!/_4$ teaspoon (1 g) ground white pepper
2 chipotle peppers in adobo sauce
$^1\!/_2$ ounce (15 ml) champagne vinegar
3 eggs, beaten

Salt and pepper
10 ounces (300 ml) canola oil
1 small shallot, peeled and diced
1 tablespoon minced garlic
¼ cup (60 ml) heavy cream
¼ teaspoon (1 g) nutmeg
1 tablespoon (15 g) butter
2 cups (500 ml) cooked spinach
2 ounces (60 ml) milk

1. Combine the cumin, cayenne pepper, paprika, cornmeal, panko, flour, salt, and white pepper in a small bowl and sift with a spoon until completely mixed. Set aside.
2. Make the chipotle aïoli. In a food processor or blender, purée the chipotle peppers and a little of the adobo sauce with the champagne vinegar, 1 egg, and a little salt and pepper. With the motor running on medium, drizzle in 6 ounces (200 ml) of the canola oil in a thin, steady stream. When incorporated, the sauce should be the consistency of mayonnaise.
3. In a sauté pan, warm a little oil over medium heat and sweat the shallots and garlic until translucent. Add the heavy cream and nutmeg and simmer until thickened a bit. Add the butter and the spinach and keep warm.
4. In a bowl, beat the remaining 2 eggs with the milk and add the oysters to soak.
5. In a large pan, heat 2 tablespoons (30 ml) of the canola oil. Dredge half the egg-soaked oysters in the crust mixture and pan sear them for 1 ½ to 2 minutes on each side until golden brown. Remove and drain.
6. On four warm plates lined with coarse salt, place five shells each. Fill the shells with the creamed spinach mixture and top each with a golden brown oyster and a drizzle of chipotle aïoli.

Serves 4

Hangtown Fry

The California town of Placerville, near Sacramento, was known as Hangtown in the Gold Rush days. If you were a criminal, you didn't want to end up there. As the story goes, one doomed individual, when asked what he would like for his last meal, replied, "Oysters and eggs"— the two most expensive and hard-to-find items he could think of. It's unclear if he was able to delay his end through this ploy, or if his request was granted, or even if the story is apocryphal, but in any case the dish has assumed a prominent position in the oyster canon. Oysters and eggs are a lot easier to procure today, though the oysters of the Gold Rush— Olympias—are not. They take this omelet to another level of complexity, but it's good with any small oysters. Bacon is traditional in Hangtown Fry, onions and spinach are acceptable, but how to treat the oysters remains an issue: fry them in a light breading, fry them naked, or simply mix them with the eggs? Most cooks prefer crisper oysters and recommend frying them in light breading, but I'm a fan of mixing them with eggs, a purer approach—especially with Olympias, which already have a nice texture.

2 strips bacon
4 eggs, beaten
Black pepper
12 Olympias or other very small oysters, shucked, liquor reserved
Optional: chopped onions and spinach
Butter for frying

1. Cook the bacon strips in a large skillet until crisp. Remove, drain, and crumble.
2. If using the onions and/or spinach, add them to the hot bacon fat and cook, stirring, until wilted. Remove and set aside.
3. Mix the eggs, oysters, a tablespoon or two (15–30 ml) of oyster liquor (for saltiness), and pepper together in a bowl. Pour into the hot pan. (If you used the onions and spinach, they will have absorbed the bacon fat and you'll need to add some butter to the pan for frying.)

4. Add the onions and spinach, if you're using them, on top of the egg mixture. Cook until the eggs have set.

5. At the last moment (to preserve crispness), scatter the crumbled bacon over the top and fold in half, omelet style. Serve immediately.

Serves 2

Pickled Oysters

Pickled oysters were standard fare in every city on the Eastern Seaboard in that heady precanning era when oysters were in demand far and wide. New York City sent regular shipments of pickled oysters to the West Indies and elsewhere in the 1700s and didn't stop until canned oysters took over in 1839. But as with so many other of the old ways (salt cod comes to mind), it turns out that pickled oysters had a special charm all their own. I know at a bar I'd rather see a jar of pickled oysters to accompany my beer than pickled eggs or Vienna sausages. In fact, if I were a savvy barkeep looking to set my tavern apart from the crowd, I'd stick an ever replenished jar of pickled oysters on the bar.

My favorite pickled oysters come from the Hama Hama Oyster Company on Washington State's Hood Canal. The secret, I suspect, is putting plentiful lemons and onions in the jars at the end. Here is Hama Hama's recipe. If you don't want to make it yourself, you can also order the pickled oysters directly from Hama Hama (see "Growers Who Ship Direct").

1¼ cups (300 ml) pickling salt

1 gallon (4 l) shucked oysters

4 cups (1 l) vinegar

1¼ cups (300 ml) brown sugar

4 teaspoons (20 g) pickling spice

⅛ teaspoon (1 g) garlic powder

2 teaspoons (10 g) mustard seed

4 tablespoons (60 ml) Worcestershire sauce

8 onions, peeled and sliced

8 lemons, sliced

Canning jars

1. Add 1 cup (250 ml) of the pickling salt to $^1/_2$ gallon (2 l) water in a large pot. Add the oysters and bring to a boil. Boil until firm, then drain.
2. In a separate pan, boil 3 cups (750 ml) of water with the vinegar, brown sugar, pickling spice, garlic powder, mustard seed, Worcestershire sauce, and the rest of the pickling salt.
3. Put the oysters in a colander with a pan underneath to collect the brine. Pour the brine over the oysters. This disperses the mustard seeds and spices through the oysters. Then layer the oysters in jars with sliced onions and lemon, fill the jars with the remaining liquid, and seal tight.

Makes about 6–8 quart (or liter) jars of pickled oysters.

Oystertini

Nothing goes with raw oysters like a martini. Bombay Sapphire gin, a splash of Noilly Pratt vermouth, and a twist of lemon peel, all so cold that ice crystals flirt with existence at the surface. Drink one with a dozen Fanny Bay oysters and feel yourself slide into a crystalline realm of confused bliss. I have to thank Greg Hinton, director of Elliott's Oyster Bar, for turning me on to this particular form of bliss, but I'll take all the blame for this next outré innovation: Throw an oyster in the gin! The oyster not only does the work of the olive, providing texture and salt and visual interest, but also covers for the vermouth with its liquor—a variation on the "dirty martini." In the name of sanity, a small, dainty oyster is the way to go here. It will look a bit like a lab experiment floating in formaldehyde, which isn't so far from the truth. I like to use a lemon twist, but do what you want— we've obviously left tradition far, far behind.

2 ounces (60 ml) gin
1 raw oyster, liquor reserved
1 strip of lemon peel

1. Pour the gin and oyster liquor into a cocktail shaker filled with ice. Shake well and let sit for 30 seconds, or longer for a weaker drink.
2. Run the lemon peel around the rim of a martini glass. Strain the

gin into the glass, then twist the peel over the glass to release a drop of lemon oil.

3. Drop in the oyster and serve.

Serves 1

Lemon Oyster Shooter

The standard oyster shooter—a Bloody Mary in a shot glass with an oyster tossed in—has no redeeming feature, other than helping to keep oyster bars afloat. But the concept of mixing your booze and your oyster is not completely twisted. This version actually keeps the focus on the oyster. In place of the Tabasco, you could use a peppery vodka for a classier drink.

1 ounce (30 ml) ice-cold vodka
A few drops lemon oil
1 small oyster
1 drop Tabasco (optional)
Lemon wedge

Pour the vodka into a shot glass and add the lemon oil. Slide in the oyster and top with a drop of Tabasco. Serve with a lemon wedge. Bottoms up.

Saketini Oyster Shooter

A surprisingly clean marriage of flavors.

1/2 ounce (15 ml) ice-cold vodka
1/2 ounce (15 ml) ice-cold sake
1 small oyster
1 slice pickled ginger

Mix the vodka and sake in a shot glass. Slide in the oyster and garnish with the pickled ginger.

SAFETY

BY NOW YOU are ready to be set loose in the world of oysters. You are excited to eat oysters, eager to turn your friends into ostreaphiles, but a doubt lingers. . . . You do not want oysters to make you sick. In particular, you do not want oysters to make you dead.

Relax. If you want to make yourself sick from food, go for the bagged spinach, or any of the other raw fruits and veggies that have passed through countless hands, fields, and processing centers on their way to your mouth. Go for any salad bar in any restaurant (or any rare burger or steak). Eat on a cruise ship.

Oysters come prewrapped in a shell. Sure, that shell will have been handled by a few people, but once you remove it, you are into virgin territory. Even in a bad year, raw oysters send perhaps 200 people to the hospital with food poisoning. That pales in comparison to the food-poisoning heavyweights. *E. coli* (undercooked beef, underwashed hands) hospitalizes 2,800 and kills 80; *Salmonella* (eggs, fruit, peanut butter) sends over 15,000 to the hospital and kills 550; *Campylobacter* (poultry) eliminates another 1,000; *Listeria* (veggies, dairy products) wipes out 500; *Toxoplasma* (kitty litter and undercooked meat) kills 375; and so on, to the tune of 5,000 deaths a year and 325,000 hospitalizations. Oysters kill perhaps 10 people a year. Non–Gulf oysters kill no one.

With oysters, the only concerns are a couple of parasites that like to sneak into the oysters while they are in the water. Pay attention to the simplest of rules and you are home free.

THE R RULE

In 2006, after several years of smooth sailing, Washington State oyster growers hit a storm of trouble in the form of *Vibrio parahaemolyticus*. This bacterium, common in warm, shallow Pacific waters, doesn't bother oysters but does accumulate in them. Vibrio likes heat. It can be inside the body of an oyster at insignificant levels, and then reproduce exponentially when that oyster is left to bake at low tide on a hot mud-flat in August. Low levels of vibrio are not a problem for people, but high levels cause vibriosis—food poisoning with all the classic gastrointestinal symptoms. The state of Washington (and other coastal states) checks the water weekly for vibrio and shuts down the shellfish beds where it is detected. But somehow, in July 2006, it missed one. By the time the oysters were quarantined, several hundred people on the West Coast and in New York City were hit with two to three days of misery. *Vibrio parahaemolyticus* doesn't kill, but it is certainly no tea party.

Parse the above paragraph and the word that may leap out at you is *July. What were all these people doing eating oysters in July? Don't they know about the R rule?* Today, many people have been led to believe that the R rule is a myth. Which it is. Sort of . . .

The R rule, for those who don't know, states that you should eat raw oysters only in months that have an R in their names—September to April. It goes way back. As early as 1762, the town of New Haven, Connecticut, passed a local ordinance banning oystering during the R-less summer months. New York passed a largely ignored one in 1715. But laws or no laws, for hundreds of years people knew to avoid oysters from May to August.

Many people believe this rule of thumb was to protect *people;* that oysters were unsafe to eat from May to August. Actually, the original laws were put in place to protect the oysters. Oysters spawn from June to August, and the first rule for managing any natural population, whether deer or chanterelles or lobster, is to let the organism reproduce before you eat it.

Overall, there were three main reasons for the creation of an oystering season:

1. Sustainability. Let oysters spawn a new generation before being harvested.

2. Storage. Before the days of refrigeration, oysters would be shipped to market in wooden barrels, and spoiled much faster during the hot summer months.

3. Flavor. In May, as oysters prepare to spawn, they use up all their sweet glycogen as they manufacture gamete—eggs or sperm. Eggs and sperm don't taste very good. And after they spawn, oysters are thin and flabby and have little flavor at all. It takes them weeks to rebuild their glycogen stores and get plump and tasty again.

You can't argue with the reasoning behind these three points, but enlightened oyster eaters will counter that none of them necessarily applies anymore. Refrigeration is a no-brainer: Oysters are stuck in cold storage soon after they are pulled from the water and kept at 40 degrees or so all the way to your plate. As far as spawning is concerned, many oysters, especially Pacifics, are now triploids—sexless oysters that never spawn. So, yes, you can eat a Pacific triploid oyster in June knowing that it will be nice and fat and that you aren't robbing the world of millions of oyster progeny. With normal, sexed, diploid oysters, which still dominate in the Northeast, you need to take geography into account. The spawning rules originated in Europe, New York, and Connecticut, where waters get warm by June. But a Maine or PEI oyster is still stuck in 50-degree water in June and hasn't the foggiest notion of spawning. Sure, avoid Bluepoints and Chesapeakes (which can spawn twice in their warm waters) May through August, but enjoy Malpeques with gusto until July.

Some of those who believe that the R rule no longer applies will laugh at the ignoramuses still hewing to it. But many who were laughing in August 2006 had to stop to spend a couple of days puking, which brings up the new reason to pay attention to the R rule, a reason that may be getting more urgent as global warming turns up the heat.

The bacteria that infect oysters and make people sick thrive in warm waters. In addition to *Vibrio parahaemolyticus,* which is pretty much restricted to the Pacific (there was one mysterious case in Long Island Sound a few years ago), there is its sinister cousin, *Vibrio vulnificus,* which lives in the Gulf of Mexico and can kill those who have compromised immune systems. Vibrio normally lives in underwater mud, but when water gets warm (over 70 degrees, give or take a couple of degrees), the vibrio gets energized enough to rise into the water column, where it finds its way into oysters and other shellfish. (Fortunately for New Orleans residents and others, vibrio is destroyed by cooking, so Oysters Rockefeller is in the clear. Read more about *Vibrio vulnificus* in the Gulf Coast chapter.) Before the 2006 slip, the last time there was a big miss by the Pacific Northwest regulatory agencies was the record heat wave of 1997, when more than two hundred people ended up in the hospital.

Then there are the many red tides of the world, which live everywhere and can strike anywhere. Red tides are population explosions of toxic dinoflagellates (algae), sometimes to the point where they actually tinge the water red or brown. These situations generally involve hot summer temperatures, when everything seems to get frisky. Unlike vibriosis, which strikes about a day after consumption and causes garden-variety food poisoning, the illness caused by red tide, paralytic shellfish poisoning, can be bad. Within thirty minutes, the symptoms hit: tingling, dizziness, nausea, semiparalysis, and difficulty breathing. Occasionally, somebody dies—three in Alaska between 1997 and 2000.

Red tide is unaffected by cooking, but it is easy to spot. Shellfish beds on both coasts are frequently closed in summer due to red tide, making it a major headache for shellfish growers, but it almost never sneaks through the detection systems to poison consumers. Virtually everyone who has gotten sick from red tide in recent years (including those Alaskans) has been a recreational harvester illegally gathering oysters from closed areas, not buying them from a licensed grower.

Instances of both vibrio and red tide seem to be on the rise as global waters warm. But in response to the vibrio outbreak of 2006, the FDA and Washington State shellfish growers have revamped their management protocol. Vibrio is easy to avoid. Since it thrives only in mud or warm water close to mud, it is basically restricted to beach-grown oysters in summer, and even they can be cleared of vibrio by hanging them in deep water for a few days to let them purge. The larger, more established oyster growers are careful about this; it's the fly-by-night operations you have to watch out for. Fortunately, thanks to the new systems, and to the several hundred people who suffered for us all in 2006, we are now less likely to get sick from eating raw shellfish than ever before, even in R-less months.

Still, why *not* stick to the R rule? Regardless of all other considerations, we know that oysters taste better—plumper, crisper, fresher—from cold waters than from warm ones. So an oyster from almost any area is going to taste better in November than in July. And the difference between an oyster that is at the peak of flavor and one that is just passable is profound. Factor in the safety and spawning issues, and you'll understand why many growers don't even want to sell their oysters in the summer—they know their product is not at its best—but restaurants and, ultimately, consumers are not so flexible about seasonal products. Perhaps they should be. Do we need oysters to be available year-round? Are they just one more food that we demand be severed from its natural cycles and seasons so it can be delivered to us wherever and whenever we like? To truly appreciate something, it helps to actually *want* it for a while. I recommend concentrating your oyster consumption in the months of September through May. In June, try the strawberries instead.

THE POLLUTION CONNECTION

Yet another myth is that oysters make people sick because they are grown in polluted waters. There were certainly cases of that back in the bad old days of the late nineteenth and early twentieth centuries. Typhoid, a particularly virulent type of *Salmonella* bacterium, is spread through human waste, and can infect entire estuaries when cities dump untreated sewage directly into their waters. This, of course, characterized the entire American coast, as well as all the cities of the world, until fairly recently. Thousands of people in the United States have contracted typhoid by drinking contaminated water. Since oysters concentrate whatever is in the water, a few cases of typhoid have derived from oysters grown in bays that were basically cesspools. There has been some hysteria surrounding that issue, with people swearing off shellfish even as they went right on drinking contaminated water. By the 1920s, this wasn't an issue, because most of the oyster beds near cities were gone, the water filthier than ever.

Has any law ever improved daily life in the United States more than the Clean Water Act of 1972? Before that revolutionary legislation, it was common to see raw sewage floating in most of our rivers and harbors. This was accepted as an unavoidable part of life in a land with millions of people. Now, of course, any raw sewage spill into a waterway is cause for outrage. Though we have the impression that environmental conditions are eroding as populations grow and industry expands (and, in many cases, we're right), many of our waters are cleaner than they have been in a hundred years. This is why oysters, along with other creatures, are reappearing in places where they haven't been seen in decades.

Sure, there are still polluted waters on our coasts. Sewage is still an issue after a major rainstorm—we know this from the beach closings. The FDA and state regulatory agencies close shellfish beds during these times as well. But it takes most bays a surprisingly short amount of time—just days—to clean themselves out again and return to normal levels, and the same is true for oysters. When you filter gallons of water through something the size of a cherry tomato, you get serious turnover.

Considering the sophistication of our modern detection systems, the state of our waters, and the health-consciousness of consumers, it's safe to say that North America's oysters are as safe to eat as they have been since before its first large cities rose two hundred years ago. Given the option, I still choose oysters from remote and pristine waters, but in the same way that I choose organic vegetables over chemically farmed ones—because it feels like a good idea in the long run, not because I think it will affect my immediate health.

NUTRITION

OYSTERS ARE GOOD food. They rank with salmon, broccoli, and blueberries as nutritional superstars. Like the best seafood, they provide lots of protein, with just a hint of fat and carbohydrates for flavor. They are vitamin and mineral powerhouses. They are even rich sources of those current nutritional darlings, omega-3 fatty acids and antioxidants. Since they are near the bottom of the food chain, they have extremely low levels of mercury in their tissue, unlike higher seafood species like tuna and swordfish, making them a top recommendation of many consumer safety groups.

PROTEIN AND FAT

Protein is the building block of life. Your muscles, organs, and immune system are built of protein. It's your most important nutrient. Without enough protein, your body can't maintain itself. You need lots of protein daily. Protein also takes a long time to digest, meaning it keeps you feeling full on fewer total calories. This is how high-protein diets work; they keep people slim, muscled, and energized.

Animal foods are the best sources of protein. Often this protein comes bundled up with saturated fat, an unwanted accomplice. Saturated fats stay solid at room temperature: Think of the marbling in steak or bacon, or even chicken fat. They stay semisolid in us, too, and that's the problem. As they cake in our arteries, they cause the blockages that result in heart attacks and strokes.

Cold-blooded sea creatures can't have much saturated fat, because at the temperature of their bodies it would get much too solid. Instead, they

261

have unsaturated fat—the good kind. Unsaturated fat, the type found in plant foods like olive oil, provides a host of benefits, from reducing cholesterol and blood pressure to keeping us full on less food, because fat triggers your small intestine to send "full" messages to your brain.

Oysters, like most seafood, are predominantly protein. They have a bit of fat, and most of that is unsaturated. They also have a few carbs, in the form of glycogen, the starch that makes them sweet, but not enough to bother about. Eat them as a way of getting the life-sustaining protein you want without the saturated fat you don't.

OMEGA-3

One very special fat contained in oysters is omega-3. It helps the body perform many key functions, such as reducing inflammation, regulating hormones, and building strong brains, eyes, and reproductive systems. Some studies show that getting a single gram per day of omega-3s (the amount contained in twelve oysters) can cut your risk of heart attack in half, as well as improve the general functioning of your cardiovascular and immune systems. While oysters have less omega-3 than the champs—salmon, sardines, other oily fish, and nuts—they are still near the top of the list.

CHOLESTEROL

For decades a myth has circulated that shrimp and other shellfish were high in cholesterol and thus bad for your health. This myth persists from the time when we had only the most simplistic understanding of cholesterol. We didn't yet understand that there were good and bad forms of cholesterol. We also assumed that cholesterol in food became cholesterol in your blood supply. We now know that the correlation between dietary cholesterol and blood cholesterol is very weak. Your liver makes far more cholesterol each day than you get through food, and it makes it from saturated fat—another reason to avoid beef, pork, chicken fat, and lamb.

Using gas chromatography, we have been able to identify the

different types of sterols found in shellfish. A lot of what we thought was cholesterol turns out to be other sterols that keep us healthy. The only two shellfish truly high in cholesterol are shrimp and especially squid. With oysters, it is a non-issue.

ZINC AND COPPER

This is where things get really interesting. Oysters are freakishly high in zinc and copper, maintaining concentrations that would be toxic to most other forms of life. These aren't just the oysters downriver from the strip mine, either. Even oysters in waters with low concentrations of these metals will contain extraordinary amounts of them. They go out of their way to collect the metals from their environment.

The numbers are alarming. Beef and crab are two foods considered high in zinc. Each has about 4 milligrams per 100 grams. Eastern oysters—are you ready?—can contain 90 milligrams of zinc per 100 grams. That's two zinc lozenges per plate of oysters.

The story with copper is similar, if less extreme. Lobster is extremely high in copper, with 1.7 milligrams per 100 grams. Eastern oysters? More than 4 milligrams per 100 grams. Some oysters have copper concentrations so high that it turns them blue or green, like an old penny. (Worry not, Marenne lovers; this isn't what turns your oysters green. Somebody checked.)

Why accumulate so much metal? No one knows, but a new theory seems promising. Oysters don't distribute zinc and copper throughout their bodies. Some goes into their shells, and the rest goes into their amebocytes—the cells in the immune system that kill bacteria and other invader cells. Since zinc and copper have strong antimicrobial properties, oysters must be arming their immune cells with metallic ammo. The immune cells barrage foreign invaders with toxic zinc in a microscopic variation of "Eat hot lead!"

Can we absorb some of these same antimicrobial powers from the zinc and copper in the oysters we eat? It's possible. Zinc is essential to a healthy immune system and to the process of wound healing. And the whole idea behind those zinc nasal sprays is that the zinc will zap the cold germs before they can infect us. So far, the scientific studies are mixed. Still, it can be heartening to feel the metallic zing of an oyster on the sides of the tongue and believe that your immune system is supercharging.

On the question of taste, it's worth noting that Eastern oysters have five to ten times as much zinc and copper as Pacific oysters—which accords with most people's observations that Pacifics are sweeter, Easterns more mineral. But Easterns also have more zinc and copper than the rattlingly metallic European Flats, so other substances must be responsible for the Flat flavor, possibly iodine.

Now think about this. There isn't much zinc or copper floating around the open ocean. It all erodes from terrestrial sources and washes out to sea, where it precipitates out of solution and falls to the bottom. If oysters do indeed rely on these metals for immune defense, then the reason they cluster at river mouths and other estuaries may have nothing to do with salinity levels, as has always been assumed, and everything to do with metal availability. This would explain the unusual fact that they can thrive at such a wide range of salinities.

Don't worry about clanking when you walk away from your oyster repast. Your body is pretty good at eliminating excess copper and zinc in your diet. However, the method of elimination may not be pleasant. One of the signs of zinc toxicity—common among users of zinc supplements—is "gastrointestinal distress," so many a diner who blamed a "bad oyster" for laying him low after a night of gluttony should probably be blaming the zinc instead. In practice, it's wise to limit your oyster consumption to a dozen or two on any given day.

OTHER VITAMINS AND MINERALS

Oysters are abundant in selenium, a potent antioxidant that helps nullify substances that cause our cells to age and break down. In iron concentration they are second only to clams. They are terrific sources of vitamin D, vitamin B_{12}, magnesium, phosphorus, and manganese. All these substances play vital roles in maintaining overall health. Chances are you won't be eating enough oysters in your life for them to make a huge difference in your health. Just enjoy the fact that, when you do eat them, you are getting an extra jolt of essential nutrients.

THE BEST OYSTER BARS
AND OYSTER FESTIVALS

OYSTER BARS

There are many excellent restaurants in North America that make it a point to have top-quality fresh oysters on their menu, such as New York's Le Bernardin, San Francisco's Zuni Café, and Montreal's Joe Beef. There are also oyster bars springing up on every urban street corner, most offering three or four varieties. This list focuses on places where oysters are an obsession, and where you can count on finding many varieties. (Plus a few other places that are classics.) There's no better way to get an oyster education than to sit down at one of these premier raw bars and taste two (always two; one and you'll miss things) of each of their oysters.

ANTHONY'S HOMEPORT—SHILSHOLE BAY

6135 SEAVIEW AVENUE WEST, SEATTLE, WA; 206-783-0780

WWW.ANTHONYS.COM

Anthony's HomePort restaurants have numerous locations throughout the Puget Sound area. All specialize in fresh seafood and postcard-ready waterfront locations. All carry local oysters, too, but the restaurant on Shilshole Bay is perhaps the most oyster-centric of the bunch. (This is where the annual Oyster Games are held, after all.) The emphasis, as with most Seattle eateries, is on the local Washington oysters.

AQUAGRILL

210 SPRING STREET, NEW YORK, NY; 212-274-0505

WWW.AQUAGRILL.COM

Few proprietors are as oyster-crazy as Jeremy and Jennifer Marshall. Since they opened Aquagrill in SoHo in the 1990s, oysters have been a focus, with at least twenty-five varieties daily and expert advice on hand in the bright, primary-color dining room and bar. Aquagrill, which sells a thousand oysters a day, is the purist's oyster bar. The Marshalls get special kudos for ensuring that oysters arrive within a day of harvest; for working directly with growers; for insisting on calling oysters by their geographical names, even when trade names exist; and for keeping cooked oyster dishes to a minimum—they will fry oysters only upon request. Aquagrill has offered 210 different varieties of oysters over the years.

B&G OYSTERS

550 TREMONT STREET, BOSTON, MA; 617-423-0550
WWW.BANDGOYSTERS.COM

B&G opened in 2003 and instantly became the best oyster bar in Boston. There are always a dozen varieties of oysters on hand, with an understandable New England emphasis; they offer a handful of West Coast oysters, too. The subterranean space is a nice nod to the oyster bars of yore, though the gleaming white marble bar and cool blue-and-steel tones feel decidedly mod. The dining area is intimate, the wine list small but tailored for oysters.

CLADDAGH OYSTER HOUSE

131 SYDNEY STREET, CHARLOTTETOWN, PEI; 902-892-9661
WWW.CLADDAGHOYSTERHOUSE.COM

A joint venture between restaurateur Liam Dolan and John Bil, PEI's oyster-shucking champ, the Claddagh transformed a stuffy old fine-dining establishment into a hip oyster bar complete with reclaimed brick walls, dark-hued wooden bar, and contemporary spot lighting. It doesn't feel much like PEI, but it instantly became *the* spot on PEI for oysters. It carries eight varieties of Canadian oyster, from both coasts, including rarities such as New Brunswick Flats and Colville Bays. Bring a few friends and take advantage of the fifty oysters for seventy-five bucks special.

DAN & LOUIS OYSTER BAR

208 SW ANKENY STREET, PORTLAND, OR; 503-227-5906
WWW.DANANDLOUIS.COM

Though Dan & Louis serves a variety of Northwest oysters, the emphasis is on Yaquina Bays, as you'd expect from a business that has been supplied by its own

Oregon Oyster Farm on Yaquina Bay for nearly a century. In addition to raw oysters, Dan & Louis is famed for its oyster stew, of which it serves two varieties: one made with petite Yaquina Bay oysters and one with larger, diced Pacifics.

ELLIOTT'S OYSTER HOUSE

PIER 56, SEATTLE, WA; 206-623-4340

WWW.ELLIOTTSOYSTERHOUSE.COM

Elliot's is Ground Zero for the West Coast oyster lover. The polished, twenty-one-foot oyster bar is backed by tubs of oysters on ice, each labeled by name, place of origin, and cultivation method, and waiting to be opened when you point at them. There are usually thirty varieties on hand, virtually all from Washington or British Columbia. You won't find an East Coast oyster at Elliott's, nor too many from California or Oregon. That makes sense, since Elliott's is flanked by some of the most productive oyster waters in the world, and the oysters served there come either straight from the grower or from local purveyors like Marinelli Shellfish and Penn Cove. They guarantee that the oysters were stored at low temperature from door to door, and they do their own safety testing as well.

It's interesting to compare Elliott's with Grand Central, the other pole of U.S. oyster culture. Though both have the freshest oysters and the widest varieties, they are opposite in so many ways. Grand Central is a creature of the old Northeast, a century-old subterranean grotto to escape the grimy city outside. Elliott's is new and modern, all glass and shining wood, perched on the edge of Puget Sound with views of water, islands, and the Olympic Mountains.

Elliott's has the chutzpah to serve just frozen mignonette and lemon, not cocktail or hot sauce, as accompaniments to their oysters. You couldn't get away with that anywhere but Seattle. (Fear not, Closet Cocktail Sauce Fan; they keep a few bottles in the back, just for you.)

GRAND CENTRAL OYSTER BAR

GRAND CENTRAL TERMINAL, NEW YORK, NY; 212-490-6650

WWW.OYSTERBARNY.COM

The famed oyster bars of nineteenth-century New York were all underground. Alerted by a candlelit red cloth balloon on the street, you ducked down some stairs and into a basement filled with revelers of all social strata and with a floor strewn with sawdust, spilled beer, and oyster shells. If you want to get as close as possible to experiencing one of those, the huge, echoing cavern beneath Grand

Central is the place. The sawdust is gone, the spilled beer gets cleaned up pretty fast, and a recent renovation has made things pretty spiffy, but the oysters are still there and the tiled, vaulted ceiling gives a palpable sense of Old New York. The mix of people occupying the retro bar stools is fun to watch. There are the tourists, the businessmen killing a plate of oysters while waiting for their trains, and the habitués who dine there every single day. The Grand Central Oyster Bar has been around since 1913 and is going stronger than ever, with thirty varieties of fresh oysters and a list of four hundred oyster-friendly wines. The oysters come from all over, but the emphasis is East Coast, and especially Long Island. Some old standbys almost always on the menu include Bluepoints, Malpeques, Wellfleets, Glidden Points, Moonstones, Kumamotos, Penn Cove Selects, Westcott Bay Sweets, Pipes Coves, and Widow's Holes.

MAESTRO S.V.P.

3615 BOULEVARD ST. LAURENT, MONTRÉAL, QC; 514-842-6447

WWW.MAESTROSVP.COM

Ilene Polansky has run this gem, in the heart of Montréal's chic Plateau district, for twenty years. Nowhere else will you find a more dazzling array of Eastern Canada oysters, including a few varieties from Québec itself. Because this is Canada, among the twenty varieties is the occasional Irish oyster, which can't be imported into the United States. Polansky has the warm presence of your favorite aunt, and both the servers and the clientele are friendly, stylish, and multilingual. Patrons used to sign their empty oyster shells and nail them to the walls, but that got out of hand a few years back and now the walls are back to normal.

OLD EBBITT GRILL

675 FIFTEENTH STREET NW, WASHINGTON, DC; 202-347-4800

WWW.EBBITT.COM

The Old Ebbitt Grill is one of those institutions in D.C. where you can just *feel* the political deals going down at every other table. The mahogany and leather surroundings are intensely Old School, as you'd expect in an establishment founded in 1856. Many presidents have dined here, and many more who wanted to be president. The Ebbitt generally has the best selection of oysters in D.C., with a nice mix from both coasts, and it's one of the only restaurants in the East to carry Olympias.

THE OYSTER HOUSE

320 FOURTH AVENUE WEST, OLYMPIA, WA; 360-753-7000

WWW.OLYMPIAOYSTERHOUSE.COM

An exception on this list, the Oyster House does not serve a wide assortment of oysters. What it does have, fall and winter, is fresh Olympias straight from the surrounding inlets, as well as pan-fried Olympias, which you are unlikely to find anywhere else. Located right on the waterfront in Olympia, in a building that used to be the culling house for the Olympia Oyster Company, it is Washington State's oldest seafood restaurant.

RODNEY'S OYSTER HOUSE

209 ADELAIDE STREET EAST, TORONTO, ON; 416-363-8105

WWW.RODNEYSOYSTERHOUSE.COM

ALSO 1228 HAMILTON STREET, VANCOUVER, BC; 604-609-0080

Rodney Clark is one of the driving forces in the oyster business, with a zaniness and energy rarely matched. His Toronto restaurant has been around for two decades. His Vancouver branch is newer, but both offer a nice selection of oysters from East and West Coasts in informal settings.

SHAFFER CITY OYSTER BAR

5 WEST 21ST STREET, NEW YORK, NY; 212-255-9827

WWW.SHAFFERCITY.COM

Owner Jay Shaffer's voluble personality imbues every corner of this snazzy yet comfortable Flatiron District gem. There are the menu descriptions. (Nootka: "Deep-cupped oyster with sweet liquor, creamy and musky. Hama Hamas watch out!" Bras D'Or: "Should be on every East Coast oyster lover's wish list.") There is the ambient chatter, much of it from Shaffer himself, who is always on hand to greet guests. Most of all, there are the oysters—nearly thirty varieties. For one event, Shaffer had sixty-two. He brings them in fresh every couple of days. Freshness is an obsession: "I want them swimming all the way to my restaurant." That helps explain why this intimate place, with just sixty seats, sells four thousand oysters a week, making it the top oyster seller per seat in the city.

SHAW'S CRAB HOUSE

21 EAST HUBBARD STREET, CHICAGO, IL; 312-527-2722

WWW.SHAWSCRABHOUSE.COM

The oyster bar in Shaw's Crab House always has a dozen different oyster varieties on hand, and Chicago's proximity to O'Hare Airport means that oysters from both coasts get there fast. It's one of the few oyster bars with an even mix of Easterns and Pacifics. The live blues and jazz, handsome bar, and 1940s décor make you feel as if you've wandered into a film noir classic—not a bad sensation.

SWAN OYSTER DEPOT

1517 POLK STREET, SAN FRANCISCO, CA; 415-673-1101
NO WEB SITE

A Russian Hill institution since 1912, Swan keeps things very simple: no credit cards, no reservations, no tables, no dinner hours, no changes in quite some time. What Swan does have is one seventeen-stool, worn marble counter, a handful of fresh West Coast oysters every day at reasonable prices, and a line snaking out the door and onto the sidewalk. Swan is open 8 A.M. to 5:30 P.M., so forget dinner. Forget lunch, too; you'll wait an hour. Follow in James Beard's footsteps and go for an unforgettable breakfast.

UNION OYSTER HOUSE

41 UNION STREET, BOSTON, MA; 617-227-2750
WWW.UNIONOYSTERHOUSE.COM

Union Oyster House was already eighty-seven years old when Grand Central Oyster Bar came into the world in 1913, making Union not just the oldest oyster bar in America but the oldest restaurant, period. The mahogany bar, an original, was where Daniel Webster downed many plates of oysters. John F. Kennedy preferred a private booth, also original, which now bears a plaque dedicated to him. Don't go to Union for the oysters—they'll have just one kind, often Bluepoints—but for the history.

OYSTER FESTIVALS AND EVENTS

For hundreds of years, oysters have been that rare food with a split personality, equally at home with the prince or the pauper. On the nineteenth-century streets of New York, the wealthy spent obscene amounts of money on lavish oyster spreads, while the poor disappeared into underground "oyster cellars" for buckets of ale, oysters on the

Oysters going fast at Elliott's
Oyster New Year. (Photo courtesy
Elliott's Oyster House)

cheap, and all-night carousing. Little has changed. At gourmet restaurants and fancy dinner parties, oysters mingle with Champagne, caviar, and the rich and powerful. At the same time, they are right at home on the streets of working waterfront communities, accompanied by a keg of beer and a party atmosphere. The proliferation of oyster festivals caters to both worlds. Do you want to taste dozens of different wines and oysters in the quest for that elusive moment of bliss when the two wrap their flavors together in a perfect embrace? Or do you want to polish off endless oysters and Tabasco sauce while watching the best shuckers in the world duel each other in a frenzy of flying shells and flashing knives? Either way, the right oyster event awaits you.

ANTHONY'S OYSTER GAMES

ANTHONY'S HOMEPORT—SHILSHOLE BAY

6135 SEAVIEW AVENUE WEST, SEATTLE, WA; 206-783-0780

WWW.ANTHONYS.COM

MID-MARCH

Anthony's take on the snazzy oyster free-for-all is a bit freer than most. In addition to a wide selection of oysters and wines, there are shuck-offs, slurp-offs, oyster fashion contests, oyster poetry readings, oyster identification contests, and oyster art. Proceeds benefit the Puget Soundkeeper Alliance.

ELLIOTT'S OYSTER NEW YEAR

ELLIOTT'S OYSTER HOUSE

PIER 56, SEATTLE, WA; 206-623-4340

The Most Beautiful Oyster Contestants at Elliott's Oyster New Year. (Photo courtesy Elliott's Oyster House)

WWW.ELLIOTTSOYSTERHOUSE.COM

EARLY NOVEMBER

If you do one oyster event all year, it should be Elliott's. In a huge tented hall at the end of Seattle's Pier 56, punctuated by the sound of wineglasses shattering on the concrete floor, oyster growers from all over the West Coast offer their oysters to revelers. You'll never see so many different fresh oysters in one place. If that isn't enough, wines from Washington State wineries line the perimeter of the hall, and a massive buffet table groans under the weight of mountains of cooked Washington State seafood—Dungeness crab and smoked salmon and oyster dishes galore. There's also the hotly contested Most Beautiful Oyster Contest, with a celebrity panel choosing the most comely oyster from twenty or so entrants, and of course the dreaded oyster luge, with raw oysters sluicing down channels of ice into people's waiting mouths. It's a great evening, all to benefit the Puget Sound Restoration Fund. Tickets are a bargain at $85.

FLORIDA SEAFOOD FESTIVAL

APALACHICOLA, FL

WWW.FLORIDASEAFOODFESTIVAL.COM

EARLY NOVEMBER

The two-day Florida Seafood Festival gives the small Panhandle town of Apalachicola a Mardi Gras feel as King Retsyo (that's oyster spelled backward) and Miss Florida Seafood arrive by shrimp boat to lead the parade and the Blessing of the Fleet, when the Apalachicola Bay fishing fleet wends its way through the jam-packed marina to be blessed for the upcoming season. There is a shucking contest and an eating contest, in which contestants eat as many oysters as they can out of paper cups in fifteen minutes. Winners generally top three hundred oysters. Other events include live music, crafts booths, and the 5K Redfish Run. Best of all, there are hundreds of thousands of Apalachicola oysters on hand for the twenty-five thousand ostreaphiles to enjoy.

GRAND CENTRAL OYSTER FRENZY

GRAND CENTRAL OYSTER BAR

GRAND CENTRAL TERMINAL, NEW YORK, NY; 212-490-6650

WWW.OYSTERBARNY.COM

LATE SEPTEMBER

The premier oyster event on the East Coast goes down over two days in late September at Grand Central Oyster Bar. For $95, you can toss oysters from thirty different growers into your mouth all night, and sample wines from all across the planet, including a few from Long Island. Many of the East Coast growers are there shucking their own oysters, so it's a great chance to put a face to the bivalve.

MILFORD OYSTER FESTIVAL

MILFORD, CONNECTICUT

WWW.MILFORDOYSTERFESTIVAL.ORG

THIRD SATURDAY IN AUGUST

Milford and Norwalk have long competed to be the heart of the Connecticut oyster industry, and now they compete to have the best oyster festival. Norwalk's three-day fest is twice the size, but Milford's attracts fifty thousand people on one day, making it the largest single-day festival in Connecticut. The offerings are extensive: live oysters from various East Coast growers, live music, live artists, aquaculture exhibits, oyster boat tours, oyster-shell decorating contests, kayak races, classic car shows, giant toys, rock wall climbing and bungee jumping, and, of course, oyster shucking and eating contests.

NEW ENGLAND OYSTER FESTIVAL

NEWPORT, RHODE ISLAND

WWW.NEWENGLANDOYSTERFESTIVAL.COM

LATE SEPTEMBER

A new creation of American Mussel Harvesters, one of the East Coast's top shellfish distributors, the New England Oyster Festival is refreshingly oyster-centric, compared to some oyster festivals. In addition to a selection of the many types of oysters American Mussel Harvesters carries, you can drink Sam Adams beer on tap, try oyster and wine pairings, watch shucking and slurping events, get oyster shucking and cooking demonstrations, and listen to live music.

NORWALK OYSTER FESTIVAL

NORWALK, CONNECTICUT

WWW.SEAPORT.ORG

FIRST WEEKEND IN SEPTEMBER

Started in 1978 as a way to honor Norwalk's fishing heritage, this has turned into one of the larger festivals of any kind on the East Coast, drawing upwards of 110,000 people and doing $5 million in business. On the menu? Bluepoints, Bluepoints, and more Bluepoints, courtesy of Tallmadge Brothers. (Norwalk is the location of their state-of-the-art processing plant, as well as their fleet of wooden oyster boats.) For entertainment, there are historic boats, harbor tours, hundreds of crafts booths, skydivers, and oystering exhibits.

OLD EBBITT GRILL OYSTER RIOT

OLD EBBITT GRILL

675 FIFTEENTH STREET NW, WASHINGTON, DC; 202-347-4800

WWW.EBBITT.COM

MID-NOVEMBER

For a Friday and a Saturday night in mid-November, a thousand people a night descend on the Old Ebbitt Grill to pay about $100 apiece to sample oysters from around the country, dance to a live band, and drink a variety of wonderful wines. The wines have been chosen by a panel of distinguished Washingtonians, such as Supreme Court Justice Antonin Scalia. New Zealand Sauvignon Blancs have dominated in recent years, with various sparkling wines, Sancerres, and California Sauvignon Blancs mixed in.

OYSTER BAY OYSTER FESTIVAL

OYSTER BAY VILLAGE, LONG ISLAND, NY

WWW.THEOYSTERFESTIVAL.ORG

MID-OCTOBER

The biggest of them all, Oyster Bay pulls in a jaw-dropping 150,000 people for the third weekend in October. The oysters are from Frank M. Flower and Son, the last of the big oyster companies on Long Island. In addition to the requisite raw, smoked, fried, and stewed oysters, there are shucking events, slurping events, pirates wandering through the arts and crafts booths, a restored nineteenth-century oyster sloop, and multiple stages of live music.

OYSTERFEST

SHELTON, WA

WWW.OYSTERFEST.COM

EARLY OCTOBER

The tiny town of Shelton, located near Olympia on the spur of land that divides the tips of Hood Canal and Puget Sound, is one of the centers of Washington's oyster industry. Every October, out at the Mason County Fairgrounds, it celebrates the local bounty at Oysterfest. Unlike many fair-style oyster festivals, at this one you can sample many different oysters, including Olympias, most of which grow within a few miles of Shelton. In addition to raw oysters, there are plenty of shooters, grilled oysters, and other local seafood specialties, such as clams and geoducks. Beer and wine is provided by Washington's local producers, and live music is heard throughout the weekend. The centerpiece event is the shucking contest, which determines the West Coast champion.

PACIFIC COAST OYSTER WINE COMPETITION

WWW.OYSTERWINE.COM

LATE APRIL

Not a festival, but an event to pay attention to. Every spring, wineries throughout the Pacific Northwest compete to receive one of the ten coveted "Oyster Wine" awards, which are used by many restaurants to help them stock oyster-friendly wines on their wine lists. All entries are judged by how well they pair with a Kumamoto (probably the most wine-friendly of oysters). Panels in Los Angeles, San Francisco, and Seattle grade the wines, the results are tallied, and the winners announced in late April. Sauvignon Blancs comprise at least 70 percent of the winners, along with a smattering of Pinot Gris and bubbly. Dry Creek Vineyard's Chenin Blanc, and Sauvignon Blancs from Geyser Peak and Kenwood, are multiyear winners.

PRINCE EDWARD ISLAND SHELLFISH FESTIVAL

CHARLOTTETOWN, PEI

WWW.PEISHELLFISH.COM

MID-SEPTEMBER

A three-day "kitchen party" featuring oysters, shucking competitions, celebrity chef chowder cook-offs, traditional PEI fiddling, the Culinary Institute of Canada food pavilion, tours of oyster farms, the after-hours Shucker's Ball, and oyster specials at restaurants across PEI. Any event that gets five thousand people up to PEI in September can be considered a runaway success.

ROYSTER WITH THE OYSTER

SHAW'S CRAB HOUSE

21 EAST HUBBARD STREET, CHICAGO, IL; 312-527-2722

WWW.SHAWSCRABHOUSE.COM

LATE OCTOBER

This weeklong festival in Shaw's oyster bar offers half-price oysters on the half-shell, thirty different varieties of oysters from both coasts, daily cooked oyster specials, daily slurp-offs, and live Chicago blues each night. The week culminates in a tent party headlined by a nationally known blues performer.

ST. MARY'S OYSTER FESTIVAL

ST. MARY COUNTY FAIRGROUNDS, LEONARDTOWN, MD

WWW.USOYSTERFEST.COM

THIRD WEEKEND IN OCTOBER

The winners of all the other oyster shucking contests in this list gather in Maryland each October at the St. Mary's Oyster Festival to determine the na-tional champion, who goes on to Galway, Ireland, to compete in the world championship. It's a big deal, and the heart of this oyster festival. Contestants must shuck twenty-four oysters as quickly as possible, with time penalties awarded for nicks to the oyster or shell. The record is two minutes and twenty seconds by Duke Landry of Louisiana. An easy day trip from Washington or Annapolis, the St. Mary's Oyster Festival draws twenty thousand people to celebrate the opening of oyster season on the Chesapeake. In addition to Chesapeake oysters served every which way, features include the National Oyster Cook-Off and live music.

SAN FRANCISCO OYSTER AND BEER FESTIVAL

GREAT MEADOW AT FORT MASON, SAN FRANCISCO, CA

WWW.OREILLYOYSTERFESTIVAL.COM

EARLY APRIL

The Irish prefer stout with their oysters, and that's the focus of this fifteen-thousand-person, Irish-themed party in San Francisco each spring. All the music is Celtic, contemporary as well as traditional, and the beer comes from far and wide. There are, of course, shucking, slurping, and cooking contests.

URBANNA OYSTER FESTIVAL

URBANNA, VA

WWW.URBANNAOYSTERFESTIVAL.COM

MID-NOVEMBER

The Urbana Oyster Festival, which celebrates its fiftieth year in 2007, transforms a somnolent Rappahannock River town of six hundred people into a two-day festival grounds for seventy-five thousand from Washington, D.C., and throughout the Southeast. Many people camp in campgrounds that surround the town. Oysters—some from local boats that still ply the Rappahannock and Chesapeake—are sold raw, fried, steamed, roasted, smoked, and stewed. The town marina displays traditional oyster boats and buy boats. Other events include huge fire engine parades, shucking contests, the crowning of an Oyster Queen and Little Miss Spat, and arts and crafts exhibits.

WELLFLEET OYSTER FEST

WELLFLEET, MA

WWW.WELLFLEETOYSTERFEST.ORG

MID-OCTOBER

This classic weekend festival lures ten thousand people all the way out to Wellfleet to enjoy briny Wellfleet oysters, New England oyster chowder and clam chowder, shuck-offs, kayak races, road races, art exhibits, and lots of kid-oriented events.

GROWERS WHO SHIP DIRECT

THE FOLLOWING OYSTER farmers all ship their own oysters directly to consumers. Some harvest the oysters the same day they ship. Look for growers fairly close to you so the oysters can be ground-shipped. Overnight delivery can easily top $100 going coast to coast.

AMERICAN MUSSEL HARVESTERS, INC.

NORTH KINGSTOWN, RI; 401-294-8999

WWW.AMERICANMUSSEL.COM

If you live in New England and want to order a variety of oysters, American Mussel Harvesters should be your first stop. Their selection of New England and Maritime Canadian oysters is particularly fine, but for freshness it's hard to beat their own Quonset Points grown nearby.

COTUIT OYSTER COMPANY

COTUIT, MA; 508-428-6747

WWW.COTUITOYSTERCOMPANY.COM

The oldest oyster company in the United States, selling Cotuit oysters from southern Cape Cod.

CUTTYHUNK SHELLFISH FARMS

CUTTYHUNK, MA; 508-990-1317

WWW.CUTTYHUNKSHELLFISH.COM

Lantern-raised Cuttyhunk oysters (and beach-raised clams) from the Elizabeth Islands.

The honor-system cottage at Glidden Point. (Photo by Bill Kaplan)

EAST DENNIS OYSTER FARM

DENNIS, MA; 508-398-3123

WWW.DENNISOYSTERS.COM

Classic, briny oysters from the bicep of Cape Cod.

FISHERS ISLAND OYSTER FARM

FISHERS ISLAND, NY; 631-788-7899

WWW.FISHERSISLANDOYSTERS.COM

Always perfect virginicas from the clean waters of Fishers Island Sound.

GLIDDEN POINT OYSTER SEAFARM

EDGECOMB, MA; 207-633-3599

WWW.OYSTERFARM.COM

Glidden Point oysters and Damariscotta Belons.

HAMA HAMA OYSTER COMPANY

LILLIWAUP, WA; 360-877-5811

WWW.HAMAHAMAOYSTERS.COM

Natural-set Hood Canal oysters in several sizes, as well as smoked oysters and pickled oysters from Hama Hama's own recipes.

Boxes of Rappahannock River
Oysters awaiting shipment.

HOG ISLAND OYSTER COMPANY

MARSHALL, CA; 415-663-9218

WWW.HOGISLANDOYSTERS.COM

Hog Island Sweetwaters (Pacifics), Kumamotos, and Virginicas.

K&B SEAFOOD

EAST NORTHPORT, NY; 888-261-8161

WWW.KANDBSEAFOOD.COM

K&B is one of the largest oyster distributors in the east, and one of the few
that sells directly to consumers. The beauty of K&B is the one-stop shopping:
Consumers can select multiple varieties from all over North America.

MOONSTONE OYSTERS

WAKEFIELD, RI; 401-783-3360

WWW.MOONSTONEOYSTERS.COM

Moonstone oysters and occasionally wild Belons by special request.

OLYMPIA OYSTER COMPANY

SHELTON, WA; 877-427-3193

WWW.OLYMPIAOYSTER.COM

Olympia and Pacific oysters from southern Puget Sound.

The shell pile at Taylor Shellfish. "For years I couldn't get enough shell for cultch," says eighty-five-year-old Justin Taylor. "Now I've got a little shell."

OREGON OYSTER FARMS

NEWPORT, OR; 541-265-5078

WWW.OREGONOYSTER.COM

Yaquina Bay oysters.

OYSTERVILLE SEA FARMS

OYSTERVILLE, WA; 1-800-CRANBERRY

WWW.OYSTERVILLE.NET

Hand-picked Pacific oysters from Willapa Bay.

RAPPAHANNOCK RIVER OYSTERS

TOPPING, VA; 804-204-1709

WWW.RROYSTERS.COM

Five different Virginia oysters: Barcats, Olde Salts, Stingrays, Rappahannock Rivers, and York Rivers.

TAYLOR SHELLFISH FARMS

SHELTON, WA; 360-426-6178

WWW.TAYLORSHELLFISHFARMS.COM

One of the largest growers in Washington State, with farms throughout the region. Taylor sells all five species of oyster, including several sizes of Pacifics, plus smoked oysters, fresh clams, geoducks, and more.

WESTCOTT BAY SEA FARMS

FRIDAY HARBOR, WA; 360-378-2489

WWW.WESTCOTTBAY.COM

Westcott Bay Flats and Petites from the San Juan Islands.

WIDOW'S HOLE OYSTER COMPANY

GREENPORT, NY; 631-477-3442

WWW.WIDOWSHOLEOYSTERS.COM

Widow's Hole oysters from Long Island's East End.

UPDATES TO THE
PAPERBACK EDITION

SINCE THE HARDCOVER edition of this book came out, the world of oysters has become more exciting than ever. More unique oysters have appeared, restoration efforts are gaining momentum, and the creative explosion of oyster bars and festivals just keeps getting better and better. Here are the highlights.

OYSTERS

BLUEPOINT (GREAT SOUTH BAY)

After a century of exile, Bluepoints are once again growing in their ancestral home—Long Island's Great South Bay. Thank Chris Quartuccio, who used to make his living diving for wild oysters in Long Island Sound. A huge set of wild oysters in the sound in the midnineties led to record harvests—Quartuccio once collected 2,300 oysters in ninety minutes. These oysters were, fairly enough, sold as Bluepoints, but Quartuccio watched over the next decade as they got undercut by "New Jersey Bluepoints" and "Virginia Bluepoints." Recently, Quartuccio decided to restore the name to greatness, using a unique facility near the Fire Island Inlet in Great South Bay—a one-hundred-foot, freestanding dock built right into the bay, with a chipper-looking cottage right on top. The oysters grow in trays around the dock and deliver the full-salt assault that made Bluepoints famous in the 1820s, along with fascinating pine and anise notes most apparent in spring. At market size, they are transferred to a wet-storage area in the town of Blue Point itself. Delivered straight to Manhattan restaurants, they are the genuine article.

DENNIS (CAPE COD)

Dennis, a town on the flexing bicep of Cape Cod, grows some of its most quintessential oysters—briny, rich, and supple, like a well-seasoned tenderloin. Grown by John and Stephanie Lowell of East Dennis Oyster Farm, these deep-cupped bivalves give you everything you'd expect from a Wellfleet—more reliably. In fact, they won Best Oyster at the Cape Cod Oyster Festival, vanquishing some famous competitors.

DRAGON CREEK (MARYLAND)

Coming from Nomini Creek on Maryland's Eastern Shore, with a salinity of about 15 ppt, Dragon Creeks are very mild oysters in the classic Chesapeake style. What they lack in salt they make up for in freshness, nice four-inch size, good plumpness, and pretty, creamy shells. Hand-delivered by the grower, Bruce Wood, they are available only in select Alexandria restaurants, including Hank's Oyster Bar. Wood is as enthusiastic about the Chesapeake Bay as he is about his oysters, and he works hard to restore water quality, collecting the shells from the restaurants that serve Dragon Creeks and returning them to his waters, where new oyster reefs can begin to replace those that were overharvested centuries ago.

EUROPEAN FLAT (BOTH COASTS)

Although growers continue to struggle to raise Flats, several superb examples have turned up recently. Look for Samish Bay Flats from Washington (amazing crunchiness, pleasingly restrained flavor), Okeover Inlet Belons from British Columbia (quite a deep shell for the species, with a gently metallic, tongue-tingling taste), and Moonstone Belons from Rhode Island (prehistoric and softball-sized, with an ancient, coppery patina to their bricklike shells and an intensely coppery flavor; not for the faint of heart, but when you tangle with a Moonstone Belon, you know you're alive).

FISHERS ISLAND (LONG ISLAND SOUND)

Fishers Island, just off the Connecticut coast, has been one of the most important oyster hatcheries for decades. Many of the best oysters on the East Coast are grown from Fishers Island seed. But the oysters that grow out on the island are proof that the genes are perfectly suited to the local *terroir*. Every year, Steve and Sarah Malinowski select one hundred rock stars from their one million full-grown oysters to serve as broodstock for the next generation. Every year, the oysters get more perfect. After twenty-five years of this, the Malinowskis have an extraordinarily deep-cupped oyster on their hands.

Fishers Island oysters come as two-year-olds, petite three-year-olds, and large three-year-olds. The two-year-olds are sweeter, but I like the springiness of the large three-year-olds, due to their substantial adductor muscles. What you notice about a Fishers Island is the strong brine (31 ppt), the strikingly clean finish, and the sweetness, which reliably kicks in around chew #5. It's not a strong flavor, but it's a zesty one that makes you immediately want another. The clean finish is characteristic of oysters grown in lantern nets. Never touching mud, they don't acquire any earthy or mineral flavors. They spend most of their lives in a protected brackish pond where the Malinowskis keep a whopping seventeen thousand nets, pulling them by hand every three weeks to let the sun kill any fouling and to make the oysters strengthen their shells. A day later, they go back in. When they reach market size, they're salted up in the mouth of West Harbor, which gets a good slug of savory Block Island Sound seawater.

KATAMA BAY (MARTHA'S VINEYARD)

Famously sandy Katama Bay, home of postcard-perfect beaches, separates Chappaquiddick Island from the rest of Martha's Vineyard. Katama, which means "crab-fishing place" in the original Wampanoag, is a shellfish bonanza. Clamdiggers and scallopers cruise its shallow waters, and oysters sit happily on that nice, solid substrate and get scrubbed clean in the currents, accounting for their bleached shells. The flavor mixes intense brine, as you'd expect from such Atlantic parts, with a sweet-cream roundness that is mysterious and wonderful, making these some of New England's finest.

MYSTIC (CONNECTICUT)

Like a spruce-lined snowscape, the green and white ridges of Mystic oysters scream winter in New England to me. Grown by the Noank Aquaculture Cooperative in Fisher Island Sound, off the Connecticut coast, Mystics are as pretty an East Coast oyster as you'll ever see. For that we can thank Steve Plant, who resists shortcuts as he grows them. Steve starts them in bags, like most oyster farmers, but then he nestles them onto clean, hard, managed beds for a year or more. With plenty of elbow room, the oysters get almost round, cup up nicely, and produce strong shells, unlike some other oysters in the vicinity. The salt is just right—enough so you notice, but not so much that you're immediately casting about for liquid relief—and the sweetness lingers. Like most northeast oysters, they peak in November and December, but Steve believes they are at their next best in June and July—pre-spawn. I'll let Steve try to convince you: "Some people get turned off by an oyster with full gonad tissue. I myself find them delicious . . . rich and creamy tasting."

NEW POINT (VIRGINIA)

On six acres of Dyer Creek, one of the most remote peninsulas in Virginia, Jack White grows the most beautiful and robust oyster on the Chesapeake. Lovingly tended by White, New Points develop indestructible shells that seem almost like bottomless pits: The oyster keeps going down, down, all the way to the end of the curving cornucopia. The shells look like they were designed by Matisse: tender pinks, purples, and greens—colors common in Pacifics but rarely so apparent in virginicas. The oysters, as meaty as any I've tasted, have a mild flavor and the yellowed ivory flesh common to southern oysters. That mild meatiness made them the best fried oysters I've had. The oysters are named for the New Point Comfort Lighthouse, the only thing that sticks farther into the Chesapeake than White's pristine tidelands.

White, whose eponymous great-grandfather worked three thousand acres of oysters with a fleet of twenty-five skipjacks, is one of the driving forces behind the Chesapeake's Oyster Gardener program. His goal is "a billion in the bay before I die."

SNOW HILL (MARYLAND)

Grown north of Chincoteague in the Maryland end of Chincoteague Bay, Snow Hills are improvements on the famous Chincoteague Salts. Farther up the bay, they get a little less ocean water, giving them a perfect (to my taste) salinity of 28 ppt. They also deliver a yeasty sweetness reminiscent of New Brunswick's Beausoleils. The whitish-brown shells are strong and paisley shaped. Snow Hill is a famous old Maryland oyster appellation, so it's nice to see it cranking out the bivalves once again.

WINTER POINT (MAINE)

Called "the Burgundy of oysters" by Daniel Boulud, Winter Points are as deeply flavorful as any virginicas I know. These four-inch oysters, grown in Mill Cove, near Bath, are filled with brine and brothy umami richness. That rich, bitter-almond finish is influenced by the clay seabed of Mill Cove. The shells of Winter Points have a beautiful black-and-white fan pattern, tinged with green algae. More important, they are nice and strong, owing to the fact that the critters spend their last stage of life toughening up on the bottom of Mill Cove. Before that, they are started in upwellers on the surface, and then transferred to racks and bags just off the bottom of the cove. The family that farms Winter Points has been working these oyster grounds for more than three hundred years. The growers cut the ice with saws in the winter and harvest with bull rakes. Give a little moment of silence for their fortitude the next time you eat Winter Points in February.

OYSTER BARS

HANK'S OYSTER BAR

1624 Q STREET NW, WASHINGTON, D.C.; 202-462-4265

1026 KING STREET, ALEXANDRIA, VA; 703-739-4265

WWW.HANKSRESTAURANTS.COM

The best oyster fun to be had in D.C. is at Hank's Oyster Bar, which opened in 2005 in Arlington and in 2007 in Alexandria. Hank's reliably has a half-dozen ultra-fresh oysters on hand. The proprietors, Sandy Lewis and Jamie Leeds, go out of their way to create a warm and welcoming atmosphere. Look for their special events, including the not-to-be-missed March oyster festival.

HOG ISLAND OYSTER BAR

FERRY BUILDING MARKETPLACE, SAN FRANCISCO, CA; 415-391-7117

WWW.HOGISLANDOYSTERS.COM

It's hard to beat holding down a bar stool in the Ferry Building, staring out at San Francisco Bay, savoring the freshest oysters, and watching the tourists throng by. Hog Island features its own varieties here, straight off the farm, but also a nice mix of West Coast oysters. The last time I was there they even had Olympias.

NEPTUNE OYSTER

63 SALEM STREET, BOSTON, MA; 617-742-3474

WWW.NEPTUNEOYSTER.COM

Look around this tiny North End pearl and you're convinced you are in a Paris bistro. The dominant colors are white and glass. The oyster selection is chalked on the mirror behind the bar. The pressed tin ceiling casts a glow. But the menu is unmistakably New England. Neptune carries a dozen different oysters nightly, most from the Northeast. They also serve an interesting mignonette made with Prosecco instead of vinegar—much less acidic than a typical mignonette, which may or may not suit you. Owner Jeff Nace, who was the wine buyer for Olives for twelve years, is as good as anyone I've met at pegging the perfect wine for your bivalves. The ambience of Neptune Oyster plays into the pleasure. The colors on the oyster trays—the chalky shells, the lights refracted in ice—are perfectly mirrored by the room. Sitting high on a bar stool, with that dreamy glow all around, gives the impression that Neptune Oyster is where ostreaphiles who are very, very good get to go when they die.

THE OCEANAIRE

WWW.THEOCEANAIRE.COM

I haven't listed restaurant groups in this book, but I must make an exception for the Oceanaire because they get all the little touches just right. When you walk into any of the sixteen Oceanaires (San Diego, Seattle, Denver, Minneapolis, Houston, Dallas, Indianapolis, Cincinnati, Charlotte, Miami, Orlando, Atlanta, Washington, D.C., Baltimore, Philadelphia, and Boston) you stare straight at a semicircular, gleaming metal raw bar packed with the freshest oysters. The Oceanaire chefs I've met have a terrific depth of oyster knowledge, as well as great enthusiasm. In many of the cities they inhabit, they are the best oyster spot in town.

THE OYSTER COMPANY RAW BAR & GRILLE

202 DEPOT STREET, DENNISPORT, MA; 508-398-4600

WWW.THEOYSTERCOMPANY.COM

I have a special place in my heart for restaurants that serve their own oysters. That's the case with this Cape Cod gem, called "the best oyster bargain in Massachusetts" by the *Boston Globe*. Owner Gerry Bojanowski keeps the twisting zinc bar piled with his own Quivet Neck oysters, as well as several other local varieties. But go for the Quivets, farmed in a little nook of Cape Cod Bay near Dennis that is surrounded by conservation land. They have a delicious pearlike tang that is highly unusual in a virginica.

RYLEIGH'S OYSTER

36 E. CROSS STREET, BALTIMORE, MD; 410-539-2093

WWW.RYLEIGHS.COM

Baltimore, with its strategic spot at the head of the Chesapeake Bay, used to be the queen of oyster towns, with more shucking houses than any other. But its fortunes declined along with the Chesapeake oyster. Today, the last of the great packing houses, Harris Seafood on Kent Narrows, must shuck Gulf oysters to make up for what the local waters can't provide. But when it comes to oyster bars, Baltimore is reviving. That renaissance took a huge leap forward with the birth of Ryleigh's Oyster in 2007, across the street from the famous Cross Street Market. The décor includes a gigantic hand-painted map pinpointing the locations of many of Ryleigh's favorite oysters. Eight varieties are on hand on any given evening.

OYSTER FESTIVALS

ARCATA BAY OYSTER FESTIVAL

ARCATA, CALIFORNIA

WWW.OYSTERFESTIVAL.NET

MID-JUNE

If Kumamotos are your drug of choice, then this fest will top your yearly highlight reel. Mounds of Kumos, as well as Pacifics, from nearby Arcata Bay are served raw and every which way to nearly twenty thousand people in the feathery fog of midsummer northern California. Shucking contests, live music, offerings from local breweries, and lots of kids' activities complete the festival scene.

COMOX VALLEY SHELLFISH FESTIVAL

COMOX MARINA PARK, COMOX, BC

WWW.COMOXVALLEYSHELLFISHFESTIVAL.CA

MID-JUNE

The incredible bounty of Vancouver Island—both above and below the waterline—is on display at this new festival. Local shellfish growers, winemakers, and farmers team up with celebrity chefs for a weekend of extraordinary good eating.

PEMAQUID OYSTER FESTIVAL

DAMARISCOTTA, MAINE

LAST SUNDAY IN SEPTEMBER

Boats piled high with thousands of Pemaquids—one of the world's best oysters—appear on the wharf of the charming town of Damariscotta every late September for this festival that raises money for local schools and environmental organizations. The Pemaquids can be had raw, baked, and stewed, and they can be washed down with local Pemaquid Ale. Live music and boat tours of the oyster farm complete a dreamy fall day in Maine.

SCHLAFLY STOUT AND OYSTER FESTIVAL

THE SCHLAFLY TAP ROOM, ST. LOUIS, MO; 314-241-BEER

WWW.SCHLAFLY.COM

MARCH

St. Louis's best brewery flies in oysters from both coasts and matches them with its three stouts—Nitro Irish, Oatmeal, and Kaldi's Coffee—plus music and shucking contests in this decidedly Gaelic-tinged festival.

OYSTERRATA

THE OYSTERINI, REVISITED

After I put a recipe for the Oystertini in the original edition of this book, I received a letter from a man demanding credit for having invented the "Oysterini," as he calls it, at a party at the Goddard Space Flight Center in 1960. Apparently the Oysterini reached its apex in 1976 at a Jet Propulsion Laboratory party celebrating the successful landing of the Viking Mission on Mars. Can NASA's shimmering success record in those halcyon days, and its subsequent decline during the later, Oysterini-less period, be coincidental? I think not. In any case, let the record hereby state: Dr. Gil Levin, the Oysterini is all yours.

THE OYSTER INVITATIONAL CHALLENGE

In April 2008 in Providence, Rhode Island, twenty all-star virginicas competed for the title of Best Tasting Oyster in a major blind tasting. Many of my favorites, including Moonstones, Watch Hills, Island

Creeks, Pemaquids, Katama Bays, Mystics, and Totten Virginicas, threw their hats in the ring. The judges included such bivalve virtuosos as Peter Hoffman of Savoy and Sandy Ingber of Grand Central Oyster Bar. The Totten Virginicas stood out—they had a fruity umami depth rare in Atlantic oysters—but they came in second, beaten out by Island Creeks, whose crisp, zesty brine was apparent even in April, a tough month for northeast oysters. The next heat will be a fall event; until then, Island Creeks reign supreme.

THE FIRST APPETIZER

In late 2007, paleoanthropologists discovered a cave on the southern tip of Africa that provided "strong evidence that early humans displayed key elements of modern behavior" much earlier than previously thought. The evidence showed that 164,000 years ago—rather than 45,000 years ago, as previously thought—humans were already exhibiting creativity, symbolic thinking, and sophisticated use of technology. The evidence? Shellfish remains, stone knives, and ochre for marking cave walls. The scientists don't know what those ritualistic symbols might have been, but you and I can recognize a proto–raw bar when we see one. "It is possible," said the team leader, "that this population could be the progenitor population for all modern humans." They'll get no argument from me.

OYSTER RESTORATION TAKES OFF

Perhaps the most exciting news is that oyster restoration is taking hold in virtually every coastal area as more and more people learn to harvest the oyster's power as an ecosystem architect. The Puget Sound Restoration Fund recently enhanced more acres of Olympia oyster habitat, expanded its shellfish gardening program, and laid the groundwork for a new community shellfish farm. In July 2008, it led an expedition to the remote corner of Vancouver Island to observe the most extensive and untouched bed of Olympias remaining in the world. Having this community as a model will help all oyster restoration projects understand what they're shooting for. In the Chesapeake, restorers are learning to outsmart the cow-nosed rays by creating artificial reefs that provide shelter for the spat. The New York and New Jersey Baykeepers organization boasts hundreds of "oyster gardeners" who are raising oysters along their waterfront, not for eating but to restore habitat in Raritan and Jamaica Bays. The University of Georgia's Adopt an Oyster Reef Program is encouraging volunteers to reestablish oysters along the muddy substrates of the Southeast. South Carolina's Department of Natural Resources has a similar program.

In Florida's Indian River Lagoon, the same waterway where I encountered my first wild oysters, the Nature Conservancy is working with thousands of volunteers to restore oyster reefs along acres of coastline. The volunteers attach cultch to mesh mats, line the lagoon with the mats, and anchor the mats with weights. Wild spat set on the cultch. Without the mats, the cultch gets washed above the waterline by boat wakes and the spat die. Rooted by the mats, these oyster communities can self-stabilize and provide habitat for all the juvenile life in the estuary.

Looming over the estuary is Turtle Mound, the only hill of any kind along the Florida coast. It's all oyster shells, left by the Timucuan people a thousand years ago, and it speaks to the potential fecundity of the ecosystem. My son and I spent a spring day gazing across the lagoon from Turtle Mound, then we rented a canoe to look for live oysters. There they were, just like when I was a kid. With any luck, some boy will gather a few for his lunch in another thousand years.

ACKNOWLEDGMENTS

Foremost thanks to Edward Behr, publisher of *The Art of Eating*, for helping me hatch the idea for this book and for being a touchstone of advice and wisdom throughout. *The Art of Eating* is the last great food magazine in America, and Ed is an editor of heroic acumen.

Professionals in the oyster and food industries have been astoundingly generous with their knowledge and time. They include: Jeremy Anderson, John Bil, Brett Bishop, Craig Bleeker, Joe Buley, Travis and Ryan Croxton, Joth Davis, Matt Dimatteo, Robin Downey, John Finger, Bernard Friedman, Seth Garfield, Mike Garvey, Eric Hellner, Greg Hinton, Bill Holler, Sandy Ingber, Adam and Lissa James, Ian Jefferds, Ed Jones, Tom and Becky Kehoe, Chris "The Palate" Labrusciano, Tommy Leggett, Gary Madden, Tom Madsen, Harold McGee, Geoff Menzies, Mike Osinski, Betsy Peabody, Angelo Picozzi, Ilene Polansky, Jon Rowley, Barb Scully, Jay Shaffer, Roberta Stevenson, Bill Taylor, Reg Tutthill, and Mike Voisin. Special thanks to John Holzapfel for lending a total stranger his collection of rare oyster books, to Arlene Balcewicz at the Long Island Maritime Museum for burying me under historical documents and photos, and to Bob Rheault for providing fascinating and in-depth answers to my questions and for making sure I had my technical facts straight.

Two fine journalists, Marialisa Calta and Jeff Cox, had blazed parts of this trail before me and were kind enough to show me their paths. Without Marialisa, I'd never have discovered Colville Bay oysters, and without Jeff it would've taken me a lot longer to taste my first Oly.

Many people have written books on the subject of oysters, but only two have nailed it. Without Eleanor Clark's *Oysters of Locmariaquer* and

Mark Kurlansky's *Big Oyster*, my understanding of oyster history would have been much spottier.

My agent Stephany Evans was enthusiastic and savvy about this project from the beginning and made its initial stages amazingly effortless. My editor Amanda Katz was keen, understanding, and willing to go above and beyond the call of editorial duty. The incomparable Maya Baran made sure that the book was noticed by someone other than my editor, my agent, and my mother. Peter Perkins served as my advance California scout, and Peter Holm gave me better maps than I deserved.

Covering so much ground requires crashing on a lot of couches. Thanks to Heather Blackie, Heidi Blackie, Cathi Buni, Monica Callan, Rebecca Cole, Tamar Cole, Maryan Elder, and Bill Kaplan for being my traveling support team. And I'm sorry about all the shells.

This book might not exist if Dad hadn't taken the kids to Stormy's way back when. And it certainly wouldn't exist without the daily good nature of Mary Elder Jacobsen or the willingness of Erick Jacobsen to understand why Daddy had to go away again to eat more oysters. Thank you all.

OYSTER INDEX